Penguin Handbooks
Organic Gardening

Lawrence D. Hills was born in 1911 and began his forty years
of practical horticultural experience when he was sixteen. He
wrote his first book mainly in R.A.F. hospitals before being
invalided out on D-Day, and is now one of Britain's best-known
writers on organic gardening. He was gardening correspondent of
the *Observer* for eight years, and then of *Punch* and the
Countryman. He now writes for, and is Associated Editor of, the
Ecologist and *Compost Science* (U.S.A.). His many publications
include *Fertility Without Fertilisers*, *Down To Earth Gardening*
and *Grow Your Own Fruit and Vegetables*. He also writes
newsletters and reports for the Henry Doubleday Research
Association. He is Director of this largest body of organic gardeners
in Britain, which he founded in 1954, and has recently completed
a world-wide tour of its overseas groups. He has frequently
appeared on television, and has lectured and broadcast on the
radio in Great Britain, the United States, South Africa, Belgium,
France, Australia and New Zealand.

Lawrence D. Hills is married, with no children. He says that he
'considers that the ever-increasing membership of the Henry
Doubleday Research Association is family enough for anyone'.

Organic Gardening

Lawrence D. Hills

Illustrated by Christine Robins

Penguin Books

Penguin Books Ltd,
Harmondsworth, Middlesex, England
Penguin Books,
625 Madison Avenue, New York, New York 10022, U.S.A.
Penguin Books Australia Ltd,
Ringwood, Victoria, Australia
Penguin Books Canada Ltd,
2801 John Street, Markham, Ontario, Canada L3R 1B4
Penguin Books (N.Z.) Ltd,
182–190 Wairau Road, Auckland 10, New Zealand

First published 1977
Reprinted 1977, 1978

Made and printed in Great Britain by
Cox & Wyman Ltd, London, Reading and Fakenham
Set in Monotype Plantin

Contents

1 *Organic and Inorganic*

An organic gardener is one who has given up chemical fertilizers, pesticides, fungicides and herbicides; some change on ethical grounds to stop pollution harmful to birds, bees and men, others to save money, since it is easy even at today's vegetable prices to spend more on chemicals than you can save when growing your own food. Whatever the reason, there are many gardeners who would like to be 'organic' and this book is written to help them to garden in this way.

The difference between 'organic' and inorganic fertilizers is defined by the way in which plants *feed*, and this cuts across the generally accepted idea of what is 'natural'; for instance, plants insist that wood ashes are a mixture of chemicals, but basic slag, which is ground-up blast-furnace linings, is considered by roots to be 'organic', like the thousands of tons of plant food minerals in every acre of fertile soil. If we are to begin with a definition of this difference, we must start with some plant biology.

A plant needs food, exactly as human beings do, though plant food is quite different. The method of feeding adopted by the entire plant is two-fold, partly by way of the roots, and partly by way of the leaves. The food taken in by the roots consists of particles of mineral nutrients, which must be in solution, otherwise they cannot be absorbed by the root-hair cells.

Plants have three ways of feeding through their roots. First, along every root there are constantly produced, minute, transparent hairs which live for only about three days. As they die they release proteins and carbohydrates on which friendly bacteria feed, and in the process make plant food minerals available for absorption by the living rootlets. This they do with the help of root secretions, just as our digestive juices do with those human equivalents of feeding roots called 'villi' which line our intestines.

Second, there are a number of helpful fungi that live with one end of their 'bodies' reaching in through the bark of the larger roots, extracting sap and energy-providing food, and the other gathering phosphates from the soil which they pass on to the plant that feeds them.

The third way is up the mighty transpiration stream that can take 90 gallons of water to the top of a 40-ft tree in the course of one sunny day and one warm still summer night. In this case, the roots absorb moisture containing mineral nutrients directly from the soil, without the interaction of bacteria or fungi. The nutrients are then extracted as required and the remaining moisture moved up the plant to be transpired through the leaves.

When we feed our crops with soluble chemical fertilizers (inorganics), like nitrate of soda, superphosphate or sulphate of potash, we use only the third method, the transpiration stream, which supplies plant food minerals fast but wastefully, for most of them wash quickly out of reach. If we use organic fertilizers such as bone-meal, these are broken down only slowly in the soil and stay within range of the fungi and root hairs; they are of such a nature that bacteria and fungi can use them in their own life process, whereas the inorganic nutrients cannot be so easily used.

So, organically grown crops are fed slowly with compost, manures and organic fertilizers, also with ground minerals such as rock phosphate which duplicate the normal mineral fragments in the soil. These materials, unlike inorganic fertilizers, can be absorbed by all three systems of feeding, and this is the crucial difference between the two methods of cultivation.

WHY GARDEN ORGANICALLY?

First, the seas that dried up in the past, leaving chemical deposits now used for fertilizers, were very few, and the raw materials for chemical fertilizers are therefore just as exhaustible as North Sea oil. Nitrogenous fertilizers can be made from nitrogen in the air, but this takes power – about 5 tons of coal-equivalent for every ton of fertilizer – and even nuclear energy is no answer. Why should we convert the world's fertilizer reserves into soluble forms and waste them down the farm drains into the sea where their recovery will take more power than we can afford? When we apply 5 cwt of potassium chloride to an acre of land that already has about 50 tons of it in the top 9 inches we are wasting plant foods which would be better employed growing food for hungrier people on less fertile soils.

Then there is the question of cost to the individual gardener or farmer. In 1976, many good organic farmers made as much as 50 per cent more profit to the cow than their inorganic neighbours, because they did not buy the concentrated cattle feeds, fertilizers and chemicals that have increased in price so immensely in the last three years. Organic farming is more efficient than organic gardening, because there is no garden equivalent of the grazing cattle returning manure to the ground. None the less, many thousands of organic gardeners and allotment holders have saved money by giving up chemicals. The gap is even more startling when we compare greengrocers' prices with the value of what we grow in our own gardens. And when we consider wholefood shop prices, which are higher still, it becomes quite clear that the best way to enjoy fresh foods grown without chemicals is to grow them yourself.

In addition to cost, many people are concerned about the dangers of toxic pesticides building up in our body-fats from the first day of our lives. So far paraquat has killed about 100 people in Britain. The organo-phosphorus compounds, developed from nerve gases fortunately not used in the Second World War, have killed over 6,000 people in Japan, and though the organo-chlorine compounds, of which DDT is the best known, have killed no one in Britain, the less well-known chlordane has led to deaths in the U.S.A. These substances are even found in the fat of penguins down by the South Pole. The name 'organo' means that they are synthetic substances, with molecules almost, but not quite, like those of organic ones. Because of this, nature cannot take them apart for recycling, and they break down slowly into other materials, some of which can be as poisonous as the originals. When organic gardeners have to use a pesticide to save a crop, they use substances of vegetable origin, such as nicotine, which, although it is a deadly poison, breaks down quickly in the soil into safe compounds, and spares friendly insects such as ladybirds and hoverflies. These safe substances do not build up resistant strains of pests, like the DDT-resistant malaria mosquitoes now found in almost every tropical country.

Many people simply enjoy the taste of good food. The best testimony to the superior flavour, higher vitamin level, better balance of minerals and lower moisture content (meaning better nutritional value for the same weight of foods grown) is given by the satisfied customers. They may be following fashion to some degree, but there is also some concrete evidence that they are right. Not much, however, because the 'organic movement' has only a tiny fraction of the money for research that is available to, say, the food-processing industry. Many years ago, a panel of members of the Henry Doubleday Research Association found that 28 out of 32 tasters put chemically grown potatoes last for flavour. Wheat is difficult to tell apart, though organic farmers can taste the difference between a wholemeal loaf made from fresh-ground, inorganically grown wheat and one made from the same wheat variety off their own farms. After all, no chemical test can measure the difference between one vintage wine and another.

Even if wholefood is supplied direct from an organic growers' cooperative, it cannot be as fresh as produce that has only travelled the length of your garden path. All vegetables and fruits start losing vitamin C as soon as they are gathered, and the shorter the trip to the kitchen, the more vitamin C they have left. This applies just as much to deep frozen vegetables and bottled fruits as to fresh crisp lettuces and thin-skinned tomatoes.

Those people who buy vegetables find increasingly that more money buys less taste; this is not necessarily just because they are older, and everything tasted better when they were in their twenties. Commercial varieties are now bred for uniformity, appearance in the supermarket, weight to the acre, and toughness sufficient to enable them to stand up to first the journey to market and then the one to the retailer. As an American grower once said, 'If someone bred a square lettuce to fit the crates better, we should all buy it, even if it tasted like a not too clean cork!'

The amateur gardener is looking for entirely different qualities. He wants his lettuces, for example, to last as long as possible in the rows so that he can eat one a day for weeks without the last ones bolting. He does not mind if a potato has a rough skin, like Record, so long as it keeps well and tastes good. He can afford to grow tomatoes with thin skins and leave them on the plants till they are really ripe, which would mean the risk of bruising the fruit for a commercial grower with a grading machine, but means the finest quality for those who eat their own.

Above all, he can try different vegetable varieties year after year till he finds those that suit the tastes of his family, though in practice organic gardeners tend to choose the same kinds for taste and yield when grown with compost, and for hardiness and disease resistance. Yield with chemicals may be higher, but the gardener can afford to ignore the profit a farmer obtains by piling fertilizer on to his potato crop and so gaining extra weight (which is largely water). All he wants is a large enough crop to last until new potatoes come in again, even though his yield could be a matter of tons to the acre less. Quality is what counts when you grow it yourself.

AIMS FOR THE ORGANIC GARDENER

There are two ways of gardening organically. The first is to aim at raising as much produce as possible that is difficult or expensive to buy and offers the maximum cash saving. This should be the choice of those with tiny gardens, and they should concentrate on lettuces and other salad crops, including roots for grating raw, and bush fruits for fresh eating and bottling, but ignoring potatoes and the cabbage tribe, not only because these can be bought easily but to avoid the need for crop rotation. Potatoes and cabbage family vegetables are like lightning – they should never strike the same place twice, for, if they follow each other year after year, they build up pest and disease troubles.

The other system is to try for 'self-sufficiency', raising as much as possible of the family food from one's own garden, as peasants do in many countries, finding it harder work than anything we in the well-fed countries do for a living. On the other hand, with the doubled food prices of the past four years doubling themselves again in eight, or at best in sixteen (if the inflation rate can be halved), we may well have to try.

With skilled gardening and a rotation that crops through the winter, the 300 square yards of the standard allotment can produce nearly a ton and a half of food in a year. Even the 12-ft wide bed 90 ft long on each side of the path down the middle of the average semi-detached garden could grow about 900 lb. of maincrop potatoes, the crop which produces the most good food from a given area. However, apart from the need for crop rotation, we cannot live on potatoes alone, not because we should get too fat, but for lack of concentrated carbohydrates.

The Irish before the Potato Famine of the 1840s were never fat, and it was the puddings, pies and cakes of the age even before Mrs Beeton that gave John Bull his well-filled waistcoat. Potatoes – if the skins are not discarded – contain the vitamins and minerals with which to digest their starches and, weight for weight, are three and a half times *less* fattening than slimming biscuits. They also contain a good supply of proteins, but we should have to eat about 9 lb. a day each if we were to attempt to live on potatoes alone. If we really wished to be self-sufficient we would need wheat for making wholemeal bread, but this cannot be grown on a garden scale because we have encouraged birds to associate houses with food, and the sparrows would simply eat our crop before we even tried to harvest it with garden shears.

Our main requirement for self-sufficiency in a small area is something that will provide a concentrated, storable protein to replace meat, which must have the right balance of what are called 'amino-acids' – these determine its quality. Among the vegetables, the soya bean is very good and has perhaps the best balance of any of the pea and bean family, but its yield, even using the one variety which is just about hardy enough for Britain, produces only a fraction of that from hardier and tastier beans which suit our climate better.

Most organic gardeners who have room enough compromise between the two methods, keeping up the potato supply (because once you have eaten organically grown you cannot endure the chemically treated product), growing beans for flavour and to keep up the soil nitrogen content, and growing as much as possible of the food they really enjoy and would otherwise spend most on. There is no waste of space worse than growing something that nobody likes, and every family must find out its own 'value-for-space' crops through the years.

2 Compost, Leafmould, Manure and Peat

The first three of these are all 'manures' in the true sense of the word, because they supply not only food for plants, but also humus for the soil. Humus is decayed organic matter broken down first in the compost heap and then in the soil itself by bacteria, fungi and other micro-organisms to which it supplies vital nourishment. By feeding in this way, they break down the organic matter further until it becomes black and finely divided, and is called humus. Humus is very important to the soil: it separates the soil grains, absorbs and retains moisture, and makes all soils more easily worked. In other words, it improves the soil structure so that not even the most inorganic of gardeners can grow crops without it. Peat is almost entirely humus and contains only tiny quantities of plant food, so it is not, strictly speaking, a manure.

COMPOST AND COMPOST HEAPS

In the past 'compost' had a different meaning, and there is still confusion between potting soil mixtures like the John Innes composts, and the compost heap made by the gardener, even though quite often all he or she actually makes is a rubbish heap that dries to a home for woodlice and the basis of a bonfire. A real compost heap should get so hot that it cooks and kills weed seeds, destroys disease spores, concentrates plant foods while keeping them in the forms that are most readily used by crops, and converts garden and household rubbish into humus.

The first essential for a good compost heap is an air supply, because the heat is produced by air-breathing bacteria as they work on the compost materials, and they need oxygen in order to live. Next, there must be a source of food for the bacteria; this is obtained from a mixture of compost materials and what is called an 'activator'. This mixture is a source of nitrogen and phosphates which build up the numbers of bacteria in the order of billions, so that they will convert rubbish to humus as quickly as possible. There are many activators: some are bacterial cultures which (in theory) provide a picked team of bacteria that can obtain their nitrogen sufficiently fast from the protein in the plant materials to ensure their breakdown, but generally speaking the best are organic manures of one kind or another. In some systems, layers of soil are added to the heap in order to supply a starting stock of bacteria, but there are always plenty in the roots of weeds, and the less soil in a heap the better, for you cannot expect any heap to cook weed seeds inside lumps of cold clay.

A well-made compost heap should reach at least 140°F. during the first few weeks. After this first heat is spent, another group of helpers takes over, mostly microscopic fungi, but also a useful bacteria called *Azotobacter chroococcum*. This is a freelance nitrogen 'fixer', and it finds conditions so good in a half-decayed compost heap that it can 'fix' on and add as much as 26 per cent more nitrogen than there was in the activator and compost material with which it was started. Compost can be made in two months in summer, but autumn heaps need until spring before the stage arrives when they are cold and the worms move in, which shows they are ready for use.

Compost heaps also need moisture; without it the bacteria and fungi cannot do their work and the heap simply becomes a dry, haylike mass, providing a home for wasp-nests and woodlice. At the other extreme, too much wet results in a slimy, foul-smelling mound, fit for nothing.

The essentials, then, for making good garden compost are: air, a source of nitrogen and phosphates for the bacteria, sufficient heat, and moisture. The most difficult to supply is the required degree of heat – plenty of fresh green vegetative material is needed for this, and smaller gardens may not always be able to produce enough.

The Carbon-Nitrogen Ratio

To every part of nitrogen in average garden rubbish there are between 30 and 70 parts of carbon. In good compost the ratio is between 10 and 12 to 1, the same level as in fertile soil. So in making compost heaps, we are bringing the proportions of substances containing these two elements down to the best carbon-nitrogen ratio ('C:N ratio' for short) for crop growing.

The ideal C:N ratio for the bacteria and fungi that recycle organic wastes to plant foods and humus is 25:1. This is why an activator is needed in the compost heap: to bring the available nitrogen up to a level that will start the process of decay. The herbal activators such as Q.R. and those containing bacteria probably act by releasing nitrogen from the proteins in sappy weeds with a close C:N ratio, doing this fast enough for quick heating. A good compost heap can hold up to 26 per cent *more* nitrogen than went in with the material and activator because of the free-living nitrogen-fixing bacteria that use some of the energy from the carbohydrates to gather more from the air.

If the C:N ratio is too high, say 100:1, the composting process either will not start or will continue to waste carbon dioxide for a long time, taking valuable nitrogen and phosphates to do this. (Garden rubbish dug straight into the ground without composting will similarly take nitrogen and phosphates from the soil, thus robbing growing plants.) If the C:N ratio is too low, say 2:1 as in fresh pig or poultry manure, the nitrogen will be wasted by evaporating off as ammonia and other gases. (Manure should be stacked to minimize this wastage.) The C:N ratio is therefore important – on it depends compost quality and quantity.

Making a Compost Bin

Many gardeners make wooden compost bins. These hold the heat in well, reduce the need for turning and keep the pile tidy while it decays. A good size has two compartments each 3 ft square and high, which will hold a cubic yard of material each. For one box you need:

186 ft of plank, $\frac{1}{2}$ in. thick, 4 in. wide, sawn into the following quantities: 9 6-ft planks; 27 3-ft planks; 18 2 ft 10 in. planks;
6 4-ft lengths of timber 2 in. wide and 2 in. thick;
5 3-ft lengths of timber 2 in. thick and $1\frac{1}{2}$ in. wide;
nails;
wood preservative suitable for garden use.

17

(These dimensions are given as a general guide. The compartments could just as easily be a metre square.)

1. Brush preservative on all the wood before assembling and let it dry thoroughly. Hidden ends and corners rot most.

2. Lay 3 of the 2×2 uprights a yard apart and nail the 9 6-ft planks to the upper 3 ft of these uprights, leaving a small gap between each plank ($\frac{1}{4}$–$\frac{1}{2}$ in.).

3. Nail one end of the 27 3-ft planks to the upper 3 ft of the 3 remaining uprights: i.e. 9 planks per upright. Leave small gaps between the planks as before.

4. Dig 6 holes 1 ft deep to take the 6 uprights at the six corners of the yard squares.

5. Fit the three back uprights into their respective holes, but only fill up and firm the ground round the upright at one end. Put the front upright of the first end into its hole. Holding a brick against the back upright to take the shock of the hammering, nail the free ends of the planks of the side to the back upright. Fill in the hole around the front upright and tread it firm. Fit the middle and other end in the same way. You now have a strong wooden letter E, in plan.

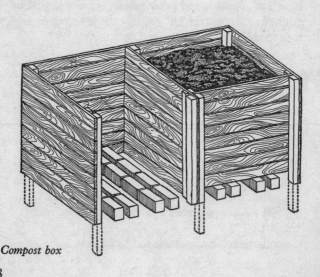

Compost box

6. The 18 2 ft 10 in. planks are used to make up the removable board fronts. These fit into slots made by nailing the $2 \times 1\frac{1}{2}$ in. timber about $\frac{3}{4}$ in. in behind the front uprights. Three are needed to make the slots on both sides of the middle divider.

This standard bin is usually called a New Zealand Box because it was invented in that country. It does have drawbacks. First, wood is increasingly expensive and the many hardboard, chipboard and plywood substitutes are neither weatherproof nor strong enough for compost bins. Secondly, making the bin demands the ability to saw

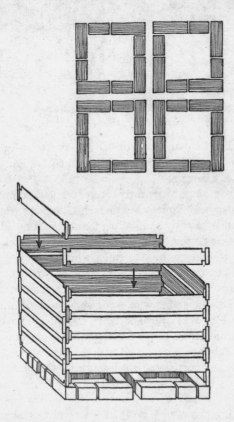

Huker bin with layout for brick air channels

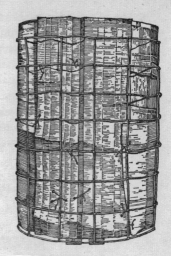

Californian cylinder with layout for brick air channels

straight, hammer hard and use a drill. But with second-hand timber available and carpentering ability even at a fairly low level, the New Zealand Box is a bargain.

Those without skill in carpentry can make the Californian Composter, invented by a Captain Macdonald, U.S. Navy (retired). To make one composter, buy a roll of pig fencing 14 ft by 4 ft. This is extra strong wire netting with large square meshes. Hook each end of one piece together to make a stout cylinder 4 ft high. Line it with opened-out cardboard cartons, stout brown paper such as cattle feed bags, or four or five thicknesses of a good quality newspaper, sewn firmly together with string and a packing needle.

This type of bin is of course portable, and though the lining will need renewing at intervals, the fencing will last longer if its rather poor quality galvanizing is coated with a black bitumen paint, as used for protecting corrugated iron from rust in the open.

Filling a Compost Bin

Start by setting two double rows of bricks or brick-ends on the ground inside each compartment, 2 in. apart and 2 ft between pairs, running from back to front where the last bricks protrude under the bottom planks of the loose fronts. Cover these with coarse and stemmy material, such as hedge clippings, cabbage stumps smashed with an axe back, or the undecayed surface of an earlier heap. These will prevent lawn mowings and soft weeds from blocking the air channels.

Then add 8 in. of garden rubbish, excluding prunings and woody material, but including kitchen wastes, with not more than 10 per cent of well-wetted paper and nothing metal, plastic or bone. Woollen rags are excellent, cotton will rot in time, but exclude nylon or any other man-made fibre. If large quantities of mowings are available, do not use them in bulk but mix them with other material, even going out to cut weeds on wasteland if necessary.

On the surface of this layer spread your manure, which is far better value used as an activator than dug in. Any manure will do (preferably fresh), even the cleanings from a parrot's cage – in fact, the best of all is pigeon manure. It should be spread in a layer $\frac{1}{2}$-in. thick. The manure section later in this chapter (pp. 33–6) gives full details of what kinds are now available and their advantages and disadvantages.

Pile on another 8 in. of material and scatter enough slaked lime on the surface to whiten it. The object of this is to prevent the heap from becoming too acid for the *Azotobacter* bacteria to enjoy. (A heap of mowings by the side of the lawn will become too hot to put your hand in within a few hours, as a result of the action of several sorts of common fungi whose spores blow everywhere. But it will soon become a cold and slippery mess for lack of air and also because it has become too *acid*, and has thus made bad silage instead of good compost.)

Next add another 8-in. layer of material, more manure, another material layer, lime again, and so on, till the bin is full and the contents cease to sink. Press the layers down lightly as they are added.

Those who have wood-fire ashes can use $\frac{1}{4}$-in. thick layers of these in place of the lime, because wood ashes contain calcium, and several of the chemicals into which their potash is converted are alkaline. Peat ashes are also good. But coal, coke and anthracite ashes are useless and spoil the heap because they consist mainly of silica and alumina, with sulphate compounds and a number of other minerals which can be damaging to plant roots.

The Californian heap is filled in the same way, but can be started with a ring of bricks set hollow side down, and air channels crossing each other in the middle. The cylinder of pig netting stands on top and is lifted off to another site when the compost material stops sinking, indicating that the lower layers have finished decaying. The undecayed upper layers can then start the new heap. In California the heaps are moved all round the garden, so that the drainings from them enrich a different place each time, for with a drier climate it is necessary to hose them thoroughly from the top at intervals. In Britain the water from teapot emptyings, etc., in the compost bucket is usually enough.

Stakes to provide vertical air channels are important where large quantities of lawn mowings can be obtained from parks or sports grounds. Drive three or four stakes, about the thickness of a broomstick, in a line down each air channel inside the bin, then fill the bin up with mowings and as much other material to go with them as possible. When the heap is finished, pull out the stakes, leaving holes to puff steam like your breath on cold mornings. Double the quantity of lime on the layers containing mowings, because they become much more acid.

If you are making compost for the first time, it is a good idea to exclude the roots of weeds such as docks, thistles and couchgrass until you are sure of getting the heap to heat up as it should. Such roots should be freed from soil and spread on wire netting or expanded metal with air space underneath till they dry enough to snap like sticks. They will then break down in the compost heap, though they would not have done so inside clods of clay. Generally speaking they should go in the middle with other material. Cabbage and Brussels sprout stems should be smashed on cement with an axe back. But the roots of clubroot-infested cabbage tribe plants should always be chopped off and dumped in the dustbin, for though blighted potato haulm or rusted groundsel can go safely in the heap because both are killed at $120°$F., which any good heap should hold for days, clubroot spores are tough and tiny. No heap has heat enough to 'cook' through a distorted root perhaps 2 in. thick that may contain 26 per cent of these clubroot spores, each of which can live for nine years in the soil.

Those who complain of woodlice in their heaps have let them become cold and dry. The answer is to turn, and soak with Household Liquid Activator (p. 24), which is always the best tonic for a tired heap.

Activators

There are many proprietary activators, such as Fertosan and Q.R., for those who cannot get organic manures, and a host of chemical makes used by inorganic gardeners. A compost-heap activator is a material containing food for the bacteria and is usually a concentrated organic fertilizer, though a bulky organic manure can also be used. Fishmeal and dried blood will produce excellent heating but are very expensive, and so is seaweed meal. The best way to use the latter is in the proportions of 25 per cent added to 75 per cent of dried sewage sludge, the mixture being scattered at the rate of 4 oz. per sq. yd on each layer of compost material, as both the seaweed and the sludge contain calcium. This produces rapid heating, for the seaweed acts as a very impure version of the agar jelly used for bacterial cultures in hospitals, and makes the bacteria multiply while the nitrogen and phosphorus in the sludge give them plenty of food very quickly.

When I am making a compost heap I start it exactly as described, but with a bottom coarse rubbish layer about 1 ft thick. I pile my material outside the heap where my inorganic neighbours also dump theirs. Every morning I empty the compost bucket from under the sink on to my heap and cover the kitchen wastes with several good forkfuls of garden rubbish. The kitchen contribution includes potato peelings, eggshells, tea leaves, dandelion coffee grounds, fruit peel, apple cores and everything that will decay except vacuum cleaner dust. This used to be widely recommended, but today even blanket fluff, which used to be wool, is mainly man-made fibre, and so much lead from petrol blows or treads into modern houses that this dust can contain as much as 500 parts per million. There is no point in adding extra pollution to your soil for such a small gain in material.

Line the compost bucket with *newspaper*, because the ink is made mainly from carbon black and paraffin and is only about 12 p.p.m. lead. Do not use colour supplements and magazines because these can contain up to 4,000 p.p.m. lead in yellow and red inks. The glazed paper, too, does not rot down well, and the reason for limiting the paper to 10 per cent is to prevent nitrogen robbery.

The activator costs nothing, and is available to everyone. After forking on the compost material I pour a bucketful of what is tactfully called Household Liquid Activator over it. This is a mixture of 1 part urine to about 3 parts of water. Organizing one's family affairs to provide this useful mixture has more advantages than cash saving and simplicity. Like all mammals we pass the surplus potash from our bodies in our urine, and this is why there is only a trace of this vital plant food in sewage sludge. It has all gone down to the sea in the effluent, where it grows algae no one wants on its way through our polluted rivers.

Our bodies need relatively little potassium compared with the quantity that there is in our food, and this should be returned quickly and naturally to the soil from our livestock and ourselves, so that the same potassium molecules are used over and over again. If we continue to drain it all away to the sea, our soils will run out of available potassium, just as the Chinese soils would have done had the Chinese invented water sanitation instead of composting, more than four thousand years ago.

Because the carbon-nitrogen ratio is high enough, the use of diluted urine on compost heaps involves no smell from ammonia wasted into the air, and the form in which the nitrogen is present favours some remarkably good cellulose-breaking-down bacteria, while conditions in a compost heap are unfavourable to the bacteria concerned with human disease. The contents of bucket lavatories can also be used as compost activators, covering each addition with plenty of vegetable waste, for Elsan fluid is an excellent disinfectant; it does no harm in the heap because it consists mainly of phenols and there is a special type of soil bacteria that breaks these down harmlessly.

Managing a Compost Heap

Those who are interested can buy a hot-bed thermometer, as used by mushroom growers. With this, they trace the progress of their heaps from the headlong rush to heat up, sometimes to over 180°F., which is the temperature used in electric soil sterilization, in the first ten days, and then down to air temperature in three to four weeks. For the best quality compost and a quick finish so that the spring heap is ready for use before midsummer, shovel it out of the bin after this first heating and cooling and back again after replacing the cleared air channel bricks, and perhaps adding something readily decayed like some more lawn mowings.

This will produce a far better breakdown, because all the un-rotted material from the edges is mixed into the middle, and a new air supply brings back the fast-working bacteria to do the work instead of leaving it to the slow fungi that need no air. By turning, it is possible to put at least two charges (complete fillings), perhaps three, through the compost bin if you have enough material. How-ever, a heap made in the autumn, say October, with the results of a garden clean-up, will take till March or April before it is ready to use, because decay is always slowest in winter. Its quality will be improved by turning it during February. Many gardeners never turn, for, with a good bin to keep the drying winds off, compost can heat right up to the sides; furthermore, if your problem is quantity of material you may not have enough for more than two charges a year.

Covering

It is sometimes suggested that a heap should be covered with soil like a potato clamp, but this involves hard spading and gives little gain in heat insulation and water exclusion. The best covering is a square of old carpet cut to fit the top of the heap, nailed along the back of the bin with roofing felt nails, and to a stake on its front edge so that it can hang over the front and be rolled up when new material is added. Heaps can also be covered with plastic sheeting, but generally the steam from the heating condenses on the underside and makes the heap too wet. Where heaps are too dry, use a polythene sheet for a few days, otherwise use carpet into which the water will soak and dry away from the top, and which holds in the heat so that higher temperatures can be achieved.

Fitting raised uprights to those at the front of the bin, and nailing a cross-piece along their tops, makes it possible to rig up a corrugated iron roof sloping to the back, to keep off winter rain. My own first heap was built like a lean-to shed, and rather dominated my garden, but it was a lovely bin and cats used to sleep on top of it, enjoying the warmth when turned out on winter nights.

OTHER COMPOSTING SYSTEMS

Brian Furner Heap

The simplest composting system of all is the Brian Furner, named after its inventor. Pile your garden rubbish in a long stack up to 5 ft high and as much wide. Cover it completely with 500-gauge black polythene sheeting, and let it heat up naturally without any activator, air supply or turning. It will heat as a result of the fungal action best known in lawn mowings, condensing the moisture in the cold hours of the night and early morning, and using up what heat energy it has in constantly recycling the water.

This process breaks down compost heap material amazingly well, but because it cannot heat up enough to kill weed roots and seeds, these should be excluded, and so should kitchen wastes because of the rat risk.

A Brian Furner is a cheap and easy way of dealing with a large quantity of rubbish, and if the heap is made with air channels beneath it and a normal activator, but covered with polythene to keep off the wind and rain, good compost can be achieved, especially if it is turned in the spring. Large, thick polythene sheets, of the type used by builders to cover up the hole in the roof when they go off for a long weekend, are now nearly as expensive as the wood needed to build a New Zealand Box, so the best cheap way round this is to cut open the polythene fertilizer bags found on every modern farm and stitch them together with a trigger stapler to make a 'patchwork quilt' large enough to cover the heap. If it is possible to obtain a discarded carpet and use it whole, this will produce even better compost if it is large enough to weight down against wind. The best carpets for this purpose are the modern nylon ones, which cling to dust and dirt by electrostatic action, but wear almost indefinitely, perhaps longer and better as compost heap covers than on floors.

Proprietary Compost Containers

There are now many proprietary compost containers. One of the first of these was the Rotol, which is a fluted cone with the top cut off and replaced with a lid, about the size of a plastic dustbin. It is filled from the top with garden rubbish and kitchen wastes, and can run without air or an activator, though many gardeners stand it on a brick base with crossing air channels like the Californian Composter. It heats up like a Brian Furner heap, on fungi, but the condensation runs down the flutings and keeps the moisture to the sides to that it can achieve high temperatures in the middle.

Because the process is anaerobic (without air), the heap can get so acid that inside the bin there will be found thousands of vinegar flies – these are quite harmless. When the compost ceases to sink, move it like the Californian type to a new site, starting it off with the undecayed upper portion. This kind of container, and others like the Rotocrop, are ideal for those without carpentry skills, and for small gardens, because they will swallow large quantities of refuse tidily and without trouble, but the compost quality is not as good as from the traditional hand-made heap. On the other hand, so many people make bad compost that their ease, good breakdown, and simplicity make them of value to beginners and reluctant gardeners.

The worst of the ready-made compost bins is the 'rat trap', like the old-fashioned wire cage type, which keeps the compost tidy, but exposes it to all the winds that blow. These are better used as incinerators than compost containers, though they could be used for drying out weed roots. They can be lined with cardboard or paper to keep the heat in, but are much more expensive than the Californian Composter. When choosing a container, buy only a make that has been on the market a long time and is still selling, like the Huker, which is a New Zealand Box made of seasoned elm, built up with interlocking corners so that it travels as a bundle of sturdy slats that fit together and avoids some rail charges. This was the first compost bin to be rated a 'best buy' by *Which?*.

LEAFMOULD

Making Leafmould

Dead leaves should be stacked to rot separately, and never included in a compost heap because they do not have the carbohydrates with which to heat it. These have almost all been returned to store in the twigs to make next year's leaves, together with most of the minerals. What is left consists mainly of hemi-celluloses and lignins, and provides lasting humus in the soil. It lasts because the plant foods and energy material are locked up by tannins, so that it stays in the soil, providing the moisture-retaining and soil-crumb-separating effect for the longest period. In terms of fuel for the soil it is like a petrol pump that will only sell half gallons at a time.

In the past, head gardeners would *buy* only beech and oak leaf-mould, because these contained the most tannins and therefore gave the longest lasting humus in borders, potting soils and kitchen gardens. If it was a case of using their own, they made it from every tree in the garden, when leafmould provided the humus to go with stable manure, and valued it because it also provided plant foods in slowly released form.

Burning leaves is a shocking waste in any garden, and because councils are the worst wasters of all, it is sometimes possible, either by direct arrangement with the road man, or by writing to your town hall, to get loads of street-swept leaves delivered. Even if these are

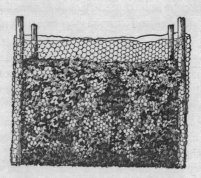

Leafmould enclosure

plane and chestnut, they will still decay to good leafmould with time and good stacking.

Leafmould making is an entirely different process from making compost because it employs only fungi, those which normally break down deep-drifted leaves. So a compost heap made in the autumn from leaves mixed with compost material is an awkward hybrid, for the activator has nothing to work on and the lime layers are difficult for the fungi to deal with. Compost takes at most six months to make, while leafmould needs two years to decay, and three in the case of chestnut or plane leaves.

Level the site for the leafmould heap, which can be done in deep shade under trees, drive in stout, well-creosoted posts at the corners and intermediate ones every 4 ft if your heap is a large one, and staple $1\frac{1}{2}$-in. mesh wire netting round it. The object of the enclosure is to prevent the leaves blowing round the garden and keep them in a solid and tidy block, so that they all decay together as if they were deep drifted in a forest, not merely thinly spread under trees in parkland. By the second autumn the heap will be firm enough for the stakes to be moved for the next leaf harvest. It will have consolidated sufficiently not to disintegrate without support.

Remove any dead branches or cigarette packets if your leaves are street-swept, and pile the leaves high, treading them as you go, unlike compost heap making, until the enclosure is full. If the summer is hot and dry, it pays to soak the heap with the hose, but otherwise it needs no attention, only time to decay. Five cubic yards of stacked leaves will make two of solid humus in about two years, ready to chop down with a spade for use wherever lasting humus is required.

Using Leafmould

On sandy soils where it can be dug in, leafmould made one autumn can be dug in the next, together with lime at 4–8 oz. a square yard to help the roots break down some of its organic matter for plant foods. Garden compost is still necessary, for it is far richer in plant foods, but leafmould makes the compost go much further. Its great value is that, for the cost of thinking ahead, one can have sufficient humus to dig in generously enough to make a real difference to sands, chalky soils or heavy clays. A barrowload to 2 square yards is not too much for any garden.

Almost any large garden which has had a gardener is likely to have piles of good leafmould, unused, which should be dug in generously. This vintage leafmould breaks down very small, and so is ideal for mixing in potting soil in place of peat, and as a surface mulch for strawberries.

Perhaps the best forcing system for rhubarb uses leafmould or even fresh-swept leaves. After weeding and clearing up in the autumn surround the rhubarb bed with 1-ft high wire netting made by snipping the 2-ft wide roll (the narrowest now made) down the middle with shears and stapling it to short, stout posts at 3-ft intervals. Fill the enclosure with the leaves, packing them in firmly. When the tips of the rhubarb show at the surface, pull away the leaves and gather the welcome, pale and tender stems, which will have a finer flavour than those forced under buckets or drainpipes. The part-rotted leafmould can later be removed and dug in elsewhere during the summer.

Trees feed themselves with humus from their own leaves. This is why foresters do not sell leafmould, and the leaves we sweep from our lawns or from under street trees are an excellent surface food for fruit trees. Drive in stout pegs at the corners of a 4-ft square round the trunk of a tree and staple foot-high netting round them. Then drive in another four stakes to hold a 1-ft wide square round the trunk, and fill up the space between the two with dead leaves or leafmould. The object of the inner square is to keep the leaves away from the trunk, so that the tree will not be tempted to send out roots from above the bulge where it was grafted, which will 'undwarf' it if it is on a modern dwarfing stock. Young trees are usually given this treatment the autumn after planting and the leaves left on for three years more. Old apple trees, or any that are weak or hungry, which shows in small, brightly coloured apples, also appreciate four or five forkfuls of rotted manure put round them before the leaves go on.

The only disease that is carried by dead fruit-tree leaves is apple and pear scab (*Venturia inaequalis*). Use the leaves of *other trees* under your fruit as a precaution. If your trees are growing in small beds in a lawn and you have a rotary grass cutter like a Hayter or Flymo, run this over the leaves as they lie on the grass to break them into fragments small enough to be taken under by the earthworms. To these useful creatures the 95 per cent of the scab spores that overwinter on dead apple and pear leaves are the equivalent of mushrooms on toast. Those who do not have this type of mower should sweep their leaves in the normal way, and tuck them away in the middle of the leafmould heap to rot harmlessly.

Leaves are a tree's weapon against grass, so they must be swept if we are to enjoy lawns under them. Those who have a stately home where leaf sweeping and wheeling is a costly burden can use this mowing trick when most of the leaves have fallen, to save time and help the worms build up humus under the lawn. Most gardeners, however, need all the leaves they can get to make the leafmould that can end their humus shortage. It is a criminal waste to burn the leaves and then buy peat to replace their humus.

Instant Leafmould

Street-tree leaves must be swept and carried to the dump or incinerator at the expense of the ratepayer, so each should demand his share. Those who have new gardens on sandy soil, or have nothing but subsoil left by the builders, can build up humus quickly by spreading a 6-in. coat of raw dead leaves on the surface and hiring a rotavator to turn them under. The machine will chop the leaves small and distribute them through the top foot of soil where, even if they have some decaying left to do, enough air will get to them through the sand to break them down safely by spring.

This kind of service is advertised in local papers and, even though the cost per hour may seem high, the wages demanded by anyone willing and strong enough to dig in those leaves would be far higher. Where the ground is poor, manure will be needed as well, but this will be still more costly. A load of leaves from the council has the advantage of cheapness, so you can pile on plenty.

MODERN MANURE

Every experienced gardener will say that the problem with manure

31

is that you cannot get it, and that if you do find some it is poor stuff and costs a great deal. This is, broadly speaking, true, for farming systems change and it is impractical nostalgia to talk of 'well-rotted stable manure' as though London were still full of hansom cabs.

The dung from broiler calf houses, cowtels, barley beef units, sweatbox piggeries, broiler houses and laying batteries is an unwanted by-product which is fertility degraded to pollution. It is usually washed by high pressure water jets from under the slatted floors on which pigs and cattle stand in these agricultural production lines, and becomes a slurry which farmers may pay large sums to have treated at the local sewage works – they are rightly and heavily fined if they discharge it into a river and reduce this to a stinking Styx. Slurry cannot, of course, be used by gardeners, for it can only be delivered by large road tankers and the smell, apart from the complications of spreading a manure which consists of about 95 per cent water, would infuriate neighbours.

Battery poultry manure is now dried and mixed into compound feeds for cattle and pigs, which is safer than it sounds because the heat destroys both bacteria and antibiotics. Drying is another way round the manure disposal problem of the agricultural production lines, which process into factory farm products the fishmeal and soya beans that could feed the protein-starved children of hungrier countries. Hot air is blown through the dung, which contains no straw to provide a bulk of humus, so that it can be ground, bagged and sold. There are many of these proprietary organic manures on the market, clean, dry and odourless because so much nitrogen has gone up the chimney of the drier, but they remain very expensive sources of the plant foods and humus they contain.

There is, however, the advantage that a 56-lb. bag is more easily wheeled into a suburban garden than 5 tons of old-fashioned steaming, strawy manure shot on to the pavement. These bags are likely to contain the organo-chlorine compounds used to control ticks, flies and other pests on the factory farms. The drying process will have concentrated them so, before buying any of these dried manures, ask the makers for a pesticide analysis, especially of lindane, aldrin and dieldrin and their breakdown products.

Manure dealers still exist and they may have bargains, provided their suppliers are still using old-fashioned methods, but organic farmers no more sell manure off the farm than their grandfathers did – it is too valuable on the land where it belongs. The risk is that manure from cowtels, where dairy cattle live without ever setting foot in a field, will have been stacked with only enough straw so that it can be stacked on a lorry with a foreloader. It then becomes something like manure silage when dug in, and can stay undecayed right through a winter and spring.

Choice of Manure

Straw-based Deep-litter

The best buy is straw-based deep-litter compost from poultry. Poultry urine is the dab of white on the dropping, and this contains ammonium carbonate which feeds *Hutchinson's spirogaete*, a powerful bacteria which breaks down cellulose and produces the heat to dry the poultry manure and keep the chickens warm. This is a composting process, and if the houses were not kept well ventilated the birds would be suffocated by the carbon dioxide from the bacterial bonfire.

The plant foods in the straw are added to those in the manure, and the ammonium carbonate, which is what makes raw poultry manure 'fierce', is used up breaking the straw down to humus. Good deep-litter is always dry, and the drier the manure the less water you pay to transport and the more plant foods on the load for your money. Allow about one 2-gallon bucketful a square yard, which is roughly 30 tons an acre, and dig it under in the autumn or spring. It is already composted, so you can use it as it comes.

Wood Shavings and Sawdust Deep-litter

Wood shavings are often used for deep-litter, especially for broilers rather than laying hens. Their drawback is that the woodwork factories that supply the shavings use extractor fans, which suck up small ends of wood and a great many chips from mortice joints. Though the bacteria can break down sawdust, and shavings up to blotting paper thickness, these larger fragments stay unrotted. If they are dug under the bacteria will go on trying to break them down, causing nitrogen robbery that may mean infertile areas lasting for years.

Shavings and sawdust have C:N ratios of about 500:1 (see pp. 16–17). This is a long way from the 10:1 of compost with which this chapter began – even if the sawdust is rotted as brown as coffee it will still be near 180:1. However, if there is a pile of deep-litter stacked and going cheap it is worth having the test for C:N ratio done (this is known as a Black and Wakeley test). Ask for one 'excluding lignins', because these do not steal nitrogen, and also for an organo-chlorine-compound test if you are worried about pesticides. (The address of an analyst for this is given in the Appendix, and because this test is quite expensive, it is only worth having for a big load.) If the C:N ratio is satisfactory this type of litter can be used, digging it in as soon as obtained.

Mushroom Compost

The easiest manure to buy is spent mushroom compost, which usually consists of wheat straw, dried blood, horse manure and ground chalk all composted together. The heat from the composting has gone to warm the mushrooms, so the straw is well broken down. The mixture looks like well-rotted manure, and can be used at once. Though the mushrooms will have taken most of the nitrogen, it is good humus and many organic farmers, including Arthur Hollins of Fordhall Farm fame, have built up their starting stock by taking the whole output of a mushroom farm. Many mushroom farmers use organo-chlorine compounds against fungus gnats (others use safe derris and pyrethrum), so those who wish to keep their soils pesticide-free can send samples to the analyst mentioned to make sure.

If ground chalk has been used in mushroom compost, it is of value because it limes the soil, but it can also be a problem. A 56-lb. bag of slaked lime has perhaps half a square mile of surface area in all the countless millions of tiny grains, so it is available quickly and easily spread through the soil. Mushroom compost may contain the chalk in large lumps with very little surface area which can break down slowly, yielding too much lime in their immediate area. So insist on seeing a sample and watch for lumps – the smaller they are the better. Because soils need only enough lime to keep them neutral (see pp. 49–50), you must be careful about using mushroom compost year after year, for this can mean too much. Some mushroom growers use gypsum in the compost, and as it has a neutral reaction, there is no difficulty with the alkali in it.

Horse Manure

The best real manure you can buy is from the increasing number of riding schools, stud farms and pony owners all over Britain. The large stable or stud farm usually has a contract with a mushroom farmer, but individual horse owners and small establishments will often have some to spare, which they are glad to get rid of, while they buy peat and chemicals. Sometimes a dealer knows of a load, but a local paper advertisement will generally locate anything in your area.

Horse manure is usually available when you do not need it, but snatch what is offered and hoard it as gardeners did in the past, when every car was a carriage and pair, and every lorry a dray. The ideal site for a manure stack is against a 6-ft high wall, with a cement base sloping back towards the wall. Pile up the manure, which should have as much straw in it as possible, against the wall, treading it firmly, because the aim is to *exclude* air to prevent heating, entirely unlike making a compost heap. If too much air gets in, the white mycelium of a fungus called 'fire fang' develops, which reduces the nitrogen level. If this was found in the past, the remedy was to spread the manure out to cool and to water it with a mixture of 10 gallons of water and 1 lb. of salt until thoroughly moist before re-stacking.

Build the heap into a rough triangle so that it can be protected from the rain by sheets of corrugated iron leaning over it against the wall. If you use polythene you will get the Brian Furner heap effect and make it too wet, and it is as well to see that the corrugated iron does not touch the heap to ensure that any condensation runs all the way down the inside to the bottom. It is better to nail up a wooden framework and build the corrugated iron sheets into a rough lean-to shed so that no plant foods are wasted by being washed out in the rain, and the corrugated iron does not go blowing thunderously round the garden some wet and windy night. After six to nine weeks

35

rotting under a rainproof roof, horse manure or cow dung plus straw in quantity will be ready to dig in. Fresh manure, however, can always be used as a compost activator – there is no need to rot it first.

Pig Manure

If you are lucky and find a friendly farmer who will bring trailer-loads of real, old-fashioned, strawy pig manure with a real old-fashioned smell, you will have the problem of ungrateful neighbours complaining about the ammonia and other volatile gases they are enjoying for nothing. This needs the very reverse of a compost heap, for you are not trying to lower the C:N ratio, which is already low enough, or to gain heat to kill weed seeds. You are merely trying to retain as much of the plant foods and organic matter as possible, without deliberately wasting the excess nitrogen which is annoying your neighbours.

Have a circular pit dug 8 in. deep with the soil stacked round the sides, ready for the arrival of the manure. Stack a layer of this 1 ft thick, then 3 in. of the topsoil, then more manure, then soil and so on in a cone-shaped heap, digging more surface soil from round the heap, if there is not enough. Protect the cone with corrugated iron sheets leaning against it, or with opened-out polythene bags stapled together, because there is not going to be much of a condensation problem.

The topsoil is added to provide another very common bacteria, *Nitrosomas europaeus*, the best denitrifier, which breaks down the ammonia to gaseous nitrogen (which has no smell) and water vapour, a process which supplies its own energy. The action will not waste all the nitrogen, but if you add *lime* layers as if you were making a compost heap, the result will be a release of ammonia and then the neighbours really will complain. In any case, fresh pig manure can be too rich in nitrogen for immediate use on the land, and this mixture of soil and manure will be very rich in plant foods and humus in six to eight weeks.

Seaweed

Although seaweed is not a manure in the same sense as one of the animal manures described in the previous few pages, it does come within the definition of a manure in that it supplies humus and plant foods. The British Isles are fortunate in having a considerable coast-line, from most of which seaweed can be obtained, the best types being the ribbon-like laminarias and the bladder-wracks. These are common and easily obtained from the sea shore.

Seaweed is an extremely valuable source of plant foods, including the vital trace elements, also vitamins, hormones, alginates and other substances useful to plants and to man. It is best used composted and then dug in, though it can be spread on the soil surface while still fresh and wet and then dug in; it is particularly useful on sandy soils. It can also be mixed into the general compost heap.

Compost Activator Manures
Activator manures are the ones which supply food for the bacteria, fungi and other micro-organisms which break down the organic matter of a compost heap.

As the following table shows, these manures fall into two classes: the ordinary manures which are low in nitrogen, and the high nitrogen type, all provided by the small stock likely to be kept by gardeners or self-sufficiency smallholders.

	Nitrogen %	Phosphate %	Potash %
Horse	0.7	0.3	0.6
Cow	0.6	0.2	0.5
Pig	0.5	0.3	0.5
Sheep	0.7	0.3	0.4
Goat	1.44	0.2	1.0
Chicken	1.1	0.8	0.5
Rabbit	2.4	1.4	0.6
Pigeon	5.84	2.1	1.77

Goat manure is perhaps the best general manure of the lot,

because the goat is a browser rather than a grazer (i.e. it feeds on the leaves and shoots of trees and shrubs rather than grass), and its droppings are rich in recycled minerals. Those who keep a goat can either accumulate their manure in store, like horse manure, or use it as the activator layers of their compost heaps. Rabbit manure is also excellent for this, rather better than when dug in because it is low in potassium, but the finest activator manure of all is pigeon droppings. These are so rich in nitrogen that they cannot be dug in without overloading the soil, so pigeon keepers are usually glad to get rid of them. Gardeners who would like a first-class activator manure should look for their nearest pigeon club in the list of local organizations, or write to *The Racing Pigeon*, 19 Doughty Street, London WC1, if there is nothing in their neighbourhood.

Some crops, such as comfrey, will take pigeon manure fresh, but all these manures are better value when used in compost, in layers up to 1 in. thick, by those who are lucky enough not to have to economize. If powdered gypsum can be obtained, this can be scattered at the rate of about 1 oz. to 2 lb. of pigeon manure, or just on the surface of the pile after cleaning out, to stop any smell developing and dry the material to a considerable extent, as well as holding on to the otherwise wasted nitrogen. The main point, however, is to make sure that the pigeon fancier keeps the droppings under cover until they can be fetched in the boot of a car, which will smell the sweeter for the gypsum. Always pack it in polythene bags.

Using Manures and Composts

Composts and manures vary in composition, depending on the weeds and other material that have gone into the heap, and on how much straw was mixed with the manure. The following table gives a rough guide to the balance of plant foods, but does not give the organic matter content, which varies according to the quantity of soil on the weed roots.

As you can see, compost has an analysis like a farmyard manure but is much higher in potassium, so it is better balanced and a richer source of humus. In the different sections on vegetables there are individual directions for manuring, but as a general rule manure should go on in autumn or spring. In the past, a farmer grow-

TABLE OF COMPOST AND MANURE ANALYSIS

	Water %	Nitrogen %	Phosphate %	Potash %
Fresh Strawy Cow Manure	66.17	0.54	0.31	0.67
The same after rotting	75.4	0.59	0.45	0.49
Rothamsted Average F.Y.M.[1]	76.0	0.64	0.23	0.32
Mushroom Compost	53.14	0.80	0.63	0.67
Deep-litter Compost, Straw	50.20	0.80	0.55	0.48
Average Indore Compost[2]	76.00	0.50	0.27	0.81
Comfrey Compost	68.00	0.77	0.29	0.92
Brian Furner Compost	47.8	0.67	0.31	0.50
Household Liquid-Activated Compost	46.29	0.80	0.29	0.41
Compost – Huker Bin	50.6	0.71	0.11	0.30
Compost – Rotol	56.2	0.88	0.22	0.36

1. Rothamsted is an experimental station where research on soils, fertilizers and manures is one of the main projects.
2. This is named after the Indian state of Indore to which Sir Albert Howard was agricultural adviser. It is a particular type of compost made according to his recipe.

ing vegetables would spread 40 tons of manure to an acre, which is about 20 lb., or a good bucketful, a square yard every three years. Gardeners would do this if they could, but usually they have only enough to feed the potatoes and cabbages generously, leaving the less greedy roots and the peas and beans to manage on the left-overs.

Manure and lime should never go on together: there is a risk of a chemical reaction which wastes the nitrogen, and this is at its highest with deep-litter poultry manure. So if your manure is fresh, it had

39

better go on in the autumn, with lime in the spring. Or you can lime in the autumn and dig in well-rotted manure in the spring. Compost can go on at any time, with or without lime, and the more you can use the better.

PEAT AND HOW TO USE IT

It has been established by both organic and inorganic authorities that if you use nothing but chemical fertilizers in any garden, the result will be a disaster. Humus is essential, and now that manure is hard to buy, inorganic gardeners buy sedge peat as a source that is free of weed-seeds, sterile and stocked by every garden shop. It is more or less neutral in reaction so it can be used in any potting soil, just like leafmould, and anyone who is rich enough can use it for supplying humus for sandy soils. The main difference, however, is that, so far as is known, it is an inferior energy provider compared with leafmould.

Peat has been extensively recommended as a 'weed-suppressing mulch'. A standard 1-cwt bale covers an area 20 ft long and 15 ft wide to a depth of 2 in. when it has been chopped small, watered with a rosed can, shovelled about to mix it and then spread over the soil. This will suppress the seedlings of annual weeds (which could be destroyed by hoeing), but not the perennial species like couchgrass, docks and convolvulus. This surface coat or mulch can be used between vegetable rows and slowly builds up humus in the upper layers as the worms take it under.

The no-digging system is based on the use of peat, for few gardeners can make enough entirely weed-seed-free compost. Seeds are sown in the spring on the surface of the soil and then covered with a layer of sedge peat 1 in. thick. Peat is low on plant food minerals, therefore liquid manures are applied extensively through the mulch while plants are growing, and fishmeal mixed with in-organic potash added before sowing. Many gardeners are hotly in favour of this system, while others would rather dig and hoe in the normal way than spend their time hand-weeding, because the blown and otherwise spread seeds germinate very well on the peat surface. There is a constant battle as well with the perennial weeds, unless these have been destroyed by one of the chemical killers. Lawn-mowings are excellent to suppress weeds and provide humus under bush fruits which are not slug-conscious, but as peat has the advantage that it is not eaten by slugs, it is the best surface coat for a strawberry bed. Spread well-soaked and chopped peat to a depth of 2 in. after planting in August or early September, and repeat the dressing the following April. This should keep down the annual weeds. The modern system of rotating the strawberry bed round the garden means that the next crop gains the benefit of the humus from three to four years' peat dressings.

Another use of peat is for storing root vegetables. It is far better than ashes or sand, with the added advantage that after two or three years, or when some damaged roots have rotted unpleasantly and may have left behind a risk of spores, the old peat can be used in the garden, and a fresh quantity bought.

Peat is an expensive substitute for leafmould, which is equally weed-seed-free and, with time enough to decay, could serve all the same purposes. We need a national campaign for greater awareness by councils and their ratepayers of the value of the autumn humus harvest from their street trees.

3 Organic and Inorganic Fertilizers

The fertilizers used by inorganic gardeners are readily soluble, easily washed out of root reach, and as exhaustible as oil. Those which are accepted by the wholefood standards of Britain and the United States, and used by organic gardeners, contain foods in a form that is available much more slowly to the feeding roots of plants and their microscopic helpers in the soil.

Both types of fertilizer have two things in common. They are increasingly expensive because they demand fuel to make and move them, and they grow scarcer and scarcer. As stock feed prices rise, fish-meal for garden use and the residues from extracting vegetable oils, like rape seed meal, come off the market and gardeners must use the fertilizers which are left, which may not necessarily be as good. Why, then, when good compost recycles the massive quantities of plant foods there are in any fertile soil, do we need fertilizers at all ?

We need them because we wish to grow crops that demand plant foods from our soils faster than their roots and their allies can make them available. Every gardener knows that tomatoes are greedy for potash – so are potatoes and gooseberries; strawberries are gluttons for phosphate. In Britain we do not have any soils like those in New Zealand from which phosphorus is almost totally absent; many of ours do, however, lack lime. But we should always try to use organic methods of supplying nutrients such as potash, phosphate and lime to our plants, since it is important to humanity as a whole that we and other similarly placed countries should leave the inorganic fertilizer reserves to countries which are unable to obtain bulky humus-containing manures, or which lack organic sources of plant foods.

SLOW-ACTING ORGANIC FERTILIZERS

The best source of lasting phosphate is *bonemeal*, an ideal dressing for a strawberry bed, spread at the rate of 1 lb. a square yard on a poor, quick-draining or shallow soil, or 8 oz. on a fertile clay. This is expensive, but it will be available over the whole four-year life of the bed, and there will be some left over for the crops that follow. The grade now available is what used to be called steamed bone flour, and because it is finely ground it is available quickly. *Coarse* bone-meal consists of bone chips about $\frac{1}{8}$-in. across. This is much slower acting and ideal for fruit trees. Though bonemeal is a good supplier of phosphorus for organic gardeners, it is nonetheless expensive, and inferior in balance and energy supply to good, well-rotted farm manure or compost.

Hoof and horn meal is even more expensive, because so many cattle are dehorned nowadays, and today's supply of hoof from riding stables cannot compare with the days when beer was delivered by gentle giants in leather aprons driving four hairy-legged horses that smelled of new buns. It contains up to 13 per cent nitrogen, and an application in winter or spring will be just starting to release it by July. The supply should then last through the following spring and summer.

Leather dust contains about 9 per cent nitrogen, and though it is hard to find today, it is an even better bargain, because the tannin hangs on to the nitrogen just as it will to that of tea-leaves. *Tea-leaves* are rather richer in nitrogen than poultry manure, containing about 4 per cent nitrogen and 2 per cent each of potash and phosphate, but all firmly locked up. Those who know they are going to plant fruit on a chalky soil should dig the holes well ahead and accumulate as much as 6 in. of tea leaves on the bottom. The best source is a café; in tea bags there is so little cellulose that it is not worth bothering about. On non-chalky soils, scatter lime on the tea-leaves to help the release, as much as 1 lb. a hole.

Feathers are another source of nitrogen, containing 15 per cent. They are excellent for all bush fruit. Dig a trench 12 or 15 in. deep and 12 in. wide along the rows, and fill up with 3–4 in. depth of trodden feathers. Sometimes feathers can be obtained from poultry farms, but at present most broiler establishments sell their feathers for treatment with high pressure steam, and for grinding for use in cattle cake. The real bargains here are old pillows and eiderdowns, which can be found on refuse dumps or bought cheaply in second-hand furniture shops. These contain first-class feathers to tread along the trenches, but beware of fillings of coconut fibre or man-made fabric wastes.

Shoddy also comes into this class, with 5–14 per cent nitrogen from the genuine wool waste that once stuffed mattresses. These are more likely to be thrown away than pillows, as the latter are now often made of long-lasting foam rubber or expanded polystyrene. If you find an old mattress going begging it will probably have holes in it. Pull out some of the filling and light it; if it frizzles, melts, and burns slowly with a smell like wool, then it is safe. Be sure that the sample of wool you burn *is* in fact real wool, for it could contain nylon. If it burns quickly with a clear flame, it is cotton or coconut fibre which can cause nitrogen robbery, while man-made fibres can produce anything, including black smoke. Shoddy can also sometimes be bought in the North where the wool industry is still centred. It is not only a nitrogen source but a moisture retainer for sandy soils. It is best dug in during the autumn so that it has time to soak during the winter; about 1 lb. a square yard was the traditional quantity ploughed in for rhubarb. There is no danger in using more if you can get it, provided you tuck it well down in the trench bottoms as you dig. Give blackcurrants a start with mattress stuffings and the effect will still show as long as ten years afterwards. Even if shoddy must be bought, it is still the best value for this crop. Blackcurrants need more nitrogen all their lives than they would normally get, and shoddy is their best manure, as it is long-lasting.

Very few sofas are now stuffed with *horsehair*, and what there is goes mainly for making plaster, but both horse and goat hair are excellent nitrogen sources, while many a barber has won prizes at village vegetable shows from the slow fertility added every time he sweeps out the shop.

FAST-ACTING ORGANIC FERTILIZERS

The best all-round organic general fertilizer is *seaweed meal*, which contains about 2 per cent each of nitrogen and potash, and a bare 0.3 per cent of phosphorus, which is an excellent balance of plant foods. It is also rich in a range of trace elements, and is therefore in demand as the best source of these in cattle and pig food. Seaweed meal is usually applied at the rate of 4 oz. a square yard as a general garden fertilizer, but it should always be dug in rather than left on the surface, because it contains quantities of sodium alginate which becomes a sticky jelly when wet. Seaweed preparations used as soil conditioners have the same disadvantage and should also be dug in.

Some writers advocate *fishmeal* as a general organic garden fertilizer, but it suffers from the same disadvantage as seaweed meal – it is used for pig and poultry food by factory farmers, and the price of even the cheapest grades is now far more than it is worth in the garden. Originally it consisted of about 9 per cent nitrogen and 7.70 per cent phosphorus, with a useful 17 per cent of calcium, but no potassium at all. Today this is added as chemical fertilizer, usually as potassium chloride (muriate of potash), either 5 or 10 per cent, but the original can still sometimes be bought, and should be used at the rate of 2–4 oz. a square yard. Like seaweed meal, fishmeal should be dug in – birds can eat it. It should go on in the spring when the crops can take it quickly. In the autumn it may go mouldy if left on the surface.

The chemical potassium chloride is used in compound potato fertilizers, and however 'organic' you may feel this fishmeal is, potatoes grown with it will have a chemical taste, as well as the wateriness and blackening common to inorganically grown potatoes.

Meat and bone meal, which contains more phosphorus, up to 16 per cent, slowly released, and 4 per cent nitrogen, is a better buy, because its calcium phosphate lasts in the soil after the nitrogen has been absorbed. It is a good tonic for an ageing strawberry bed at the rate of 8 oz. a square yard, or it can be used for crops generally at half this rate.

The quickest-acting organic fertilizer is *dried blood*, which can contain as much as 10 per cent nitrogen, though very little else. It is a tonic for tired lettuces, but even more expensive than fishmeal, because its nitrogen is in the form of protein. It should never go on later than September because it will have wasted by the spring, and can go mouldy like meat and bone meal.

Very few organically grown vegetables should need tonics, any more than organically fed people need them. Though crops may start away more slowly in the spring because they must wait for bacterial action to make nitrogen available, and all soil bacteria 'work to rule' till soils warm up to 50°F., they catch up as the year turns. It is expensive to hurry Nature, and not always wise.

Far too many organic gardeners think inorganically, and feel that they must keep paying in potash, phosphates and nitrogen to make the account book of the soil balance up at the end of the month. The best test of a soil is its crops, and so long as it goes on producing good food, it is all right. Some gardeners over-feed their soils with organic fertilizers and merely buy themselves troubles, just as some people can stuff their pets (or themselves) into ill health.

Dried sewage sludge is becoming increasingly hard to obtain in the 10–20 per cent moisture grades – these consist of odourless dark grey powders, and make excellent lawn fertilizers or compost heap activators. Because they have been dried by heat, dried sewage sludges also lose the greater part of their nitrogen up the chimney of the drier. However, the rest, which can be as high as 3 per cent, is locked into more slowly released forms than is found in the liquid distributed by tankers on farm land.

All lawns are a valuable source of good cheap mulch and compost material, but grass and weeds are relatively shallow rooting and, if you go on mowing with the grass box attached to the mower and empty the contents on to your compost heap or between the raspberry canes year after year, you will need to feed the lawn. Dried sludge, which can contain 5 per cent phosphorus as well as nitrogen, is a well-balanced lawn food, and many large football clubs buy it by the 40-ton railway truck-load. Golf clubs, tennis clubs and sports grounds of all kinds follow the advice of the Sports Turf Research Institute at Bingley, Yorkshire, and spread $\frac{1}{2}$ lb. a square yard on the grass in March, and another $\frac{1}{2}$ lb. on sandy soils in June or July.

The other garden use for sludge is as a compost heap activator mixed with 25 per cent of seaweed meal, which makes this expensive material go further and produces better heating than either material will used alone.

THE BORDERLINE FERTILIZERS

In the past every gardener used *soot*, but today sweeps are cleaner and take the soot away with them, probably for sale to add to something quite unexpected. Soot is a mixture of unburnt carbon, tars, and very impure sulphate of ammonia. Though it can be valuable to darken soils in the spring so that more sun heat is absorbed, its plant food value is very much less than a chemical fertilizer, and this fact, together with its impurities, makes it unpopular with the inorganic school who would do far better to use their chemicals pure.

Wood ashes are the organic gardener's traditional source of potassium, but they were in fact the first of all chemical fertilizers. When we burn wood we convert its potassium, phosphorus, calcium and some other minerals into oxides and carbonates, and throw away the energy and nitrogen. When an old tree falls in a forest, the fungi and the boring beetles, termites and other wood eaters recycle the minerals but *in their original forms*. This is why the primitive gardening system of burning the forest, growing crops for two years and then moving on to another patch needs about 37 acres for every individual fed. The protein supply is obtained from trapping and shooting game in the 35 acres of recovering forest that goes with every 2-acre patch, and the system is the only one so far discovered that will grow food continuously on poor tropical forest land. If the population increases, the rotation must be quicker, but then the result is in fact disaster, for the trees do not have time to replace the minerals washed away in the rains.

In Britain we do not have enough room for this system. We have small gardens, and our concern is to get the best value out of the woody rubbish that will not break down on the compost heap. *Thin* winter apple and pear prunings (soft tips of summer ones and the summer prunings of stone fruit *will* compost), bush fruit prunings, especially fruited raspberry canes, rose prunings and hedge clippings, especially yew and holly, and small clippings of privet or *Lonicera nitida* will all eventually rot in an ordinary compost heap. But any shoots about the thickness of a pencil or more will not break down. Ideally, this material should go through a compost shredder, but one good enough to convert these, together with semi-hard material such as cabbage stumps, to easily composted, chewed-up fibre is far more expensive than any gardener can afford for a mechanized tool that is only used occasionally. The best use for this uncompostable material is to burn it, hoarding it up until there is enough for a good blaze that will burn right out, leaving a pile of white ashes to shovel into a metal dustbin and keep covered until required. Twigs are very much higher in potassium content than trunk wood, so your small bonfire will leave far richer ashes than a flaring one of planks from an old tarred fence; paper contains very little potassium because it is made from conifer trunk wood. The finest wood ash is obtained from apple tree prunings, which can contain 40 per cent potassium oxide and carbonate, 20 per cent calcium oxide, 15 per cent sodium chloride, 6 per cent phosphates and 19 per cent silica. If you burn weeds with soil on the roots, the result will be red burnt earth, which is mainly silica and alumina, and about as useful as brick dust.

Though some gardeners use wood ashes as a source of quickly available potassium and sodium chloride (common salt) at the rate of 8 oz. a square yard for onions and beetroot, the best way to use them is in fact in the compost heap. Scatter them in place of the lime layers, for their calcium oxide will do just as well, and the potassium will be combined in various organic forms. If you have quantities of wood or peat ashes from domestic fires, the amounts can be increased to 2 lb. a square yard of compost heap surface, but not more, because there can be chemical complications. Manure layers are still required, however, because wood ash is not an activator. Keep the heap covered with carpet so that the potassium is not washed out by rain.

Kainit is regarded as organic by some authorities (depending on their knowledge of agricultural chemistry), and it is a good example of drawing the line between organic and inorganic. Kainit is 'salt' from a sea that dried up in the geological past and became the Stassfurt deposits in Germany, which average 59 per cent common salt, 26 per cent potassium chloride, 4 per cent magnesium chloride and sulphate, and some silica and alumina. It is still used as a fertilizer for sugar-beet, which is derived like all beet from *Beta maritima*, a seashore plant, which enjoys salt. Because kainit (named from the

Greek *kainos* or 'new' as it was in the 1840s) is usually dug and ground, it is regarded as 'natural' or organic.

The Dead Sea is also drying up, and in Israel the water, which is so full of salt that it supports swimmers like water-wings, is pumped out and sorted by crystallization, so that the potassium chloride, or muriate of potash as farmers call it, is regarded as inorganic if coming from Israel, but organic if coming from Germany. Yet both contain the same chemical, and either will give potatoes the same chemical flavour. Kainit, therefore, should be regarded as an artificial or inorganic fertilizer, especially as it can cause complications in the soil.

SOIL SWEETENERS

Lime

Lime has two functions. It supplies calcium which all plants need. It also corrects an over-acid soil.

Slaked lime, or 'garden lime' (calcium oxide), is easily bought in any garden shop, and is of value not so much to supply calcium as to keep the soil balanced between acid and alkaline-reacting, which is what most crops require. The simple type of soil-testing kit used to measure the need for lime is both cheap and useful. It consists of a kind of liquid litmus paper and a small china or plastic container to hold a soil sample. The liquid is poured on to the soil and the resultant change in its colour is matched with a colour on the chart supplied, which will show how much slaked lime will be needed, depending on the degree of acidity and which crops are to be grown. Garden soils do not live on a knife edge, especially when they are well supplied with humus, and the aim should be to keep the soil between pH 5.9 and pH 7.0, the lower figure being preferred by potatoes, strawberries and raspberries, which like an acid soil, and the higher by beet, broccoli and cauliflowers, which enjoy an alkaline one.

Slaked lime is readily available, and is therefore ideal in compost heaps and on clay soils, but *ground limestone*, usually known as limestone flour (calcium carbonate) is better on sands because it will not wash through so quickly. One good dressing of the latter will last five years, which is why it is a favourite on the farm, but it is not suitable for compost heaps. Usual dressings are 8 oz. a square yard on sandy soils and 4 oz. for slaked lime on clays, but the quantities will depend on the results of your soil test.

There are now a number of brands of ground *Lithothamnus seaweed*, dredged up off the French coast, which contain about 48 per cent calcium and 4.5 per cent magnesium, but though these are as 'organic' as coral or oyster shells, there is no extra value in them to justify the high price. *Oyster shell* as used for chicken grit is excellent to provide slowly released calcium for gardeners, because the coarser grades of ground limestone are sold only by the ton to farmers. But remember that chalky gardens want none, and clay soils also have calcium enough to need no extra supply.

Gypsum

Both wood ashes and kainit contain common salt, and when this is used on a clay soil, it can produce the same kind of permanent stickiness that is found in sea-soaked land, or where nitrate of soda (or sodium nitrate) has been used for a long period. There is an exchange of sodium with the calcium in the clay molecules, which is a disaster for the soil structure. Britain first saw this effect in the reign of Henry VIII, when the needs of potassium-demanding hops were supplied with ashes from wood-burning London. The answer to this stickiness, from Roman experience, was ground gypsum (calcium sulphate) at the rate of 4–8 oz. a square yard, which was just as effective when used after the sea broke in and flooded Essex and Suffolk farm land in 1952.

It is possible that some extra sticky clays may be the result of wood ashes, kainit or nitrate of soda being used in the past, and where this hydrated sulphate of calcium (i.e. gypsum) can be obtained, the Roman recipe is worth trying. It used to be recommended for old kitchen gardens that had been over-manured for many years, a highly unlikely situation today. Gypsum is mined in Derbyshire.

Ground Minerals

The basic difference between ground minerals and inorganic fertilizers is that the former will not be washed away quickly through the soil. Though the minerals need power to grind them, they are simply a more generous supply of the fine particles of plant foods that the roots and their helpers have evolved to use. There is no point, however, in spending money for grinding, packaging, transport and profits to add a little more of what is already in your soil, unless you are certain that there is a total lack of something. Chapter 15 gives a description of deficiency symptoms (often mistaken for plant diseases). Ground minerals are the best way to correct serious shortages, and need to be used perhaps once in ten years or even less frequently. Those who use inorganic fertilizers instead have to use them almost every year to by-pass the normal feeding system.

Ground rock phosphate is allowed by wholefood standards, because it stays. Superphosphate is not, because it is soluble and washes away. Basic slag is a borderline case. The original blast-furnace linings, which constitute basic slag, held about 15 per cent phosphorus and 40 per cent calcium, which made them an excellent fertilizer for growing clover on Welsh and Scottish hillsides depleted of calcium and phosphorus by centuries of sheep farming; modern methods make more and better steel, but worse slag. The composition of slag varies with the ore that is being smelted, and some can be as low as 5 per cent in phosphates as well as there being a risk from toxic metal content. If phosphorus is short, buy rock phosphate, which will be expensive but can contain 20 per cent or more of what you want. Bonemeal is easier to buy and better value still.

In America and on the Continent, organic gardeners buy ground potassium-containing rocks, but in Britain we do not have deposits of the richest types, while the weight and hardness of the granites and felspars mean heavy transport and grinding costs. The iron and potassium silicate called glauconite, known as 'greensand' in the U.S.A., holds 6–7 per cent potassium and about 7.5 per cent magnesium. This is not, however, the geological formation that extends across Surrey and Kent south of the chalk downs, which is in fact a lime-free sand enjoyed by pines and rhododendrons.

There is scope for detailed research on the sources of ground minerals, their rate of release in the soil under various conditions, and their value as supplements to organic methods on deficient soils. But with the scanty knowledge at present available, organic gardeners should be suspicious of all ground minerals and industrial by-products offered as sources of plant foods and trace elements.

4 Green Manure and Compost Crops

Every gardener should know the difference between plants and weeds. Most weeds have seeds designed to germinate over a long period, with perhaps 20 per cent coming up in the first season and the rest giving rise to the old saying, 'One year's weed, seven years seed', by appearing year after year. A green manure crop is one that grows as fast as a weed, retaining the nitrogen the soil bacteria have gathered and bringing more plant foods into circulation, *but* is without the delayed-action seeds that come up among the vegetables next year.

Annual Lupins

Lupins belong to the pea family, the *Leguminosae* or legumes, and so have nitrogen-gathering bacteria in the lumps on their roots. They also have the most effective phosphorus-gathering fungi reaching out from their roots, and this is why they are the favourite green manure for sowing before planting a new strawberry bed. When they are dug in they not only supply nitrogen and humus, but also quickly available phosphorus for the roots of the newly planted strawberries.

The green manure lupin is *Lupinus angustifolius*, with small, slender blue spikes rather like those of a tree lupin. It is also called the Bitter Blue Lupin, because it contains a bitter-tasting alkaloid that rabbits dislike, and which makes the large seeds distasteful to birds. Sow them singly in dibber- or finger-made holes 1 in. deep, 6 in. apart, with 1 ft between the rows, between the first week in April and the first in August. This gives time for two crops in the same season. They are ready to dig under when the flower buds can be seen but are not showing blue, because if they are left longer the fibres that grow to support the seed pods can be the cause of nitrogen robbery. An ounce of lupin seed should sow 70 ft of row.

The wide spacing makes it easy to hoe off the seedling weeds as soon as the lupins show, and they will not be too tall for a second hoeing. The April sowing can be left to grow up to 3 ft high, to flower and make fat seed pods; they are ready to gather when they turn grey and split, to keep for next year's green manure. The stems can be cut with shears for compost, and cabbage tribe plants put in without digging to take advantage of the firm soil and a share of the plant foods. The greatest advantage can be had from cutting the lupins in early July and planting Brussels sprouts in the undug ground.

Lupins take about eight weeks from sowing to digging under, and if strawberry plants can be booked for delivery in the first week in September, it is possible to sow another crop of lupins immediately after the July cutting, so that the strawberries can have a double quantity of phosphorus. Another trick with the April sowing is to sow sweet corn in the seedling lupin rows in May and leave them to grow on, enjoying the nitrogen and phosphates when the lupins are cut in July. Sweet corn is also greedy for phosphorus, and shortage shows in purplish streaks on the leaves.

Because lupins are legumes and therefore nitrogen gatherers (see p. 53), they can be dug in and a vegetable crop sown immediately after them, but if they stay in till they have flowered and are stemmy, they should be cut and removed for compost. Sowing and planting can then take place among their stubble. Their roots are better value for nitrogen left in the soil than put on the compost heap.

Winter Tares

The disadvantage of lupins is that they can be grown only in spring and summer, when all small gardens need the room for vegetables. The only time that most gardens have space empty is in winter, and the value of winter tares (*Vicia spp.*) is that they are a legume that will gather nitrogen in this spare time. They are also better at holding down weeds than lupins, which grow up on one tall stem instead of spreading.

Sow the sizeable seeds of the tares 3 in. apart, with 6 in. between ½-in. deep furrows – this ensures that 1 oz. will sow 80 ft of row. Sow them in August or September to grow through the winter, and dig them under in March or April before spring sowing and planting, or sow in March or April to dig under in June or July. It is a good idea to sow alternate rows of lupins and tares and dig them in together, but it makes hoeing to keep weeds down less easy, with rows only 6 in. apart.

Dig in the tares before they flower, unless you wish to leave a row to set tiny, pea-like pods and save your own seed. Tares are good food for goats and rabbits, which is why they should be wired in if there is any rabbit risk.

Grazing Rye

One of the most satisfactory winter-grown green manure crops is Lovaspatoni Grazing Rye. This is sown between August and early October, and dug under in March or April when it is about 2 ft high. It is not a legume, but it is dug in when it is high in protein, and therefore there is no risk of nitrogen robbery. But leave it till the stems develop and the ears look like slender barley, and the result will be a disaster. Rabbits are also fond of rye, so it should be wired in like tares, if they are likely to attack.

Rake the ground level, ideally no later than the end of September, especially in the North, scatter the rye-like grass seed at the rate of 1–2 oz. a square yard and sprinkle on enough fine soil to hide it. Where birds are extra fierce, take out furrows 1 in. deep and 3 in. apart, sowing the seed along each, aiming at a spacing of 1 in., and cover it. This saves seed, but takes longer to produce a very even plot. Either way the rye will be up in about ten days and grow through the winter like a fast lawn, ready to dig in with a sharp spade, tucking well into the trench bottoms.

If you leave some undug, it will come into ear about July and be ready to harvest in late July or August, when the lowest grains are shed from the light brown ears. Cut it with shears and hang it up over newspapers in the shed or garage to dry till the seed can be shaken out ready for sowing. Use the straw and the plants with soil shaken off the roots on the compost heap. Put a nylon net on posts over your seed rye crop, or the birds will clear it as soon as it is ripe.

The old idea that gardens should be left rough dug through the winter 'for the frost to break up the soil' is now debatable and, especially on a sandy soil, the real problem is that plant foods are washed out in wet winters. It is said that the web of roots that a rye plant makes would stretch for half a mile if all were placed end to end, and this is what retains the minerals, and is so useful in quick-draining soils. (Seed obtainable from Henry Doubleday Research Association, Bocking, Braintree, Essex.)

Mustard

The green manure crop that everyone knows is mustard, not the kind that goes with cress, but the agricultural one which is much cheaper. This is sown broadcast, on ground raked level as for rye, at the rate of 1 oz. a square yard. Cover thinly with sifted soil, and it will be up fast, ready to dig in when it looks like slender tomato plants and has buds only just showing. Though it has enough protein at the soft and sappy stage not to cause nitrogen trouble, it has the fatal drawback of belonging to the family *Cruciferae*, the cabbage family, and so being a potential source of spreading clubroot. Therefore it is not a green manure to use year after year, especially as it is only a summer crop and adds no nitrogen to the soil. It is, however, the basis of one of the most effective cures for wireworm on new gardens and allotments, and this special use will be described in the next chapter.

Other Green Manure Crops

The rise in fertilizer prices, especially the nitrogen-supplying kinds that constantly need more costly fuel to make, is increasing the interest in green manuring, even among inorganic gardeners. Work is in progress to find out which clovers and other legumes can be used most effectively on a garden scale, and exactly how much of their expensive seed to sow on square yards rather than acres. Those who are interested should write to the Henry Doubleday Research Association, Bocking, Braintree, Essex, for the latest information.

Comfrey

This is not, strictly speaking, a green manure crop, but a perennial plant providing four or five cuts a year of foliage so rich in protein that it has a C:N ratio of 9.8:1, so that it is a kind of instant compost. It also provides plenty of readily available potassium. It has roots that go down 4–8 ft, which is deeper than most fruit trees, but instead of locking up the minerals in wood where only fire or fungi can release them, it keeps them all in a 'current account', as it were, ready for immediate use by crops. It is not a legume but a member of the *Boraginaceae* (the forget-me-not family), so must have nitrogen specially supplied in a simple form which can be absorbed quickly.

The botanical name for comfrey is *Symphytum uplandicum* (formerly *S. peregrinum*), a semi-sterile hybrid between *S. asperum* from Russia and the wild *S. officinale*, the herbalists' comfrey. It rarely sets seed, so is sold as offsets to be planted at any time except December and January. The leading garden variety is Bocking No. 14, which has the highest potassium content and resists both rabbits and the rust which is its only disease.

The comfrey bed should be in full sun and, as it will last about twenty years, choose a place where it can stay undisturbed. Take care to remove all perennial weeds (see the next chapter for a 'rogues' gallery'), and give it a good start with mattress shoddy or any manure, even pigeon droppings, at the rate of 2 lb. a square yard. Plant the offsets 2 ft apart each way with the tops of the growing points about 2 in. under the surface, since they can dry out and die in a rainless spring.

A spring planting should be hoed to kill annual weeds, have any flower stems removed in June or July, and be left to grow larger and larger till the foliage dies down at the end of October. Dig between the plants in November to remove grass, which is the worst weed in comfrey, and in later years, on sandy soils, if a soil test shows them to be acid, spread 4–8 oz. of slaked lime to the square yard every other autumn. In the spring and again about June, if possible, scatter pigeon or poultry manure on the surface and fork it in, or any other fresh manure you have. A 2–4 in. thick coat of spent mushroom compost is also an excellent weed suppressor and food while the bed is young, and watering with Household Liquid Activator (p. 24) at the rate of roughly 1 qt a plant is a useful way of providing cheap nitrogen for a crop that needs this faster than compost can supply it. The first cut should be ready in April when the plants are about 18 in. high, and can be used in potato trenches (p. 95).

The following table shows the comparative freshweight analysis of comfrey and other manures:

	Water %	Nitrogen %	Phosphorus %	Potash %	C:N Ratio %
Farmyard Manure	75.0	0.6	0.3	0.5	14:1
Russian Comfrey (wilted)	75.0	0.74	0.24	1.19	9.8:1
Indore Compost	76.0	0.5	0.27	0.81	10:1

If comfrey is composted, it can take eight barrowloads to make one barrowload of compost. When it is merely cut and wilted, every four barrowloads of fresh foliage means about three of material with the analysis in the table. This has more than twice the potash of first-class farmyard manure, a little more nitrogen, and less phosphorus. It has doubled the yield of potatoes compared with the 'no manure' plots in replicated trials.

The mineral balance stays fairly constant through the season, according to the following average analysis from all the comfrey varieties grown by the National Institute of Agricultural Botany at Cambridge:

Dry Matter Basis					
	7 April %	15 May %	27 June %	7 July %	6 Sept. %
Potash K_2O	7.95	5.94	7.44	8.25	7.83
Phosphorus P_2O_5	1.25	0.72	1.15	1.01	1.05
Calcium CaO	1.86	2.70	1.81	2.65	3.10

Comfrey is a plant food collector. The foliage is *not* a source of humus, for it grows so fast that it has no time to build lasting hemicelluloses and lignins, and very little vegetative material is left from the long narrow 'compost heaps' formed in effect by every trench. Therefore wilted comfrey in no way replaces compost, which provides lasting humus and energy, but it does give a readily available organic potassium fertilizer to be used for crops that need it. An established bed will produce roughly 2 cwt of cut comfrey a season in four to five cuts from a dozen plants.

Other cuts of comfrey through the summer can be used as mulches, as mentioned later under individual crops, and used for liquid manure.

Comfrey Liquid Manure

This can be made at any time of year, but the autumn brew is useful early in the season, and for house-plants and in the greenhouse. The standard recipe is 14 lb. of cut comfrey in a 20-gallon fibreglass water butt. This should be raised on bricks so that a can will go under the tap. Stuff in the foliage, fill up with a hose, and leave the tub to ferment with the lid on it for about a month. The floating comfrey will blacken and decay, and there will be a clear brown liquid to draw from the bottom that is ideal for watering on tomatoes when they are setting their first truss. The first cut from a comfrey bed planted in September will be ready by June in time for the tomatoes, and to give them weekly feeds.

Analysis of the liquid shows about three times as much potash, almost the same quantity of nitrogen, and about half the phosphorus as in a standard chemical tomato feed, so it is as well to half fill the can with water before topping up with comfrey liquid manure. When the level in the tub gets low it can be tipped up, the residue added to the compost heap, and a fresh load of leaves added. The 20-gallon water butt is easiest to handle, and a battery of three provides a steady supply, but use plastic or fibreglass containers, as old oil drums or other substitutes which can rust result in excess iron oxide in the water.

Comfrey is very easily increased by division in spring – pieces of the roots alone will produce new plants. If necessary a comfrey bed can be killed with a solution of ammonium sulphamate at 1 lb. to 1 gallon of cold water, applied with a rosed can to 100 square feet in spring. Those who are interested in the medicinal, agricultural and nutritional aspects of comfrey are referred to Appendix 2 (p. 234), and for ammonium sulphamate stockists to Appendix 1 (p. 233).

Compost Material Plants

The cheapest and easiest way of growing compost material, rather than green manure, is to buy ½ lb. or so of the common striped sunflower seed sold in pet shops for parrot food. Sow each of these 1 in. deep and 1 ft apart each way in staggered rows, any time between March and June, and pull up the sunflower plants as soon as they are 4 ft high. Shake as much soil as possible off the roots and pile them on the compost heap. Never leave them to soar higher and higher, with flowers as big as dustbin lids, for the stems will be over 2 in. thick and far woodier than Brussels sprout stems. It is better to grow two or even three 4-ft-high crops than to amaze the neighbours with plants that look in at the bedroom windows and can only be sectioned with a saw. Though it is easy to cut down the plants two joints above ground and get four slim shoots from each, the resulting stump will be uncompostable and hard to shake free from soil. The seed is so cheap that it pays to sow and sow again, when every sowing crowds another crop of annual weeds to death.

Sunflower stems are excellent to mix in with lawn mowings, which can often be obtained free from parks, sports grounds or tennis clubs. Check that at least two mowings have been given since the last dressing with a selective weedkiller. Composted alone they make a slimy mass, but as a surface coat, or mixed with sunflower or other bulky foliage, they are a welcome extra well worth fetching for any garden.

If you have over-manured, as many gardeners do, with poultry manure or any fresh bargain load like wet sewage sludge or a real bulk of pigeon manure, sow sunflowers to use up the excess plant foods, and convert them to compost material. Many annuals have been tried as compost growers, and *Lavatera trimestris*, *Gillia capitata*, *Malope trifida grandiflora* and *Phacelia tanacetifolia* all produce bulk as well as beauty and bee fodder, but none is as good as the cheap and easy sunflower at building lasting humus from unwanted space.

5 New Allotments and Gardens

In 1918 we finished a war with $1\frac{1}{2}$ million allotments producing £15 million worth of vegetables every year at 1918 prices. Today we need those allotments just as much to grow the food that inflation is pricing off our plates. There were 1,887 people on the waiting list for allotments in Bristol alone in 1975, an estimated 10,000 in Greater London, and totals over the thousand in most British cities. Yet, according to the society Friends of the Earth, there were 20,000 acres of derelict land in London, and almost every local authority has land lying idle, waiting to become either part of the 70,000 acres a year that motorways have swallowed during the past decade, or the car parks and civic centres we can no longer afford.

Building land prices mean that every new house has a tiny garden, but civic fashion dictates that every estate shall be surrounded with broad acres of grass, mown at the expense of the ratepayers. Therefore there is an ever-increasing demand for allotments, which will grow still more as food prices double and redouble. Every year thousands more people realize that the more food they grow themselves the nicer it will taste, and the more money they will have left over for other necessities.

CAMPAIGNING FOR ALLOTMENTS

The legislation concerning allotments dates from the 1920s, though at the moment of writing it is threatened with modernization. Under the Allotments Act of 1922 an 'allotment garden' must not exceed 40 poles or 300 square yards in area, and must be 'wholly or mainly cultivated by the occupier for the production of vegetable and fruit crops for consumption by himself or his family'. A keen gardener can, however, apply for extra, up to but not more than a quarter of an acre (1,210 square yards), which will give room for plenty of bush fruit for jam or bottling. Borough, urban district, and parish councils are under a *statutory obligation* to provide allotment gardens for all suitable persons, provided the application is made by six registered parliamentary electors or ratepayers residing in their districts.

So the first step for anyone who has a garden with room only for a clothes line like a metal umbrella and a square yard of sand box for a toddler, is to find out from the public library or town hall if there is a local allotment society. There may easily be 500 people in front of you on the waiting list, so collect another five ratepayers and *demand* allotments. Point out to your council that their *duty* under the Allotments Act of 1908 is to provide allotments for 'all suitable persons'. They have provided *some* suitable persons with them, but not *all*, not by a thousand, or whatever the local figure is. Before launching an attack on the local council it is worth having a thorough search for derelict land, finding out as much as possible about each area, including how long it has been empty, and how many plots of 300 square yards it would provide.

There is no need to form a society, but in some ways this is easier, and there are simple and legal specimen constitutions and rules which will save hours of arguing, available from the organizations listed in Appendix 1 (p. 231). In any event, write to your local paper inviting support from the public, and tell them what you have done. One individual or even six can easily be argued down by the town hall staff, but a letter in the local paper will make them take notice, while local radio or T.V. publicity can have a positively melting effect.

Under Section 35 of the 1908 Act, 'rooms in public elementary schools can be used free of charge with the consent of any two managers for the purpose of public discussion on any question relating to allotments'. So write to the headmaster or headmistress of your local comprehensive school, which has replaced the elementary school of 1908 but inherited its obligations just as our new area councils have taken over the duties of the old local authorities. Hold your first meeting free under the Act, and tell the reporter from the local paper that this is your right under the Act which has not yet been repealed.

The Allotments Act of 1925 gave local authorities the right to obtain land for allotments either by agreement or compulsion, in the last case hiring it for not less than fourteen years or more than thirty-five, with power to renew at the end of the period. Under the Community Land Act of 1975 it looks as though area councils will hold large areas of land awaiting development, which they can be compelled to use to fulfil their legal obligation to provide allotments. Plots can be let to tenants on a yearly agreement with six months' notice on either side. Unless there is a special agreement that a minimum of three months' notice shall apply if the council wants the land for housing, the six months' notice must expire outside the cropping season, that is, on or before 5 April, or on or after 29 September.

THE ALLOTMENT SITE

Local authorities and residents are sometimes hostile to allotments, regarding them as hideous eyesores. This is mainly because of the makeshift sheds of corrugated iron, plastic, flattened paint tins, tarred paper and second-hand timber, especially old doors, that sprinkle the patchwork of plots, each one cultivated by an individual enjoying the freedom to grow what he likes.

Standard, ready-made sheds, bought wholesale and kept well painted or creosoted, providing storage for tools and shelter from a sudden shower, are an answer attractive to local authorities, and the council could well pay for them and include the cost in the rent. Under the 1925 Allotments Act, councils do not have to show a profit on their allotments, which are a service to the community as a whole rather than to the residents whose gardens overlook them, and they can legally *lose* the equivalent to a rate of ¾p in the pound.

The best material for fencing in the site is chain-link, buried for a foot at the bottom to defeat rabbits, and extending 5 ft up concrete posts with three spaced strands of barbed wire at the top. The latter should slant outwards to make the posts unclimbable. This fencing should go right round the site. The cost can be cut in towns where rabbits are unknown, making the buried foot of fence unnecessary. It could come down still further if it were possible to use 3–4-ft high pig netting, strained on well-bitumenized steel posts, but ask any allotment holder about vandalism and he will tell you that this is the main problem; an unclimbable fence is the only answer, justified in the long run by the increasing value of the food behind it.

A strong enough campaign could secure a permanently fenced site, with a standpipe for water for every 2 acres, sanitation, and car and bicycle parking space. This would be an asset to any town, increasing in value through the years, and costing no more than an adventure playground or a small park to establish, and far less to maintain.

Garden Sites

Very few sites are ideal. All have disadvantages, but no soil is so horrible that something will not grow in it, given hard work and good humus. The sites to refuse are those shaded by trees and robbed by their roots, or the large gardens often offered for temporary cultivation, where it is not possible to get a lorry load of manure within reasonable barrow-wheeling distance.

A letter to the local paper may bring several offers of gardens too large for their owners. These often have the great advantage of high walls or other rabbit-proof fencing, and a water supply from a creaking iron pump that sucks from a tank filled by rain from the roof. They may, on the other hand, be full of worn out, unpruned apple trees, or have a lean-to greenhouse with non-standard glass and rafters so rotted that any attempt to paint or replace panes will bring them crashing down with the first weight on the ladder. They may also be so thickly hedged with restrictions that they are unworkable. The owner probably wants to keep the garden cultivated without paying wages, or to restore a derelict wilderness to help sell the house. So it should be made quite clear that, while rent can be paid in vegetables at an agreed proportion of greengrocers' prices, any mowing, edging, hedge-clipping or flower-bed-weeding should be at the local hourly rate for jobbing gardeners.

The essential is to have a 'gentleman's agreement in writing' (this is a legal term and applies also to any agreement with a lady), which loans the land either for a set term of years or with six months' notice according to the terms of the Allotments Acts. It must set out the rent to be paid, bind the tenants to leave the land as they found it (for example breaking up and removing any concrete bases for sheds), and lay down conditions on such questions as access and parking for cars and bicycles, dogs, transistor radios, water supply, fruit trees and tree-felling. Any garden which has gone downhill for an elderly owner, whose last gardener died ten years ago, will be starved of plant foods and humus, and needs a good load of manure plus tools, barrows and youth to wheel it in. Buy new tools rather than argue about borrowing forks worn as short as fingers, and broken-backed spades. Such an agreement should be prepared by a solicitor, whose fees will be low because it will not involve the sale of freehold land with inquiries to establish title and the planning position. This is a bargain in saving arguments afterwards.

The most important point in any agreement is on tree-felling. A cooking pear whose blossom has been a tower of delight through forty remembered springs cannot be replaced once it is spread flat as a dropped glove, but remember, if it stays, there are no vegetables that will thrive in dry shade under trees. On any site take out as many trees as possible, unless of course they are modern varieties in full bearing. Any tree-felling should remove the stumps completely rather than leave them as a source of suckers. Woodmen 'fell' trees, but gardeners have to extract them like teeth. Though anything above a foot in diameter should be left to a professional, old fruit trees are within the scope of garden methods.

Start by sawing off the branches to leave a tall stump at least a third of the height of the tree. To lower the large branches, use a strong rope long enough to allow you to stand well clear. Then dig a trench about 1 ft wide, 2–3 ft from the trunk, and about 2 ft deep for a large apple, cutting through each root as you come to it with a sharpened axe. Tie the rope tightly and firmly near the tip of the tall stump and pull, then release, repeating this rocking action until the stirring of the soil in the trench bottom shows where roots remain to be cut; the levering action of the rope tied high on the sawn trunk will break the taproots and the tree will come down.

Two adults should be able to fell a tree up to a foot across the trunk at ground level, and few old apples grow larger than that, but they must take their time and keep together. One man pulling the rope and the other chopping in the trench can mean a broken back for the latter if the tree comes down suddenly and fast. Many hands make light work, but they mean danger unless there is someone in charge and giving the orders, not everyone pulling and talking at once, and a child with a pram in the wrong place.

Never fell a walnut tree. They have no real pests or diseases, live up to 150 years, and their wood is costly for furniture and gunstocks. They take fifteen years from planting to produce the first real crop of nuts, which is why they are rare, but walnuts ripened on the tree are a revelation to those who have only eaten them kiln-dried. Spare also the the horizontal trained pears round the paths and the fan-trained cherries, peaches, apricots and nectarines on the walls, for these can have a value in fruit beyond anything you can plant. Make it clear *who* is to have the fruit and who is to prune them, because their roots may well take so much from the manure and compost you add that they are a burden.

Other Sites

The wide areas round modern council estates, which take up land enough to give everyone a full-sized garden, are usually subsoil smeared flat by earth-moving machinery; they will build fertility slowly as the mowers cut the grass for the worms to take under, recycling the nitrogen the clover has gathered and taking energy from every blade. Tower blocks cut down the sunlight with their shadows, and again the bulldozers and scrapers will have left a disaster area in the soil which will take a long while to restore.

All over Britain there are areas reserved for new schools, cemeteries, playing fields, roads, car parks, awaiting planning permission for something, or lying long, narrow and idle beside derelict railway lines. All these could make allotments or single gardens within bicycle range of city centres. There is no reason why allotments should all be on one site, and an Organic Gardeners' club could take over perhaps a dozen, just as an Angling Club may be fishing tenants of many flooded gravel pits.

Clearing the Site

Even if a site is obtained privately, perhaps reserved for a factory extension, it is possible to arrange for a council lorry to collect the rubbish, from bottomless buckets to broken baths, that any empty land accumulates, provided it can be stacked near the gate. Thick nettle beds can mean piles of coal ashes below. Shovel these into polythene fertilizer bags to be taken away with the rubbish, for they are a blend of lifeless minerals and sulphur, a burden on any garden.

Buy or borrow a second-hand motor scythe or large rotary rough grass mower, and set all the eleven to fifteen-year-olds in the gardening group mowing in turn and raking up the weeds for the compost bins (see p. 18), which should be the first building on any organic garden. Place the bins near the gate, with room to bring a small lorry to them, because it may later be possible to get leaves and other material in bulk.

Nettles, thistles, cow parsley, hemlock and rosebay willow-herb are the first colonizers of derelict land and subsoil. Their roots go deep and far to select fresh minerals to bring into circulation. Cutting them concentrates this fertility and kills the weeds more effectively than any spray, if this is done before they flower and seed. Wait till the weeds are tall enough to offer a bulk of compost material, mow, then wait six weeks and mow again. Even docks can be killed by cutting closely three times a season. Bracken can be destroyed by three mowings a year, if these are done when the new fronds are just uncurling, and as the fresh fronds hold up to 2 per cent potash and, like nettles, are rich in calcium, they are splendid compost material.

Look over the land carefully for rushes, which show poor drainage, and horsetail (*Equisetum*), which means subsoil near the surface. If a site with both these weeds is offered by a council as an alternative to existing allotments, refuse it, unless they have it drained by a land drainage contractor. Draining a field is no job for anyone's spare time, which is better spent on cultivating a more promising site.

Never have an allotment or garden site ploughed so as to destroy the basis of the paths, leaving the hard work of breaking down with forks the tough strips of inverted soil full of weed roots. If the land is full of bird sown briars, blackberries and thorn bushes, hire a contractor to clear it rather than attempt it by hand. It will need a tractor and monkey-winch to rip out the thorns, a chain to tear out as much as possible of the blackberries, and a heavy cultivator behind the tractor to rip up their roots. Then plough a foot deep, spread 2 tons of ground limestone or dolomite an acre if a test shows lime to be needed, and use heavy barrows to break up the ploughed strips.

This operation will be expensive, but it is better to get an estimate for the whole job, and hold whist drives to raise the money, than spend week-end after week-end making small clearings in the wilderness while enthusiasm evaporates.

Wireworms and Their Control

Every new allotment- or garden-maker will learn about wireworm when this pest eats holes in all his potatoes, his carrots and most root crops, including tulips and other bulbs. The wireworm is the larva of the click beetle (*Agriotes lineatus*). This is light brown, shiny, and slender, $\frac{1}{2}-\frac{3}{4}$ in. long, with a bunch of legs at one end. Click beetles lay their eggs between May and July in grass roots, and the larvae take from three to five years to become beetles, starting off small and white and eating only decaying vegetable matter. They are eaten by so many garden friends, especially the larvae and adults of ground beetles, that only about 15 per cent reach greedy maturity at the rate of $2\frac{1}{2}$ million an acre – 8 million is a bad infestation. They moult their leathery skins about nine times during their long lives and they are 'off their feed' till this is accomplished. Their routine is to feed from early March to the end of May, rest and moult in June, eat again from July to October, and then go down deep in the soil for the winter, away from hunting rooks. If you can make a start on your garden or allotment in March or April, you can catch up to 80 per cent of them in the top 2 in.

If the allotment site is grassland, decide on the position of the main path, which should be wide enough to take a 1-ton van filled with mushroom compost bags (about 10 ft), and allow space at the far end to turn it. The paths between plots should be 30 in. wide to allow for mowing, and it pays to buy a good mower with a grass box, letting the person whose turn it is to mow keep the mowings for compost or surface mulching.

Then strip the turf from your marked-out plot, and stack it grass-side down on cut-open polythene fertilizer bags or old asbestos or corrugated iron sheets. The wireworms will stay in the heap eating grass roots, but cannot burrow down and escape into the soil below because they are blocked by the metal or 500-gauge polythene. The stack will decay to good loam, suitable for replacing greenhouse soil or for potting.

A version of this trick which combines composting with wireworm beating is to start with a two-turf-thick layer on the polythene and build up the sides to two feet high, leaving a hollow in the middle. Empty kitchen wastes, especially tea leaves and potato peelings, into this space, obtaining extra from cafés if possible, and cover it after every addition with two thicknesses of upside-down turf to keep off birds and dogs. The potato peelings and other wastes will provide such rich feeding for the wireworms that they will become beetles in three years instead of five and fly off to lay eggs on grassland. Some will lay on the grass paths on the allotments, but most beetles go a considerable distance before laying.

By mid-June the wireworms will have stopped feeding and the middle of the heap will have sunk with decay. Then add 3 in. of soil and plant marrows or outdoor cucumbers in the sheltered hollow. It will be possible to break up the turf stack 'compost heap' by the following spring, but many gardeners keep it for several years as a combined marrow bed and kitchen waste disposal unit, to be dug down and spread as a source of humus and good soil.

If the allotments were broken up mechanically and there is no turf to stack, or if you missed the March-April 'wireworm rise', wait till between late May and mid-July, and sow mustard as described on p. 56, but let it grow as tall as it will, because the object is not building humus or feeding bacteria, but wireworms. The largest and greediest will feast on mustard foliage, pupate, and then wake as beetles in the spring, while the others will stay down eating instead of attacking the potatoes in the summer. Dig the mustard under before it gets a frost on it, and before September ends. The soil of new gardens and allotments has no clubroot spores, so there is no reason why the process should not be repeated.

If entry to the allotment site is so long delayed that there is not even time for mustard, wait till next season. Instead sow broad, french, runner and haricot beans, peas, kale, parsnip and spinach, all of which wireworms dislike. If you sow carrots or plant potatoes, they could be ruined. There are a number of trapping tricks described in Chapter 17 which are also effective.

Couchgrass Control and Cultivation

The wicked white roots of this worst weed grass can be controlled as part of the lay-out operation. Strip the turf and stack it evenly, if you find no wireworms. Grass side down, even without kitchen wastes, it will decay to good soil for future spreading. Then dig several trial holes spaced over your strip, going down 1 ft deep, first to see how far down the good brown soil goes, before you come to the lighter coloured subsoil, and secondly to see if there are any joined white couchgrass (*Agropynon repens*) roots. It looks like this:

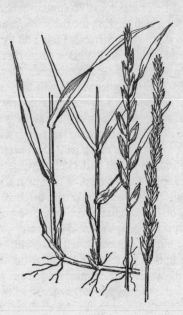

Couchgrass

There are many local names for couchgrass, such as twitch, squitch and scutch, etc., and the sharp pointed roots can pierce potatoes. Whenever it is seen in the course of routine cultivations, it should be dug up and spread to dry for compost, or burnt.

The results of the trial holes will show the cultivation needed, and every member of an allotment society should dig his own (not just leave it to the Hon. Secretary), because the soil depth and weeds are going to vary.

Then hire a man with a rotavator, for you need a powerful machine that will save weeks of digging, as well as breaking down the soil evenly and finely. As the machine will be needed only for breaking the hard ground when you start, it does not pay to spend over £500 on a big one. But you *do* need a mower for paths and compost weed cutting, which will go on all the season. Contractors usually charge travelling time, so it pays to have all the plots cultivated together, but what each needs depends on the results of the trial holes.

The lucky gardener will have found no couchgrass and have a foot of good soil. He needs his plot turned over twice, so the machine can get down the full foot, ideally with a few days between cultivations. This will give the local robins a good chance to peck up the odd 15 per cent of wireworms, and many other soil pests. Then, if a soil test shows the need for lime, spread as much as 2 lb. of ground limestone or 1 lb. of slaked lime to the square yard, ready for the final rotavation, which will distribute this evenly through the soil.

If the gardener is luckier still, he will have obtained a load of mushroom compost to be turned in, providing humus and plant foods, with sometimes a bonus of lime. If he is wise, he will have decided which end of the plot will have the first potato bed, and will have left this unlimed. A shallower soil will need only one cultivation, with any lime spread straight on the soil surface. It is better with two, to provide a level plot ready for sowing at once.

If couchgrass roots are found, wait for dry weather before doing any cultivating, until about June, and then cultivate three times at three-week intervals. The machine will chop up the roots and leave them in the soil which is 'puffed' full of air so that they dry out. The second and third attacks go deep enough to destroy the lot. Remember that wet soil and/or rain will encourage the couchgrass, together with a number of other unpleasant weeds, including creeping buttercup. This process means a delayed start, but it is valuable for killing couchgrass.

Other Wicked Weeds

Those gardeners who boast they 'make friends with their weeds' must be lucky enough to have only annual kinds like groundsel, fat-hen or chickweed, which are easily killed by hoeing. If you remember to hoe off these seedlings at 1 in. height often enough for two or three years they need be very little trouble. The really hateful weeds are all *perennial*, which means that their roots survive in the soil and come up next year with a flying start on your seedling vegetables.

Convolvulus, also called bindweed and bellbind (*Calystegia sepium*), has powerful white roots that go down a long way, and must be repeatedly dug up to exhaust them, though they will reappear and climb plants, shrubs and even trees by twining and strangling. It has large white bell-shaped flowers. There is a smaller species, *Convolvulus arvensis*, the Lesser Bindweed, with smaller pink or white flowers like shallow cups, which is also a twiner and strangler.

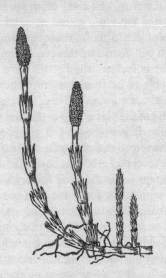

Horsetail

Horsetail (*Equisetum arvense*) is the last survivor of the Coal Age trees, with brittle stems and black underground roots. It is a weed of

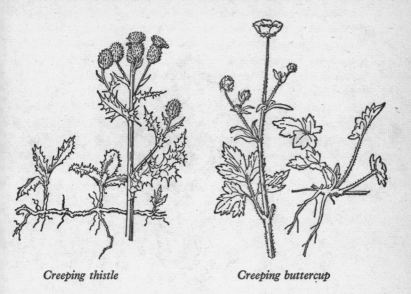

Creeping thistle   *Creeping buttercup*

poorly drained ground and subsoil, to be dug out on sight, though more humus and better drainage will drive it away in time.

Creeping Thistle (*Cirsium arvense*) has spreading white roots and is very prickly, but like all thistles it can be killed by cutting and then composted. It spreads by means of seeds blown by wind, so can arrive in any garden and should be dug before it grows large.

Creeping Buttercup (*Ranunculus repens*) spreads by rooting from the joints of its surface stems as well as by seed. This is one to hoe out as a seedling before it grows worse.

All docks including *Rumex crispus*, the Curled Dock, and *R. obtusifolius*, the Broad-Leaved Dock, should be killed by hoeing when they are small, or pulled or dug when they grow large, which is the best remedy. In February or March there is a period when they lose their grip on the ground, and they are quite easily pulled. In the past farmers would test their docks at intervals, and when the time

Dock

(which varied with the weather) was ripe they would turn out all the village women, paying them as much as three shillings a day to clear the hated weeds for burning. Docks can be dried and composted, but can also be killed by repeated cutting.

Goutweed or Ground Elder (*Aegopodium podagraria*) was introduced by the Romans (who should have known better) as a cure for gout, and in its time was a 'wonder drug' but was replaced as a cure by the drinking of Bath water. It has creeping underground stems, leaves rather similar to but smaller than those of an elder tree, and small white flowers. It is a weed of shady places, clay soils and old gardens. It can be killed by sowing *Tagetes minuta*, the

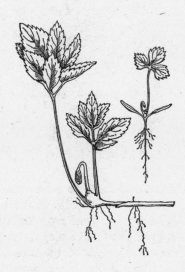

Ground elder

Mexican Marigold, thinly in furrows 1 ft apart and 1 in. deep in April, after digging out as much as possible of the ground elder's wretched roots (see Appendix 1 for a seed supplier). A portrait of the ground elder is above, and those who have it, hate it.

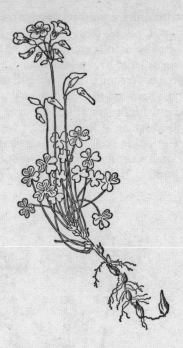

Oxalis cernua

In mild districts Oxalis can be the worst weed of all. The common species is *O. corymbosa*, introduced from Bermuda in 1757. It has leaves like a shamrock, and white roots like tiny turnips, with a cluster of wheat-grain-like bulbs sitting on the top. One touch of the fork and these will spread all over the garden. Wait till the brutes are growing well in June or July, mix up ammonium sulphamate at the rate of 1 lb. to a 2-gallon can of water, and apply the solution to 100 square feet. This is a stock method of killing horrible weeds, and the chemical becomes sulphate of ammonia and washes away afterwards, so that the ground can be sown or planted four weeks later. It will kill convolvulus, but it must not be used to kill it among cultivated plants. It is a killer, expensive but effective. (See Appendix 1 for a supplier.)

Light Starvation for Weeds

None of these fierce weeds can be killed by piling compost, peat or sawdust on them on a no-digging system, for they have enough food stored in their roots to grow through any surface coat. The latest way round the problem has proved effective in clearing creeping buttercup out of blackcurrants.

Spread six thicknesses of newspaper on the surface and weight it down with stones, so that it excludes light and starves the leaves of solar energy. When the paper grows yellow and brittle, replace it with fresh, and put the old on the compost heap. This idea has been tried with black plastic, but the wind can tear this more easily, and the moisture that condenses on the undersurface makes a perfect environment for slugs. Newspapers cost nothing, if collected from kind neighbours, and the sun and rain make them more easily rotted. There is scope for experiment under other bush fruits and between vegetable rows.

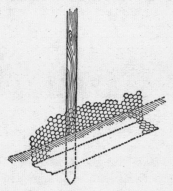

Fencing against rabbits

Rabbit-proof Fencing

The major problem of new gardens in the country, or allotments anywhere, is rabbits. Modern rabbits live mainly on the surface like hares, because myxomatosis is spread by rabbit fleas that live dormant in second-hand burrows. This change in habit means that they cannot be caught in quantity by putting ferrets down the burrows

77

and bolting them into nets. Snaring and shooting are the only effective control measures, and before any allotment is taken over, ask for the services of the local rabbit catcher. (Ask for the mole catcher as well, for these, too, can be major pests. The more humus the more worms, the more worms the more moles, and these, interesting and attractive though they are, can play havoc with seedlings.)

Chain-link fencing is expensive, but ordinary wire netting 4 ft high will serve to keep rabbits out. Put in fence posts, preferably metal, bitumen-painted to last, and easily hammered in. Dig out a strip 4 in. deep and 6 in. wide on the outside, or on grassland turn up the turf so that it folds back by this amount. Then bend the bottom of the wire so that it fits into the trench, and attach the rest to the posts, putting back the soil or replacing the turf. When the rabbit arrives, he will dig down to burrow under, find the bent portion of the netting and give up. The netting lasts a long time, provided the grass and weeds are cut along the line of the fence, for the moisture thrown out as they reach up can rust it away.

6 Crop Rotation

The art of gardening lies in using time to make space go further, fitting the seeds into the sowing months in such a way that there are crops ready round the year. In Britain it is possible to eat your own vegetables for cooking and salads, with the help of storage, but without a greenhouse or cloches, at all seasons. The secret lies in crop rotation, and every gardener has to make up his or her own, which will vary through the years as new favourites are found and the family grows up with differing tastes, though the basic principles remain the same.

One of the most important rules to remember is that none of the cabbage family should ever be planted in the same place two years running. This is because clubroot, their common disease, has so far no satisfactory cure except resting the soil till the spores die out. So the longer it is before cabbages come round again, the better. This applies to potatoes as well, one of whose major pests is eelworm, which also builds up in the soil. Potatoes are also subject to scab and blackleg, and again, the answer is rotation. Onions, too, get white rot fungus if they grow too often in the same place.

The organic gardener has a third factor to consider. His object is to keep up the fertility of his garden, while taking far more out of it than any farmer. 'Fertility' is the ability of the land to go on growing good crops indefinitely, and in Britain there are cottage gardens that have fed families for 500 years, with the aid of manure from the home farm. Today we use compost and, where there is space and time available, green manure crops as well, which are sown in the autumn to dig in and decay to humus by the spring. There is also the problem of keeping up the nitrogen content of the soil. On a garden scale this is mainly supplied by the root bacteria of peas and beans, so the more of these you grow the better.

The following plan divides vegetables into four general groups:

YEAR 1

Bed 1

Potatoes
Earlies: 21 lb. seed
potatoes (10 rows)
followed by leeks.

Maincrop: 14 lb. seed
potatoes (10 rows)
followed by broad beans.

2 rows of young
Remontant strawberries.

Bed 4

Roots
Onions
Carrots
Beet
Kohl-rabi
Salsify
Parsnips
Pumpkins
Lettuces
Radishes
Remontant strawberries:
their last year, thrown
away at the end of the
season.

Bed 2

Legumes
Broad beans
Peas, runner beans
French beans, haricot
beans.

All peas and beans
followed by young plants
of Brussels sprouts,
sprouting broccoli,
cabbage.

2 rows of strawberries,
first year of cropping.

Bed 3

Brassicas
Cabbage tribe, planted as
young plants in this bed
the year before.

Outdoor tomatoes after
the winter cabbages are
cleared.

Lettuces, radishes,
turnips or swedes.

Remontant strawberries,
cropping well.

GARDEN PATH

(1) Potatoes; (2) Legumes (peas and beans); (3) Brassicas (the cabbage tribe); (4) Roots.

Other crops, such as salad, are grown with each of these to use the space to its best advantage. This rotation should supply a family with vegetables all the year round. It also includes Remontant strawberries, which are moved round the beds year by year with the vegetables instead of staying in one place like rhubarb, bush fruit or comfrey – this system means that there is always a young strawberry bed coming into fruit, two in full production and one wearing out. (For more details see pp. 173–4 ff.)

Here is a table showing the crops in each of the four beds over the full 4-year rotation:

	Year 1	Year 2	Year 3	Year 4
Bed 1	Potatoes	Legumes	Brassicas	Roots
Bed 2	Roots	Potatoes	Legumes	Brassicas
Bed 3	Brassicas	Roots	Potatoes	Legumes
Bed 4	Legumes	Brassicas	Roots	Potatoes

Each section containing two beds is 13 ft wide and 45 ft long, designed to fit either into the two beds, one on each side of the centre path of the average 1930s-built semi-detached house garden, or (without the middle path) into the standard allotment 300 yards square. These gardens usually had 120 ft of cropping space, which would leave 30 ft at the end for bush fruit, and keep the herb bed near the kitchen door, the tool shed and the compost bin behind the garage, and the lawn crossed by the clothes line next to the house. As allotments have side rather than middle paths, the rows are made twice as broad and the sections shorter so that they fit one behind the other: otherwise you would have to tramp over one section to get to the next.

The strawberries are split and replanted in September where some of the potatoes have been on Bed 1, so that they change ends every rotation. Note that all the crops on Bed 4 are harvested by September or October, so that this leaves room for winter tares to be dug in as green manure before the potatoes. This rotation concentrates the peas and beans before the cabbage tribe, because these can be cut off at ground level and the surface weeds hoed off – Brussels sprouts especially appreciate planting with a steel-shod dibber into firm soil.

The following table is designed for those who wish to work out their own rotations. This is strongly recommended, for a wet winter week-end spent planning a rotation to fit your garden can do more to make your garden feed you than almost any gadget you can buy. It is not the vegetables you *grow* that count, but how many you eat and enjoy, and if you start with a plan you can make notes on it of the crops that produced too little and those that produced too much until you have a scheme that fits your needs.

WHAT YOU COULD BE EATING EACH MONTH

JANUARY	Sown	Planted	FEBRUARY	Sown	Planted
Beet (Stored)	May	July	Beet (Stored)	May	
Broccoli, Heading	April	June	Broccoli, Early		
Brussels Sprouts	April	June	Sprouting	April	June
Cabbage	June	Aug.	Brussels Sprouts	April	June
Carrots (Stored)	April		Cabbage	June	Aug.
Chinese Radish	July		Carrots (Stored)	April	
Kale	April	June	Chinese Radish	July	
Kohl-rabi	June		Kale	April	June
Leeks	April	July	Kohl-rabi	June	
Onions (Stored)	March		Leeks	April	July
Parsnips (Stored)	April		Onions (Stored)	March	
Potatoes (Stored)		April	Parsnips (Stored)	April	
Pumpkin (Stored)	April		Potatoes (Stored)		April
Salsify	April		Salsify	April	
Savoys	April	June	Spinach, Winter	Sept.	
Shallots (Stored)		March	Swedes (Stored)	July	
Spinach, Winter	Sept.		Tomatoes (Bottled)		May
Swedes (Stored)	July		Turnips (Stored)	Aug.	
Tomatoes (Bottled)		May			
Turnips (Stored)	Aug.				

MARCH	Sown	Planted
Beet (Stored)	May	
Broccoli, Sprouting	April	June
Brussels Sprouts	April	June
Cabbage	June	Aug.
Chinese Radish	July	
Kale	June	Sept.
Onions (Stored)	March	
Parsnips (Stored)	April	
Potatoes (Stored)		April
Salsify Leaves	April	
Tomatoes (Bottled)		May
Turnips (Stored)	Aug.	

APRIL		
Beet (Stored)	May	
Broccoli, Late Sprouting	May	July
Cabbage	July	Aug.–Sept.
Leeks	April	Aug.
Lettuce	Sept.	
Onions, Spring	Aug.	
Onions (Stored)	March	
Potatoes (Stored)		April
Salsify Leaves	April	

MAY		
Beet (Stored)	May	
Broccoli, Late Sprouting	May	July
Cabbage		Aug.	Oct.
Lettuce	March	
Onions, Spring	Aug.	
Onions (Stored)	March	
Radishes	March	
Spinach, Summer	Feb.	
Tomatoes (Bottled)		May
Turnips	March	

JUNE	Sown	Planted
Beans, Broad	Nov.	
Cabbage	Mar.	April
Carrots, Early	Mar.	
Lettuce	Mar.	
Onions, Spring	Aug.	
Potatoes, Early		Mar.
Peas, Early	Feb.–Mar.	
Radishes	April	
Spinach	April	
Spinach, N.Z.	April	
Tomatoes (Bottled)		May
Turnips	Mar.	

JULY		
Beans, Broad	Mar.	
Beet, Fresh	Mar.	
Carrots, Early	Mar.	
Cauliflowers	Jan.	April
Kohl-rabi	April	
Lettuce	April	
Onions, Spring	Aug.	Mar.
Onions	Aug.	Mar.
Peas, Early	April	
Potatoes, Early		March
Radishes	May	
Spinach	May	
Spinach, N.Z.	April	
Tomatoes (Bottled)		May
Turnips	May	

AUGUST		
Beans, Windsor	April	
Beans, French	May	
Beans, Runner	May	
Beet, Fresh	April	

83

August – contd.	Sown	Planted
Cabbage	Mar.	May
Carrots, Short	April	
Cauliflowers	April	June
Cucumbers	April	
Kohl-rabi	May	
Lettuce	June	
Marrows, Courgette	April	
Onions	Mar.	
Peas, Maincrop	April	
Potatoes, Early		April
Radishes	June	
Spinach	June	
Spinach, N.Z.	Mar.	
Swedes	April	
Tomatoes, Outdoor	Mar.	May
Turnips	June	

SEPTEMBER

	Sown	Planted
Beans, French	May	
Beans, Runner	May	
Beans, Windsor	Mar.	
Cabbage	Mar.	May
Carrots, Maincrop	April	
Cauliflowers	April	May
Cucumbers	April	
Kohl-rabi	June	
Leeks	Mar.	April
Lettuce	June–July	
Marrows, Courgette	April	
Onions	Mar.	
Peas, Maincrop	May	
Potatoes, Early		Mar.
Pumpkins	April	
Radishes	July	
Spinach	July	
Spinach, N.Z.	Mar.	
Swedes	April	

September – contd.	Sown	Planted
Tomatoes, Outdoor	Mar.	May
Turnips	June	

OCTOBER

	Sown	Planted
Beans, French	June	
Beans, Runner	May	
Beet	June	
Broccoli, Heading	Mar.	May
Brussels Sprouts	April	June
Cabbage	April	June
Cauliflowers	April	May
Chinese Radish	July	
Kohl-rabi	June	
Leeks	Mar.	June
Lettuce	July	
Onions (Stored)	Mar.	
Parsnips	Mar.	
Swedes	May	
Tomatoes, Outdoor		May

NOVEMBER

	Sown	Planted
Beet	May	
Broccoli, Heading	April	June
Brussels Sprouts	April	June
Cabbage	April	June
Carrots	April	
Chinese Radish	July	
Kohl-rabi	June	
Leeks	April	July
Onions (Stored)	Mar.	
Parsnips	April	
Potatoes		April
Pumpkins	April	
Salsify	April	
Savoys	April	July
Shallots		Feb.

November – contd.	Sown	Planted		Sown	Planted
Spinach	Aug.		Chinese Radish	July	
Tomatoes (Fresh and Bottled)		May	Kale	April	June
			Kohl-rabi	June	
Turnips	July		Leeks	April	July
			Onions (Stored)	Mar.	
			Parsnips	April	
			Potatoes		April
			Pumpkins	April	
DECEMBER			Salsify	April	
Beet (Stored)	May		Savoys	April	July
Broccoli	April	June	Shallots		Feb.
Brussels Sprouts	April	June	Swedes	June	
Cabbage	April	July	Tomatoes (Bottled)		May
Carrots	April		Turnips	July	

The next table gives condensed information on when to sow and plant, how long seeds keep, how many fill a 50-ft row (halve this to find the quantity for a standard allotment width), and very approximate yields. These vary not only with soil, season and skill, but with sowing times. It is often better value to sow roots for storing *late* so that they are nicer than the woody monsters, and fit in after something like early lettuce. The accounts of individual vegetables in later chapters give many tips for fitting in extra crops.

TABLE OF VEGETABLES

Vegetable	How long seed keeps	Seeds or roots per 50-ft row	When to sow	When to plant	Depth to sow
Bean, Broad, longpod	2 years	¼ pint	November	—	2 in.
Bean, Broad, Windsor	2 years	¼ pint	Feb.–April	—	2 in.
Bean, French	2 years	½ pint	May–July	—	2 in.
Bean, Runner	2 years	½ pint	May–June	—	2 in.
Bean, Tic, for drying	2 years	2 oz.	November	—	2 in.
Bean, Daffa, for drying	2 years	2 oz.	November	—	2 in.
Bean, Haricot	2 years	2 oz.	May–June	—	2 in.
Beet	2 years	½ oz.	Mar.–June	—	1 in.
Beet, Spinach	2 years	1 oz.	Mar.–April, Aug.–Sept.	—	1 in.
Broccoli, Heading	3 years	¼ oz.	April–May	May.–Aug.	½ in.
Broccoli, Sprouting	3 years	¼ oz.	Mar.–May	May–July	½ in.
Brussels Sprouts	4 years	¼ oz.	Mar.–April	May–July	½ in.
Cabbage, Green or red	3 years	¼ oz.	Mar.–May, July–Oct.	May–June, Aug.–Oct.	½ in.
Carrot	3–5 years	½ oz.	Mar.–June	—	½ in.
Cauliflower	3 years	¼ oz.	April–May	May–Aug.	½ in.
Celeriac	4 years	¼ oz.	March	May	½ in.
Celery	4 years	¼ oz.	Mar.–April	May–June	¼ in.
Cucumber (Burpless)	6 years	25 seeds	April–May	—	1 in.
Kale, Curly	4 years	¼ oz.	April–May	June–July	½ in.
Kale, Rape	5 years	¼ oz.	June–Aug.	—	½ in.
Kohl-rabi	4 years	½ oz.	April–Aug.	—	½ in.
Leek	4 years	¼ oz.	Mar.–April	June–Aug.	½ in.
Lettuce	3 years	¼ oz.	Mar.–Sept.	—	½ in.
Marrows	6 years	18 seeds	April–May	—	1 in.
Onion Sets	—	100 bulbs (½ lb.)	—	March	2 in.
Onion Seed	1–2 years	¼ oz.	Mar.–April or August	—	½ in.
Parsley, Turnip-rooted	2 years	1 oz.	March	—	½ in.
Parsnip	1 year	½ oz.	April	—	½ in.
Peas	2 years	1 pint	Feb.–July	—	2 in.
Potato tubers, Early	—	7 lb.	—	Mar.–April	6 in.
Potato tubers, Maincrop	—	7 lb.	—	Mar.–April	6 in.

How far apart	Between rows	Thin to	Weeks till eating	Eating period, fresh or stored	When to harvest for storing	Good crop for 50-ft row as picked or dug
4–6 in.	2 ft	—	28	June	—	40 lb.
4–6 in.	2 ft	—	16–20	June–July	—	40 lb.
6 in.	2 ft	—	12	July–Oct.	—	75 lb.
6 in.	30 in. (pairs)	—	14	July–Oct.	—	85 lb.
1 ft	1 ft	—	—	—	Aug.–Sept.	3½ lb.
1 ft	1 ft	—	—	—	August	3½ lb.
6 in.	8–12 in.	—	18–20	Oct.–Mar.	Mid-Sept.	4 lb.
6 in.	8 in.	—	16	June–Mar.	October	75 lb.
—	18 in.	1 ft	20	July	—	85 lb.
2 ft	2 ft	—	24–52	Oct.–May	—	20 heads
2 ft	30 in.	—	32–52	Jan.–May	—	70 lb.
30 in.	30 in.	—	18–24	Oct.–Mar.	—	45–50 lb.
1–2 ft	1–2 ft	—	18–35	All year	—	25–50 heads
—	8 in.	6–8 in.	12–24	June–Mar.	October	40 lb.
18 in.	2 ft	—	18–24	Aug.–Nov.	—	25–50 heads
1 ft	1½ ft	—	28	Oct.–Mar.	November	60–70 lb.
1 ft	½–3 ft	—	20–28	Aug.–Feb.	—	60 lb.
2 ft	2 ft	—	14	Aug.–Oct.	—	50–80
30 in.	3 ft	—	28	Nov.–April	—	70–80 lb.
—	1½ ft	2 ft	40	May–June	—	70–80 lb.
—	1 ft	8 in.	14	July–Feb.	—	70–80 lb.
8 in.	8 in.	—	26	Sept.–April	—	75 leeks
—	9–12 in.	6–12 in.	10	All year	—	75 lettuces
3 ft	4 ft	—	14	July–Oct.	—	40–60 fruit
6 in.	1 ft	—	20	All year	August	50–60 lb.
—	1 ft	6 in.	24	All year	September	50–60 lb.
—	15 in.	12 in.	32	Nov.–Mar.	November	All you want
9 in.	1 ft	—	32	Nov.–Mar.	November	100 lb.
2 in.	2–4 ft	—	14	June–Sept.	—	120 lb.
12 in.	18 in.	—	12	July	August	75 lb.
15 in.	27 in.	—	20	September	October	100 lb.

Vegetable	How long seed keeps	Seeds or roots per 50-ft row	When to sow	When to plant	Depth to sow
Pumpkin	6 years	14 seeds	April–May	—	1 in.
Radish	4 years	¼ oz.	Feb.–Aug.	—	½ in.
Radish, Chinese	4 years	¼ oz.	July–Aug.	—	1 in.
Salsify	2 years	½ oz.	April	—	1 in.
Savoy Cabbage	5 years	¼ oz.	April–May	July–Aug.	½ in.
Shallot	—	2 lb.	Feb.–Mar.	—	2 in.
Spinach, Summer	2 years	1 oz.	Feb.–Aug.	—	1 in.
Spinach, Winter	2 years	1 oz.	Aug.–Sept.	—	1 in.
Spinach, New Zealand	2 years	1 oz.	April–May	—	1 in.
Swedes	2 years	½ oz.	April–May	—	½ in.
Sweet Corn	2 years	1 oz.	April–May	—	1 in.
Swiss Chard	2 years	1 oz.	April–May, Aug.–Sept.	—	1 in.
Tomatoes, Outdoor	3 years	¼ oz.	Mar.–April	May–June	½ in.
Turnips	2 years	½ oz.	Mar.–Aug.	—	½ in.

How far apart	Between rows	Thin to	Weeks till eating	Eating period, fresh or stored	When to harvest for storing	Good crop for 50-ft row as picked or dug
3 ft	3 ft	—	—	Oct.–Feb.	October	20–40 lb. plant
—	2 in.	—	5–6	April-Oct.	—	Plenty
4 in.	9 in.	—	10	Oct.–Mar.	—	50 lb.
6 in.	9 in.	8 in.	18	Nov.–Mar.	Leave in	20–30 lb.
12–18 in.	2 ft	—	28	Nov.–Feb.	—	40–50 heads
8 in.	1 ft	—	28	Sept.–Mar.	June–July	30–40 lb.
—	1 ft	6 in.	8	May–Sept.	—	40–50 lb.
—	1 ft	8 in.	10	Oct.–Mar.	—	30–40 lb.
—	2 ft	2 ft	14	June–Oct.	—	30–40 lb.
—	1 ft	1 ft	20	Aug.–Mar.	November	40–60 lb.
15 in.	2 ft	—	15	Aug.–Oct.	—	50 cobs
1 ft	15 in.	—	10–14	July–Mar.	—	40 lb.
2 ft	3 ft	—	16	Aug.–Oct.	October	80 lb.
—	1 ft	4–12 in.	6	May–Mar.	As required	40–70 lb.

7 Potatoes

The potato is our finest vegetable, in terms of supplying the greatest food value from the least space; its vitamins and minerals help digest the carbohydrates it contains, and it also has a very useful supply of protein and vitamin C. One pound of starch-reduced slimming biscuits contain as much carbohydrate as $3\frac{1}{2}$ lb. of potatoes. Perhaps the reason why so many people give up potatoes rather than biscuits and cakes when slimming is that bought potatoes are a much less attractive food. In the rotations in the last chapter, a quarter of the room in every garden or allotment is suggested for potatoes, because well-chosen varieties, grown with compost, are a vegetable to enjoy.

VARIETIES – MAINCROP

Perhaps the finest flavoured potato of all is Record, which has been called the 'Cox of the kitchen garden', with a yellow, firm flesh. It has superb flavour, far superior to the famous King Edward. It has also the lowest dry matter of any, which makes it very good for frying and salads, but its main commercial use is for making potato crisps. Its yield is lower than thirstier kinds, but gardeners know it is a maincrop variety with a first-class flavour, and do not worry about the rather rough skin that keeps it out of the supermarkets. Because seedsmen now stock fewer and fewer potato varieties, the address of a specialist supplier is included in Appendix 1 (p. 233).

Second only to Record comes the pink-skinned Desirée, a firm cooker, a good frier and potato salad variety, not as yellow but a heavier cropper. It keeps well, and is rapidly replacing King Edward as housewives learn to ask for it by name. It has the disadvantage that it is easily infected with potato scab, but as the scab markings of the skin can be peeled away this condition is not serious, though they make it less suitable for baking in the jacket.

The diseases of potatoes and other crops are discussed in Chapter 15, but resistance to them has been bred into many varieties. This work is done mainly at the Scottish Plant Breeding Station at Pentlandfield, near Edinburgh, and all their varieties have the prefix Pentland, in the same way that those from the Cambridge Plant Breeding Institute, Maris Lane, are called Maris. As a general rule, any kind with either prefix has resistance to one or other of the farm and garden problems.

These first two potatoes are maincrops, which are for lifting in September or even October to keep till new potatoes arrive, and they are bred for heavy yields. Pentland Crown is the most scab-resistant of all, and is therefore the favourite for selling in polythene bags at supermarkets, though it is almost as tasteless as Majestic, with an equally heavy yield. A better potato is Pentland Ivory, which is white and floury, with as good a yield as either and resistance to both scab and potato blight. Desirée, too, has blight-resistant foliage, so is only half as likely to be infected with this fungus disease as King Edward and has a third better chance again of escaping as Majestic. Just as even the tasteless varieties gain flavour when grown with compost, their healthy diet helps any bred-in disease resistance to defend them.

There are about 150 varieties of potato in cultivation, and those that do not resist anything but have survived on their merits from the past are still worth looking for. Kerr's Pink, introduced in 1917, has the densest haulm (foliage) of all, and because this makes it the best suppressor of annual weeds, it is a favourite for new gardens and allotments. It also crops well, keeps well, and lasts longest out of water without blackening, which makes it best for the fish-and-chip-shop trade. Golden Wonder is regarded as the best flavoured of the white and floury varieties, a rather poor cropper, but a scab resister and a favourite for baking and boiling in its skin in Scotland.

Those who have trouble with potato eelworm, which results in tiny tubers and stunted foliage which dies off early, should try Maris Piper, the eelworm-resistant variety, which is a high yielder and a good, firm-fleshed, well-flavoured potato. It has the handicap that it only resists one of the many races of eelworm, while the remainder increase, but there are new kinds 'coming off the drawing board' at

Pentlandfield that will be worth growing. The wild potato that resists eelworm also passes on quite a good flavour.

VARIETIES – SECOND EARLY

This class is perhaps best for small gardens, because they can be dug as soon as the flowers are fully open to scrape as new potatoes, or left in to grow larger till the haulm dies down, lifted in August, and stored for the winter and spring. The advantage for the gardener is that he needs only one variety for both early eating and keeping, while the quick finish gives him a better choice of winter-eating or green-manure crops than if he had planted a late-maturing potato like Arran Consul (perhaps the best keeper of all), which is dug in October.

The best second early for flavour is Duke of York, introduced in 1891, with yellow flesh, shallow eyes for easy scraping when new, and a good keeper. It is excellent as an example of compost-grown quality when scrubbed well, brushed with a little oil and baked in its jacket. Craig's Alliance is the fastest-growing of all, as quick as a real early, but finishing about the first week in August. It is a heavy yielder except in a dry year, a good scab resister, and the best in this class for those who like white flouriness for boiling or steaming more than yellow firmness for potato salad.

The best of the new kinds is Maris Peer, which is the best blight resister, an excellent scab resister, and a very heavy cropper in a wet season. Maris Page is nearly as good, but better for frying and a non-blackener, so it is replacing Kerr's Pink for fish-and-chip shops.

VARIETIES – FIRST EARLY

The famous flavour-variety is Epicure, which was introduced in 1897. It has deep eyes, which make it awkward for scraping, but it has the ability to recover fastest of all from frost, as well as a good flavour which keeps it in cultivation. Home Guard, introduced in 1942, is a better scraper, and its haulm resists cold winds, while its disadvantage of picking up any chemical taint such as naphthalene or g-BHC (now

HCH), used against wireworm, does not concern organic gardeners. Arran Pilot is a well-known variety. It is resistant only to common scab (and immune to wart disease), but builds up weight fast after flowering and though it is not renowned for its flavour, home grown taste better than the bought ones. Maris Anchor is an eelworm resister in this group, and so is Pentland Meteor. Both are white-fleshed, and quite good keepers if left in to grow large.

ORDERING AND STORING SEED POTATOES

The few seedsmen who stock a range of potato varieties soon sell out of the best, so always order in <u>November</u> before the rail trucks are made up for delivery from Scotland, where high winds blow the aphids that carry potato viruses out to sea, and make Scottish seed always the best. When you order, allow 14 lb. of seed tubers for every 100 feet of row, because though early and second early varieties go 12 in. apart and 18 in. between rows, and maincrops 15 in. between tubers and 27 in. between rows, maincrop seed is always rather larger. Open the bags as soon as they arrive, probably in late January or early February, because it pays farmers to 'chit' or sprout their potatoes, and gardeners also gain from the extra yield.

Collect from greengrocers or market stalls the grape or tomato trays which have raised corners so that they will stand one on top of the other. They are worth paying for because they will last several seasons. Then set the tubers in the trays, eye-end upwards, and stack them in a light, frost-free shed, under the staging in a greenhouse, or even in a spare bedroom, where they can stay sprouting till planting time. This varies with the season, and though Good Friday was the traditional planting date, this was merely because this was always a holiday for farmworkers and allotment holders, who planted their potatoes on their first free day. No time is wasted if the tubers stay in their trays till even the end of April, which gives time for the last sprouting broccoli and leeks to finish and the weather to turn kinder. Modern farmers build special sheds lit with strip lighting just to sprout their potatoes in at the optimum temperature of 45°F. A single year that brings a full yield when frost has ruined the unsprouted seed can pay for the whole building, so gardeners should buy early and sprout their seed, rather than chancing what the garden centre will have left on Easter Thursday.

PLANTING POTATOES

There are many ways of planting potatoes, but the no-digging one of standing the seed tubers on the surface and covering them with sections of straw bales, peat or compost is not recommended. Potato tubers swell where resistance is least, and they will come to the surface and grow green with the alkaloid solanine, which is poisonous. The fruits of the potato, rather like small green tomatoes, which are common in some years, contain even more of this alkaloid, and should on no account be eaten. Potato seeds are only used for raising new varieties because, if they were sown like other seeds, they would only have time to grow into grape-sized tubers by lifting time.

On sandy soils or where there is plenty of humus, just dig in compost of rotted farm manure, *never* lime, and make 6-in. deep holes with a metal-shod dibber at the spacing required; then push a seed potato, sprouts upwards, down each and fill in after it. This is quick and easy. But remember that on clay soils the dibber can 'puddle' the sides so that water is held in wet springs, which retards growth.

The other way is to dig a trench 8 in. wide and about 1 ft deep, so that plenty of compost can be spread along the bottom and trodden down, covered with a 1-in. thick layer of soil for the seed potatoes to stand on with their tops (not sprouts) 6 in. below ground. This sounds hard work, but it means that every year a quarter of your garden gets plenty of humus well down for deep-rooted crops, and you can use the upper layers of the compost heap and keep any weed-seeds underground, if you had trouble getting the heap hot enough to destroy them.

There are many variations on this system. On very light sands and chalk soils, tread dead leaves that have been stacked through the winter along the bottom of the trench, add perhaps 2 in. of compost, then the soil layer, and then set out the tubers. This uses less compost but more moisture-holding material, and as the trenches should be in a different place each year, your garden gradually builds up a deep dark soil that can be a pleasure to dig. There are many variations of this method. For instance the first spring cut of comfrey can be used as follows.

Cut the comfrey plants 2 in. above the ground with shears, and leave the foliage overnight to wilt. Then spread this along your potato trenches at the rate of $1\frac{1}{2}$ lb. to 1 ft of row, place your seed potatoes on top and fill in the trench. The balance of minerals in cut comfrey is roughly the same as in a chemical potato fertilizer, but with rather more potassium and less phosphorus. Though growing comfrey foliage to use as a potato fertilizer would not pay on a farm scale (farmers can make more money feeding the foliage to pigs), it grows a garden potato crop which will have a chemical fertilizer yield, but with the genuine compost-grown flavour. In cold springs comfrey starts slowly and may not be ready until May; there may not be enough growth on the plants to provide foliage to cut for early or second early potatoes. In this case the seed potatoes should be left longer in the chitting (or sprouting) trays. This wastes no time because they will grow their shoots before their roots anyway, and they can be planted when there is enough comfrey.

Sprouting in trays allows time for lawns to produce a good cut for those who have no comfrey, but grass is not such a good potato manure, with only 0.6 per cent potassium compared with the 1.19 per cent in comfrey.

Partly made leafmould, comfrey, and grass, or combinations of them all, act as long narrow compost heaps that decay with acidity. Potato scab is caused by a fungus that *dislikes* an acid soil, so it is possible to grow potatoes without scab even on chalk where it will always be worse, and where the non-resisting kinds can suffer from it until a minor problem becomes a headache.

Fill in the trenches without treading the soil (which could break shoots), and when the shoots come through, draw soil over them with a hoe if frost threatens, for if the growing points are killed, the carefully sprouted seed potatoes must go back to the beginning and start again.

95

EARTHING-UP AND DIGGING

When the shoots are 6 in. high, draw the soil towards them in a ridge, but do not cover the tips. This is called earthing-up – it kills the seedling weeds, supports the haulm, and puts more depth of soil over the tubers. Do this again about three weeks later to bring the ridges higher and destroy more weeds, and the spreading haulm will suppress the rest. This is why potatoes are regarded as a cleaning crop for soils full of annual weed seeds waiting to germinate under neglected grass. If the weather is very dry, water the trenches formed by making the ridges.

When the first early varieties' flowers are open, thrust the fork in from the side of the ridge to reduce the risk of wasting by spearing tubers, heave up and gather the hidden treasure, which will increase with every day that passes. Take a row at a time to clear the ground for the crops that follow, and dig only enough for use each day. Put the green haulm and spent seed potatoes on the compost heap (if not diseased), and spread the new potatoes on a sack in the sun for twenty-four hours to lose their earthy taste before they are eaten.

When three or four rows have been used, dig over a second time to level the ground before planting leeks, lettuce, late peas or whatever crop is to follow, and to get out even the tiniest, left-in potatoes. Potato blight can overwinter on stray tubers left in the soil. If everyone in Britain could dig up *all* their stray potatoes for just one year, the infection chain would be broken and blight would be banished, ending the problem which began in the 1840s. The immediate gain is a few more welcome earlies, and not having stray potatoes come up as weeds among your seedlings next year.

Second earlies are dug steadily across the bed, those for storing being lifted when their haulm dies down and is brown. Wait for this to happen also before you dig the maincrops which need to be fully mature, and try to choose a time when the soil is reasonably dry. Always thrust in the fork from the sides of the ridge to reduce damage, and spread out the tubers to dry and ripen in the sun for about three days. Then tip them into sacks for storage. Do not use brown paper or polythene bags, because these will sweat inside and this can start the tubers rotting. After the crop has been dug for six weeks or so, tip out and pick through, throwing away any that are rotting, and removing speared ones for immediate use, before returning the rest to the bags.

STORING POTATOES

Potatoes need a temperature of about 35°F. and darkness to keep well and avoid any risk of greening. Miniature potato clamps of the farm type will attract rats, and one of the best garden stores is a second shed with fibreglass insulation covered with hardboard or asbestos on the inside, and lined with metal round the bottom to defeat gnawing teeth. If it has windows that can be closed with hardboard secured with turn-buttons, like the blackout shutters of the past, these can be removed in spring to let in the light and the shed used for stacking the sprouting trays.

An even better method in these days of central heating is to nail stout building board over the thick fibreglass between the rafters that is used to prevent heat loss from the warm house below. This saves so much heat that roof water-tanks are usually insulated to prevent freezing. A hardboard or timber floor strong enough to take potatoes (in half-filled bags so as to save carrying a whole hundredweight up the loft ladder) is a rewarding investment, for this kind of temperature will also store apples. In the spring, however, the temperature of the roof space will go above 45°F. and the potatoes will start sprouting. If the house has a gable end, or ideally two, a builder can fit windows to open and allow a draught through, for the problem of storage is to keep the potatoes *cold* enough to last. The roof space of a garage is also good, provided the beams are strong enough to take the weight.

Potato storage room is an asset to any household, for, even if your garden is too small to grow a full year's supply, it makes it possible to buy them by the hundredweight from an organic farmer so that you can still enjoy compost-grown flavour and quality.

8 Roots

Artichokes, Beetroot, Carrots, Onions, Parsnips, Radishes, Salsify, Shallots, Turnips and Swedes

Though cooking is essential for potatoes because their starches are indigestible without it, many root vegetables are nicer eaten raw. It is possible to enjoy salads of grated roots right through the winter, with a gain in minerals, vitamins and enzymes including catalase, which is a protective factor against cancer.

ARTICHOKES

Of the two artichokes – Jerusalem and globe – the one most worth growing is the Jerusalem. The globe (*Cynara cardunculus*) gives too little return for the space and trouble it takes. The Jerusalem with its small, knobby tubers actually comes from America, is a kind of sunflower and is very hardy. Those who are not very fond of it can cut it twice a year for compost material and just dig up some roots when they are needed.

Tubers are scarce and expensive from nurseries, so the best way to start a stock is to watch your greengrocer and buy by the pound – the ordinary artichoke is a species and there is no difference between eating quality and those bought from seedsmen. There is a French variety called 'Fuseau' which is *Helianthus tuberosus fusiformis* – it has long, smooth tubers with a finer flavour. These are at present almost impossible to buy in Britain, so those who take an autumn holiday in France could well try and bring some back, rather than buying carrots, cabbage or radishes which are nearly the same as our own.

Store any tubers you buy in peat in a dry shed until February or March, the best planting time. Dig in compost or manure to give the bed a start, then put in the tubers 6 in. deep, 18 in. apart each way in staggered rows. On good soil a row 15 ft. long should produce about 28 lb. of tubers. When the plants come up, put a post at the end of each row and one in the middle with a string on each side of the 6-ft tall stems to prevent them blowing over. In the following November the stems can be cut for compost material or dried for light flower stakes. Dig the tubers as required – because they are fully hardy there is no need to dig and store. Keep the last few to grow again. Because they have no diseases they can occupy the same ground for as long as four years, though if they do stay in the same place, give some compost every season before replanting.

When digging up the crop take great care to get the little ones out, because these are fearful weeds in the crop that follows. The best yield is always from lifting and replanting every year.

The one handicap of Jerusalem artichokes is their awkwardness to peel, but they can just as well be scrubbed and boiled like potatoes and liquidized for artichoke soup. They contain inulin, rather than starch like potatoes, which gives them their typical smoky taste, and levulose rather than ordinary sugars, so they can be eaten by those who must avoid starch and sugar.

BEETROOT

There are two widely grown types of beetroot, the old round kind (globe) and the new crosses with sugar-beet (tankard), of which Cook's Delight is the best. This is so named because you do not cook it, but grate it raw and, as it is non-bleeding, a large specimen (which can be 2 in. thick and over 1 ft long) can stay in the refrigerator for slicing or grating as required. There are two others of the same type, Cylindra and Housewives' Choice, and all stand out of the ground like large red sausages, with Cook's Delight so tall that it may have only a fifth of its length in the soil. A third type, the long variety, is grown mainly for exhibition.

In the round class, Sutton's Early Bunch is about the fastest, fully grown by June from an April sowing, and about cricket-ball size by October, for storing from June sowings. Detroit and

Boltardy are also popular, while there is a yellow kind, Golden Globe, for those who like a change of colour. All these round sorts are for boiling, not eating raw.

The sowing time depends on whether you want to eat beet in the summer by sowing in March or April, or to aim at enjoying lettuces while these are easy, and keeping beetroots in store for winter – in this case sow from late May to mid-June. Like all roots, beets do best where potatoes or any other crop had compost or manure the previous year.

Make 1-in. dibber holes at 6-in. intervals along the garden line, drop one of the large seeds down each, and close in the hole with the dibber point before moving the line 8 in. and making another row of holes, placed so they come between the others. This staggering is a good idea for sowing or planting anything, for the leaves will spread in a circle and these fit together more closely and suppress weeds. It is especially useful with summer cabbages, which can sit solid on the weeds.

Beet seed looks like small yellow raspberries, for each is really a cluster, so pull out all but the best in each bunch when they have grown enough to be sure. Beet should never be allowed to run short of water. The summer beet can be lifted as required, or the whole batch taken up to make room for something fast like lettuce, and stored to eat till the autumn. The second sowing can follow in the same space, because beet have no disease that demands rotation, which brings two batches of small, tasty beet rather than one of heavy monsters. Those who want really large specimens can make a May sowing of Cook's Delight, which does not go tough with age like the round varieties.

In September or October, lift your storing beet, twist off the leaves for compost material and, after letting the roots dry in the sun, set them out on a 2-in. thick layer of dry peat on the bottom of a tea chest or other stout box, taking care that they do not touch each other. Add another 2 in. of peat and more beet, repeating the process until the roots are all stored. An anti-mouse precaution is to stand the box on 2-lb. fruit bottling jars which will be too slippery to climb, but keep the box a good 6 in. from the shed side, for mice can run up it and jump a lesser gap. Peat is the best storing medium for all root vegetables, with sifted ashes, ideally from an anthracite or coke central heating system, second best.

CARROTS

There are two types of carrot – short, fat and fast for early sowing and summer eating, and longer and stouter for storing. The favourites in the first group are Amsterdam Forcing and Early Nantes, sown in mid-March or early April for grating raw or cooking. The late or maincrop kinds are also bred for speed, for today they must be sown late to avoid carrot fly. Of these Chantenay Red Cored, Sutton's Favourite and James Intermediate are all tapered cylinders with the speed to grow 2 in. in diameter or more at the top, which is storing size, from a mid-June or early July sowing to give the best chance of avoiding the main attack from the fly. For a description and an account of other counter-measures see p. 216.

Like most roots, carrots prefer to follow a crop that was manured last year, but if this is not possible, compost and leafmould can be dug in before sowing. Two bucketfuls of compost and another two of fine leafmould to a square yard will convert even a heavy clay to carrot-quality soil, while one of each will suit a sand. Rake the soil to as fine a tilth as possible before sowing seed in $\frac{1}{2}$-in. deep furrows 8 in. apart. Mix the small seed with eight times its bulk of fine bonemeal – this stretches $\frac{1}{2}$ oz. of seed to fill 200 ft of furrows and shows up well against the soil. Close in the furrows and wait till the ferny leaves are over 1 in. long, then thin to about $1\frac{1}{2}$ in. apart. When the remaining carrots are $\frac{1}{2}$ in. across the root tops, pull again to leave the others 3–4 in. apart, eating the thinnings in salads.

The fast short carrots take about twelve weeks from sowing to cooking, and several sowings can be made, each of which provides two pullings, one whole and the other grated or cooked. They are not good keepers, so the other kind must be grown for storing. Sow these in the same way, but thin to a 3-in. spacing when 2 in. high, and dig them in October. Another way is to buy pelleted seed and sow it in late May. This has a thick coat of a kind of clay, making the seeds large enough to sow singly 3 in. apart and thus, by cutting out thinning completely, avoiding the scent of crushed carrot foliage which attracts the fly at thinning time.

When the carrots are lifted, twist off the leaves for compost and leave the roots in the sun under shelter so that they dry sufficiently for the soil to flake off without washing. Look them over carefully for any holes that contain the small creamy yellow maggots which will become carrot flies, and cut these up for immediate use, for damaged roots will not keep. Then store them in peat like beetroot.

There are some lucky gardeners who may be free from carrot fly, living far from waste land where hemlock or cow parsley or other carrot fly hosts are growing. They can sow maincrops safely in May and grow heavy yields without trouble.

ONIONS

Onions, too, are afflicted with a fly (*Delia antiqua*, the onion fly), and this has driven most modern gardeners to raising theirs from sets, which are small bulbs. This cuts out the need for thinning, evades the need for the careful firming and preparation which used to mean that making an onion bed was a major operation, and brings the crop ready for lifting in August instead of risking a struggle to ripen in what could be a wet autumn.

The variety sold as sets is Stuttgarter Giant, which is a mild, flat onion. Giant Fen (globe variety) and other British grown sets are available, all more expensive, though equally mild. Sets are sold by the pound, which gives about 200. Spring onions include White Lisbon, a non-keeping kind for eating raw, and the two that are worth growing from seed, James Long Keeping and Up-to-Date, for those who like stronger onions. Those who take continental holidays can still buy Red Italian, the last survivor of the really strong onions of the past, bred to go with powerful cheese and beer that *was* beer; it lives on in countries where it competes with garlic.

Onion sets should go in from the first week in March to the second week in April. Spread lime at 8 oz. a square yard, and any compost you can spare, before digging, raking level, treading the bed firmly and raking smooth again. Onions like something solid to push against when they come out on the surface to ripen in the sun, but on heavy clays it is best to wait for dry weather so that the ground does not pack hard. Plant the sets with a dibber, 6 in. apart and 1 ft between the staggered rows, first twisting off the dry tops so that nothing shows to give a handle to the sparrows. Leave the growing point about 1 in. below the ground, and fill in the holes with the dibber point.

It pays to hoe the bed, because if weeds get large and have to be pulled by hand, there is a risk of breaking the onion stems. If you are growing for show or like extra large onions, scatter fishmeal at 2 oz. a square yard in early June, and hoe it in as a tonic. Those who aim for size by feeding with sulphate of ammonia (or soot) to supply extra nitrogen and sulphur, gain it, but at the expense of storing quality.

When the tips of the leaves yellow in August, bend the necks over at right angles to break them if they do not do it themselves, and loosen the roots with a fork to start them drying. After ten days' drying, dig up the bulbs and spread them in the sun to finish. When the foliage has withered completely, clean this off and store the bulbs in old nylon tights hung in a dry shed. They can also be hung in bunches from the eaves of a shed, or stored on a tray of wire netting hung under a garage roof.

Those who would like to try onions from seed can prepare the bed in the same way, sowing in March or early April in ½-in. deep furrows 1 ft apart, and thinning to 6-in. spacing, hoeing in the same way. The major difference is the problem of ripening them in late September, dragging them in and out of the rain on a sack in a wet autumn.

Spring onions should be sown thinly in ½-in. deep furrows 1 ft apart in August, and left unthinned to pull for salads from about April onwards, which makes them a useful winter crop for those who can sell surplus bunches to a greengrocer. If you leave a row in, thinned to 3 in. apart, you can snip off the leaf tips to add onion flavour to salads and dig the bulbs from May onwards for cooking. They will not keep long but can be eaten until October. Those who like onion leaves in salads can buy greengrocers' spring onions in April and plant them out 3 in. apart for snipping and for bulbs; this is certainly cheaper than buying onion plants.

PARSNIPS

The larger the parsnip the greater the chance of its rotting in winter from canker, so it pays to sow them as late as the second week in April to have them smaller and tastier, with better keeping qualities than from earlier sowings.

Parsnips take between three and four weeks to germinate, which is ample time for weeds to swamp them, so the following policy pays. To each 4 square yards, scatter 1 lb. of lime (if a soil test requires it) and 8 oz. of fishmeal or blood and bonemeal (if no compost is available), and dig this in. Then rake level and take out a 1-in. deep furrow with the corner of the hoe along the garden line, and set out clusters of three seeds at 9-in. intervals. Sow radishes thinly between the clusters, close in the furrow and move the line along 1 ft ready for the next row.

The radishes will be up fast and mark the rows so that the parsnips can be hoed, and by the time the radishes are ready to pull, the parsnips will be ready to thin to the best in each cluster. Dig them in November to store like beet. It is also possible to leave them in the ground and dig as required. This works best with White Gem, a new canker-resisting variety which does well from the March sowings that go in with the first radishes of the season.

RADISHES

The best summer radish is Cherry Belle, an all-red kind that takes forty days from sowing to eating and will then last four weeks in the rows without going hot and woody. Those who like a colour range in the salad can try Yellow Gold and White Icicle, which is long and tapered, but neither lasts so long from a single sowing. The winter radish for grating or cooking, to eat like a turnip with a radish flavour from November to April, is Chinese Rose, which is better than Black Spanish because it only needs scrubbing, not peeling.

Sow your first radishes in March (unless they are sharing a bed with your parsnips), in pairs of ½-in. deep furrows 2 in. apart. Sow them thinly and aim at a sowing every three to four weeks till the end of June, either one pair of rows or two, according to how much you like radishes. Most gardeners sow too many at once and waste space on woodiness, or crowd their parsnips by not pulling enough before the foliage swamps the main crop, but it is easy to fit a row in if you like them, bearing in mind that though they belong to the cabbage tribe, they grow too fast for clubroot.

Chinese Rose has roots which can be 6 in. long and 4 in. thick, producing as much as 1½ lb. to 1 ft of row. If it is sown at the ordinary radish season it runs quickly to seed, so it should always go in after midsummer, with July the best month. Sow the quite large seeds 1 in. deep, 4 in. apart and 9 in. between rows, hoeing once while they are small. They are fully hardy, need no more attention, and are not a clubroot risk.

Dig them as required and cook exactly like turnips, steaming or boiling until tender with very little water. The roots can also be sliced and fried like potato chips, or liquidized after cooking to make a radish-flavoured soup. They are most popular grated raw for salads, or cut into sticks and eaten with drinks like cocktail olives, but a great deal cheaper. Even when the Chinese radish is running to seed in April, the roots are still non-woody; it is perhaps the nicest of the winter salad vegetables, and certainly the most trouble-free.

SALSIFY

Salsify belongs to the daisy family (*Compositae*), so misses almost all pests and diseases. It is very hardy because it comes from Russia, first arriving during the reign of Henry VIII, when Catherine Parr was Queen. Dig in compost in the early spring, then sow the long black seeds in clusters of three or four at 6-in. intervals along rows 9 in. apart, and thin to one plant a cluster. Hoe them perhaps twice through the summer to keep down seedling weeds.

Dig as required from November to January, taking up every alternate row for cooking, and then cover the bed with autumn leaves about 6 in. thick, held down with wire netting, to force the roots like rhubarb. In early April, scrape the dead leaves away and pick the new salsify leaves – like those of a 'red-hot-poker' – when they are 4–6 in. long, to serve in salads or cook like spinach with an asparagus flavour. They are a welcome change from kale and sprouting broccoli, and picking can continue until May, when they will grow strong stems and flowers rather like those of sweet sultan. Dig the spent roots then, and pile the plants, stems and all, on the compost heap, or feed them to chickens or rabbits, for they are rich in calcium and iron. The iron is obvious in the red stains on one's hands after handling salsify leaves, but this comes off easily with washing in *cold* water.

Salsify leaves should be cooked fast with very little water, as spinach should be, and the water itself can be added to soups for the flavour and minerals gathered by this deep-rooting vegetable. The roots should be washed, cut into 1-in. lengths, and simmered for twenty minutes or until tender. They can then be baked in the oven, grilled with cheese on top, or fried in corn or sunflower seed oil. Another way is to rub the cooked roots through a sieve, mash them up with butter and fry with egg and breadcrumbs, or make them into a vegetable soup. Salsify has a distinctive taste, due to the iron it contains, which has earned it the name of Vegetable Oyster.

SHALLOTS

Those who need something much milder than onions, for peeling without tears, can grow shallots. Prepare the ground as for onion sets, and buy the large offsets in February. Plant them firmly at this time, with half their depth out of the ground, 8 in. apart and 1 ft between rows. They may need hoeing once or twice to keep the weeds down before the leaves turn yellow in June or July.

Dig them then, spread in the sun to dry, remove the dead foliage and split them up into offsets to store in a dry shed like onions. Each bulb will have from six to nine offsets, and some of these can be saved for replanting next February. Though the rest are usually pickled, they can be used as smaller and milder onions.

TURNIPS AND SWEDES

Greengrocers' turnips are as hard and heavy as cannonballs in the scales. Those that are grown fast and small from frequent sowings in organic gardens are tennis-ball size for cooking and grating raw, with leaves that are as rich in vitamins A and C as broccoli. The most popular varieties are Golden Ball and Early Snowball.

Sow first at the end of March to have the first roots ready in May, in $\frac{1}{2}$-in. deep furrows 1 ft apart, then sow again in May, June and August, the last sowing being for winter storage. Thin to 4 in. apart, cooking the leaves with little water as though they were spinach, but thin to 9–12 in. for winter-stored turnips. Those who like turnip greens can wait four weeks after sowing and then either pick the leaves like spinach or clip a length of row with shears 1 in. above the roots. Leave it to recover while you eat the rest of the row, and new young leaves will grow in successive crops. Turnips are often stored like beets, but they can stay in the ground all winter to be lifted as required. Golden Ball has considerable resistance to clubroot, but the others must go in the cabbage part of the garden rotation.

Swedes are even hardier than turnips, and the variety Purple Top can stay in the ground for lifting as required anywhere in Britain, thriving in the most exposed places. They are slower growing than turnips, and a sowing in April at the same spacing as turnips will supply them for summer and autumn eating, with another sowing in June to last through the winter. Thin them to about 6 in. apart because their foliage is larger (though not so good as a green vegetable as that of turnips). Those for winter storing should be thinned to 12 in. They provide golden-yellow colouring for winter grated salads, and make a good soup when boiled till tender and liquidized with about an eighth of their bulk of cooked onion or shallot. Thin the mixture with milk, add butter or oil, with herbs to taste, then reheat and serve.

9 The Leaf Vegetables

Broccoli, Brussels Sprouts, Cabbage, Cauliflower, Kale, Lettuce, Spinach, Swiss Chard

Leaf and flower vegetables provide folic acid, which is one of the most important of the B group vitamins because it is essential to general health and digestion. It is present in large amounts in liver, but up to 70 per cent of it can be destroyed in cooking, or thrown away in the cooking water. It is missing from most tinned and frozen foods, and the best way to take it is in raw leaf vegetables. These also provide excellent roughage, and a diet that includes plenty of these is the finest cure for the constipation that goes with white bread, white sugar and chips with everything. A gluben-free diet has ample fibre in leaf vegetables without whole wheat.

BROCCOLI

There are two kinds of broccoli: the 'heading', which is like a hardy cauliflower and is described later in this chapter, and the 'sprouting', which is one of our hardiest and most valuable green vegetables, with some resistance to clubroot, which makes it perhaps the most useful of the cabbage tribe. Purple Sprouting is the best – the flower and stem shoots are ready to pick in January and can go on until May, finishing in time to be followed by outdoor tomatoes. White Sprouting is not so useful, since it usually provides only one crop of tiny cauliflower heads among the leaves in spring, instead of growing a long succession which can be picked until the buds open into yellow flowers.

Sow sprouting broccoli in April in ½-in. deep furrows in a seed bed, aiming at 1 in. between seeds. Though seed is cheap and the packet will be a fat one, the thinner you sow the better the plants will be. When the seedlings are 4 in. high, dig them and snip the tip off the main root so they grow more fibrous roots when they are transplanted 4 in. each way in a waiting bed. This is an area in the cabbage tribe rotation space where they can stay until other crops release their room, and it is an important part of the organic gardener's routine, because he is trying to fit as many crops as he can into a small garden. In June or July (or about four to six weeks after transplanting), dig up the waiting plants and cut their leaves across with a knife, halving most of them, but missing the growing point. This reduces the leaf surface, so that they have less of it breathing out water when the roots are broken and not absorbing water, and it makes it possible to move the cabbage tribe when the plants are very large. It is usually easy to buy young plants of sprouting broccoli and other members of its family, but they are always available earlier than your room is ready, and at the best time for your rotation the plants are sold out. If you have spare space, you can plant at the earlier times given in the table in Chapter 6.

Broccoli like firm soil, so if possible they should follow peas, beans, lettuce, spinach or anything that does not need to be dug, so that the weeds can be hoed off the surface for planting without digging. If they are to go in a new garden or allotment, strip the turf for stacking, scatter 1 lb. of slaked lime a square yard (if required according to soil test results) for rain to wash in, and put broccoli in the undug soil. If they must follow potatoes, tread the soil very firmly.

Use a steel-shod dibber or a trowel and make large holes to take the young plants 18 in. apart each way, to allow room to walk up and down and pick between. Water the plants well after firming the soil over the roots, and if they must be moved in hot dry weather, cover them with newspaper held down with brick-ends during the day time for the first two days while they take hold of the soil. If the plants grow tall on a rich soil, drive in stakes that come 30 in. out of the ground, and tie the tall stems firmly to them, because the sail area of big broccoli is enough to break the roots in a strong wind.

In the winter and early spring and on through the time when green food is short, pick the broccoli shoots as the sprout heads show colour, taking the central ones first, with about 6 in. of stem. Never strip a plant completely but leave some of the shoots to extend. Do not damage the leaves, because they are working to feed the plant, even in winter.

BRUSSELS SPROUTS

The best-known Brussels sprout variety is Cambridge No. 5, ready for picking from December until March. Citadel is a larger version, and Peer Gynt is a smaller variety to start the crop in October, replacing Cambridge No. 1. There is also a cross with a pickling cabbage called, simply, Red, which has a different flavour as well as a striking colour. All can be eaten raw in salads as well as cooked.

Their cultivation is exactly the same as that of sprouting broccoli, but they are even more prejudiced in favour of firm ground. Soft ground results in 'blown' sprouts later, as does lack of water when young plants. Reserve the space where the early peas were for them, or plant them in June without double transplanting *between* the broad beans, so that they make a start in shade, before the beans are cut down and the weeds hoed off.

Do not keep the stumps for extra spring greens, because the favourite wintering place for cabbage pests, especially the mealy cabbage aphid and cabbage whitefly, is on these stumps. Take them up, chop off the root and burn it or dump it in your dustbin in case of clubroot, then bash the stem on concrete with the back of an axe to turn it into compost material, or so that it can lie in the bottom of pea trenches and slowly convert its woodiness to lasting humus. This applies to all cabbage family stumps.

Always *dig* rather than pull these stumps, because if one has clubroot, the swollen and rotting root mass can break off, leaving up to 26 per cent of its spores to last nine years in the soil. Once again, remember to clear any bed from the end, to leave the ground ready for the next crop. The commonest waste of room in a small garden is a piece undug and unsown waiting for a scattered half dozen of something to finish.

CABBAGE

In terms of food production from a small area, cabbages are one of the best bargains, weighing from 2–6 lb. each, or an average of 1 cwt for twenty-five plants. With careful selection of varieties it is possible to eat cabbages, cooked or raw, all the year round, and if it were not for clubroot our winter food production would shoot up, as they can replace leeks, green manure or bare soil.

The following table gives some nutritional values for the cabbage family:

Milligrams per 100 grams

	Calcium	Phos-phorus	Iron	Vita-min C	Folic Acid	Vitamin A Inter-national Units
Broccoli, raw	122.0	59.0	3.30	100.0	50.0	9,000
Broccoli, cooked	160.0	53.0	1.52	100.0	15.0	5,000
Brussels sprouts, raw	27.0	121.0	2.23	100.0	50.0	400–600
Brussels sprouts, cooked	27.0	45.0	0.63	65.0	15.0	400–600
Cabbage, raw	45.0	26.0	0.50	60.0	20.0	150
Cabbage, cooked	58.0	45.0	0.63	60.0		80–170
Cauliflower, raw	122.0	60.0	1.43	70.0	30.0	100–150
Cauliflower, cooked	23.0	33.0	0.47	3.0	15.0	30–90
Kale, cooked	197.0	72.0	2.54	51.0	15.0	7,500
[Lettuce	43.0	42.0	0.56	8.0	20.0	4,000]

Lettuces have been included because although they are at the bottom of the list for vitamin C, their great value lies in not belonging to the cabbage family and not therefore being subject to clubroot. Only those who have room to rest their soil for long periods, or have never had clubroot, can afford to replace lettuce with summer cabbage. Aim always at concentrating the cabbage tribe so that each section of your garden only grows them one year in four.

With a large garden, or without clubroot, the first cabbages to sow in March are Summer Monarch and Velocity, bred to eat raw as well as cooked, both far nicer than Greyhound or Primo which are the common kinds usually offered as plants. Aim at $1\frac{1}{2}$ in. between seeds sown in $\frac{1}{2}$-in. deep furrows 12 in. apart. Dig up the seedlings when they are 3 in. high, to leave a plant every 12 in. in staggered rows, and replant the dug up seedlings at the same spacing.

Velocity will be ready in about ten weeks from sowing, and Summer Monarch in twelve, but the latter is a better-flavoured variety, and the seed is always more expensive. So it pays to sow the seeds in threes at staggered spacing 1 ft apart, and remove all but the best when this is certain. The transplanted seedlings will mature about three weeks later than the others, which lengthens the cropping time, so a second sowing in May will carry the supply on till the end of September.

In May, sow Autumn Monarch and Winter Monarch, or Winningstadt and Christmas Drumhead, and move the seedlings to waiting rows ready to plant 18 in. apart each way in late August and September when the early and second early potatoes are cleared. These cabbages will finish in January, and can be succeeded by January King and the delicious red cabbages which are far too good to pickle with vinegar, which destroys vitamin C. Stockley's Giant is one of the best of these, but almost every seedsman has a red variety which will last on until March.

Another type for these difficult months is the savoy, which is the kind of cabbage with crinkly leaves. Ormskirk Rearguard is perhaps the best to stand from Christmas till as late as April. Sow in May and plant $1\frac{1}{2}$–2 ft apart each way, in staggered rows in July and August. These need plenty of room because they can rot if they touch each other in winter.

In July sow Sutton's April, which is nicer eaten raw than the old Flower of Spring, or Ellam's Early, for eating late March to early May, to fit in before outdoor tomatoes. They need spacing like savoys and planting in late September and early October, after the maincrop potatoes are dug.

CAULIFLOWER

Cauliflower seed is expensive, so it pays to buy a set of varieties, date the packets, and sow them for succession, a few from each. All The Year Round can start the season, sown in April and again in late June, in the usual ½-in. deep furrows. When the seedlings have four cabbage-like leaves, transfer them to their cropping position and set out 18 in. apart and 2 ft between rows.

Cauliflowers are less easy to grow, however, than sprouts and broccoli, and it is important to keep them growing fast, to be ready in late August and September. After three weeks scatter dried blood at 2 oz. a square yard round each plant, not on the spaces between. Comfrey liquid manure (see p. 59) is also appreciated. If they follow the first potatoes to be dug, which gives them plenty of compost, tread the soil well before planting, for they need the firmness.

In late May sow Veitch's Self-Protecting, or one of the other self-protecting kinds which used to be called 'broccoli', ready to plant out 2 ft apart each way in August, to eat until Christmas. At the same time sow the new Newton Seale, or Sutton's Snow-White, and plant out at the same time, for spring eating.

Though bought cauliflowers and broccoli are sold with few leaves attached, just the white curd in the middle, the leaves are just as good food value and should be cooked separately or together with the flower, for they form half the crop.

Though *sprouting* broccoli has some clubroot resistance, the cauliflower types, like cauliflowers themselves, have none, and the root damage from the disease cripples them so badly that one cannot save anything at all from the wreck.

KALE

The kales grow the most minerals and vitamins for winter with the least trouble. They have more resistance to clubroot than sprouting broccoli and, on an alkaline soil and with little manure, they grow tough and sturdy to face the wind and rain in even the coldest northern gardens. Their problem is that few people are really fond of their flavour, and the leaves are leathery rather than crisp in salads.

The nicest way to cook them is as follows. Coat the bottom of the pan with oil, add half a cup of milk, and bring to the boil. When the milk begins to rise up the pan throw in the shredded kale, put on the saucepan lid and shake so that the shreds of kale are coated with the boiled milk. Turn down the heat and simmer for 7–10 minutes. The object is to seal the vitamins inside with the milk proteins and improve the flavour. This method can be used with all old leaves of cabbage family vegetables, but the kales gain most from it.

The nicest of the kales is the new Pentland Brig, from the Scottish Plant Breeding Station (like so many famous potatoes), which is ready for picking from the end of January till early April. Earlier kales, for eating from November to the end of January, are the Dwarf Green Curled and the Scotch Curled (like whisky, kales are Scotch, not Scots), which look like giant parsley. Sow in April or May and transplant $2\frac{1}{2}$ ft apart and 3 ft between rows in June or July.

Kales do not like double transplanting, so the best way to fit them into a crowded garden in June or July is to plant them either in existing lettuce rows, or in the furrows where these are sown, for the plants will stand above the low-growing lettuces, which can be cut under them. On new allotments kale can be planted where the turf has been stripped, gaining from the extra firmness of the ground, and the fact that it resists wireworm. There is space to sow or plant a row of late lettuce between the kale rows; clear it before the kale casts too much shade – it can grow 4 ft high.

Pick the shoots where the leaves join the stems, just like sprouting broccoli, and though the leaves can be eaten, never strip a plant, but keep it growing. The remarks about bashing the stems for compost or putting in pea and bean trenches apply to kales too, not only for humus but to knock out the hibernating pests. All kales are good winter green food for poultry, and Thousand Head (asparagus kale) or Hungry Gap (rape kale) can be grown in the same way especially for them, though their larger leaves are on the coarse side for most tastes.

LETTUCE

Gardeners and allotment holders do not look for the same qualities in their lettuces as growers and greengrocers. We need lettuces which last to cut one at a time week after week from as few sowings as possible: they want them early and all ready together, to catch the best price and clear the field.

Perhaps the best garden lettuce is Sutton's Windermere, an improvement on Webb's Wonderful. It has large frilly leaves, well spread for maximum vitamin C, thick midribs to hold firm in drought and make an average plant a solid pound weight of salad, and the ability to give about six weeks' eating from a single sowing. If you prefer the plain-leaved cabbage type rather than the frilly kind, choose Buttercrunch, which lasts almost as well as Windermere, even in dry summers. The most popular upright or cos lettuces are Lobjoit's Green, Little Gem and Winter Density, which can be sown in summer (as well as in the autumn) for a winter supply in mild districts.

Scatter bonemeal at 4 oz. a square yard before the first sowing of lettuce in March, or meat and bone meal if the soil is poor, unless the ground had compost for the previous crop. Dig and rake level, then sow the Windermere variety thinly in $\frac{1}{2}$-in. deep furrows 1 ft apart. Thin the seedlings to a foot between plants in staggered rows, transplanting the thinnings to the same spacing, and they will be ready a fortnight later. Sow again in early May, in mid-June and mid-July to keep up a steady supply till the end of September. Bolting (running to seed) is less likely with the modern varieties, but watering well will also help to keep it to a minimum.

How many rows you sow each time depends on your appetite for lettuce, and it is very easy to waste space on too many, but because they are *Compositae* (daisy family), it is perfectly safe to sow the June or July batches where the March one finished. If you grow nothing but lettuce for years, diseases can build up, as market growers find. To extend the season further, sow Winter Density in July and again in August for autumn and winter eating.

Ordinary cabbage lettuces can go 9 in. apart each way, while cos can be 6 in. apart and 9 in. between rows, but Windermere is so large that it needs the extra space. Though the cos lettuce varieties are supposed to be 'self folding', it is better to gather the leaves together and put a tie of wool or a rubber band round them about a quarter of the way down from the top, to blanch the inner leaves and achieve the delightful pale green crispness that always makes this type more expensive to buy in the shops.

Winter Density, sown in August, has the advantage that its leaves are well clear of the ground and safe from attack by slugs. Sow in September in the South for a batch to come through the winter and heart in the spring. It is also possible to move them into a cold greenhouse after the tomatoes are cleared, for eating before the seedling sowing rush starts.

It is possible to buy seedling lettuce in March and have a batch ready as early as May, and the favourite variety for this is All The Year Round. Plant it 8 in. apart each way. In town areas, the best policy is to cover the rows with wire peaguards to keep the sparrows off, for they will destroy all early seedlings. Those who have trouble with mildew, which builds up from growing lettuces too often, can grow the mildew-resistant Avondefiance, a good ordinary cabbage type.

SPINACH

The ingredient that gives spinach its flavour is oxalic acid, which has the quality of locking up the iron and calcium in the foliage, together with more from our bodily reserves, as oxalates. So, though the spinach family is rich in these useful minerals, in terms of our bodies it contains less than none. On the other hand, its members are immune to clubroot because they belong to the beet family (*Chenopodiaceæ*), and are very easy vegetables to grow for those who like them. They can be enjoyed all the year round from the smallest garden.

The most useful variety of summer spinach is Cleanleaf, the kind which holds its leaves highest away from the mud splashed by rain. The first sowing can be made in February or March, in clusters of three or four seeds 6 in. apart and 1 in. deep, with 1 ft between rows. In April the first young leaves will be ready to pick and eat raw in salads, long before the very first lettuces. As they coarsen and become bitter-tasting, the leaves are less attractive raw, and are better cooked. Later sowings at three-week intervals until August will keep up the supply until September, each sowing taking about five weeks to grow from seed to picking, giving three weeks eating from each. In August, sow Longstanding Winter Spinach at the same 1-ft row spacing, but with 8 in. between clusters, and thin them to single plants, staggered so that they are less likely to touch. This should be a very much larger sowing than the others, because they will not grow fast in winter.

Pick only a few leaves from each plant so that none are overworked, and remember that a great basketful of leaves cooks down to very little, so the average garden using all its winter room for spinach should be able to support a family of addicts and starve out their clubroot through the years.

PERPETUAL SPINACH

This is only relatively perpetual, because it can provide a year's spinach leaves from only two sowings instead of a long succession of them. It is a rootless beetroot, with a less strong spinach flavour because it is a little lower in oxalic acid. Sow it in 1-in. deep furrows 18 in. apart, spacing the large seeds in pairs at 1-ft intervals, and thinning to the best when this is certain. Make the first sowing in March or April for the summer, and another in August or September for winter and spring.

Pick by bending the leaves down till they break off, not cutting or pulling, in case they bleed. Cut out any flower stems that grow, especially through the summer, and never strip a plant. Always sow enough so that there are plenty to share the burden.

NEW ZEALAND SPINACH

This is an entirely separate genus, *Tetragonia expansa*, a trailing plant, of which the small leaves at the tips of the shoots are eaten. Sow the large seeds in groups of three, 2 ft apart each way and 1 in. deep, after soaking them for twenty-four hours in water, because their hard cases make them slow to germinate. Sow in May when the soil is warmed, or in April under cloches, as advised later for pumpkins (p. 131).

Hoe between the plants till they get ahead of the weeds, and pick the top 2–3 in. off the shoots when they have grown 8 in. long. This picking continues from June or July, right on until the first hard frost, when the mass of branching stems can be dumped on the compost heap. New Zealand spinach never bolts, and the tips can be harvested more quickly than any other kind. It can be cooked as a green vegetable, or made into good soups with a liquidizer.

SWISS CHARD

This is another rootless beetroot, but with tall leaves from 1–2 ft long, and giant white midribs, often 4 in. wide, which provide a bulk of carbohydrate and a change from cabbage in winter both for the kitchen and the soil. There are both red and green-leaved varieties of this hardy winter vegetable (also called Seakale Beet and Leaf Beet), but there is not much besides the colour to choose between them.

Sow in April or May 1 in. deep in clusters of three 1 ft apart, with 15 in. between rows. Thin to the best in each cluster and break the leaves off downwards as they are required. Sow again in August or September for the winter crop. Manure or compost can go on before the April sowing, but not before the later one as this may make the plants too large and soft to stand the winter.

Snip the leaf portions away from the midribs and cook them in their own juice for 10–15 minutes. They are a separate dish from the white midribs, which should be sliced across into 2-in. lengths and simmered slowly for 15 minutes with chopped onion and a lump of butter or margarine. The ribs can also be cut into 1-in. sections, steamed till tender and then fried like chipped potatoes.

Swiss Chard is perhaps the most satisfactory of the winter spinaches because it stands well clear of the ground, has no enemies other than slugs, and you can go out on a cold day and quickly gather enough leaves for a meal, above any snow, instead of spending far longer picking a winter or perpetual spinach that cooks to very little.

The Oxalic Acid Question

The problem with the beet family, of which spinach is a member, is that they contain so much oxalic acid that it could be dangerous to those who eat too much. The following table sets out the position:

	Milligrams per 100 grams				
	Oxalic Acid %	Vitamin C	Calcium	Iron	Vitamin A International Units
Spinach	0.8920	59–75	595	4.0	8,400
Spinach, New Zealand	0.6500	62.00	890		1,400
Beet Leaves	0.9160	34–50	94	3.55	21,000
Swiss Chard	0.6600	38.00	87	4.02	2,800
Fat-hen	1.1100	85.00	990		19,000
Rhubarb (cooked)	0.5000	15–20	440	0.28	100
Lettuce	0.073		43	0.56	4,000
Broccoli Leaves	0.0054		122	3.50	

The weed fat-hen can be eaten when it is a seedling about 6 in. high by those who are short of green vegetables, but in 1945 it poisoned some displaced persons living in bombproof shelters in Austria and eating only the fat-hen that grew among the ruins. There is a risk of calcium shortage, especially among children, from eating quantities of spinach. Rhubarb *leaves* hold very much more oxalic acid, and should *never* be eaten, though the stems are safe.

There is a new low-oxalic-acid spinach, Monnopa, for sowing instead of Cleanleaf as a summer spinach, but it is without the bitter flavour which gives spinach its taste. Maybe some day there will be a low-oxalic-acid Swiss Chard, perhaps with a different flavour altogether.

10 Peas and Beans

Organic gardeners should always grow more peas and beans than inorganic, because these legumes replace bought nitrogen fertilizers with a 'home-grown' supply, gathered from the air in the soil by the bacteria in their roots. This nitrogen is combined with oxygen so that it can be used by the plant, receiving 'the rate for the job' in carbohydrates, just like the phosphate-gathering fungi with which we began (see p. 10). The energy that the leaves of pea tribe crops pass on to their bacteria is far less than the fraction of the five tons of coal or equivalent it takes a factory to make a ton of fertilizer, but it is used more efficiently, and it is part of the art of gardening to waste as little nitrogen as possible between one crop and the next.

In addition to growing French and runner beans to eat, pods and all, and peas and broad beans to shell, organic gardeners grow peas and beans for drying and storing. Those who have the space can grow 5–6 lb. of hardy haricot beans to 100 ft of row, replacing the many tinned vegetarian nut foods and imitation soya steaks with home-grown protein.

Today there are many people who wish to be self-sufficient on the land, but the problem is to grow enough concentrated vegetable protein from a small area to avoid the mental and physical slowing-down caused by too much carbohydrate. If you want to be a self-supporting *meat eater* you will need to have much more land (about six times as much), and do far more work, for someone will have to milk the goats, kill the pigs and castrate the bull calves.

Proteins are made up of amino-acids, and of these, ten have to be specially supplied – our bodies can synthesize the others but not these, which are all present in the legume crops. Soya beans have the best balance of amino-acids, but yield the lowest crop, and, in this country, tic and daffa beans are the most reliable, hardiest, and crop best in the least space.

The beans we can grow in Britain, excluding the soya bean which is, so far, too tender and low yielding for our gardens, fall into three groups: (1) the broad bean, and its relatives the tic and daffa beans, which are fully hardy and grow through the winter from autumn sowing; (2) French beans, including the haricot beans, which are low bushes and sown in May or June because they are not hardy; and (3) runner beans, including the climbing butter beans, which need sticks to support them and like French beans can only be sown when the risk of frost is past.

BROAD BEANS

There are two classes of broad bean, the longpods for autumn sowing and the Windsors for the spring, the latter having larger but fewer seeds in the shorter pods, and a finer flavour. Aquadulce Claudia is the favourite in the first class because it is the hardiest, but Meteor is faster and a heavier cropper, especially bred for deep freezing. The Windsors should be sown from March onwards, and Giant and Unrivalled Green are the most popular. They can be sown as late as May by those who prefer a succession of broad beans to spending their space on green peas.

The longpods are best sown in October and November, which fits them in after the outdoor tomatoes. Broad beans are greedy for potash, and unless they have plenty they can get chocolate spot fungus, which shows as brown patches on the leaves, stems, and pods. So spread $\frac{1}{2}$ lb. of wood ashes and a good bucketful of compost to the square yard and dig them in before sowing. Watering with comfrey liquid manure (p. 59) when the plants are about 1 ft high the following year is the alternative.

A pint packet of either kind of broad bean holds about 200 seeds, and they should be sown in trowel holes 3 in. deep, 8 in. apart, along a garden line. Move the line 8 in. further down the garden and sow another row with the seeds opposite the gaps, so that the plants in the staggered rows will support each other. This is usually enough support, but in windy gardens put a stake at the end of each row and one in the middle so that strings on both sides can support the plants. Allow 2 ft for picking space before the next pair of rows.

Sowing in the autumn results in plants with skins too tough for the blackfly (*Aphis fabae*), and when the beans reach about $2\frac{1}{2}$ ft high, about 8 in. of the growing tips should be cut out so that the blackfly cannot get a start. This method of defeating the main enemy of broad beans is so easy that the autumn-sown longpod type is by far the most popular.

Picking should start when the young beans inside the pods are about $\frac{3}{4}$ in. across. At this stage they can be sliced and eaten, pods and all, before these grow tough and woolly. Cut off the bean plants at ground level when picking finishes, and hoe the surface clear of weeds. Then plant Brussels sprouts, broccoli or cabbage with a dibber into the spaces between the double rows – this will be about the right spacing so that they gain the firm ground they like and the nitrogen from the left-in roots.

The Windsors are grown in exactly the same way, but they can be badly attacked by blackfly, so use one of the safe sprays described in Chapter 16. They clear rather later, ready for spring cabbages to be planted, and like longpods, their foliage makes good compost material.

Tic and Daffa Beans

These have the same shaped leaves as broad beans, but smaller and more plentiful pods that point upwards instead of outwards. Daffa beans look like chunkier and smaller broad beans with dark brown skins, while tic beans are light brown and much rounder. They are not sold in garden quantities, but they can be bought from agricultural feed merchants, who sell them as extra protein in pony rations.

Sow them 2 in. deep, 6 in. apart and with 1 ft between rows, in October or November like broad beans for harvesting in August, or in February and March for a later finish, which runs the risk of blackfly. The autumn sowing usually avoids blackfly, but the tips can be taken out in May or June like broad beans if the creatures appear.

When the pods turn black and the lowest ones split at the ends, the bean plants are ready to cut at ground level or pull up. Hang them to dry in a shed, with newspaper below them to catch any fallen seed.

When most of the pods are splitting put them between sacks and whack them with a stick, then sift out the beans, which is quicker than the monotonous job of popping the pods. Store them in screw-top jars or any rat-proof container.

Broad beans can be dried in the same way for seed. When dried, they should *not* be eaten, because they contain an alkaloid that risks a condition known as fabism if eaten in quantity. This is why they are not used for stock feed like tic and daffa beans, which are descended from the varieties that made horses 'full of beans' for centuries. If you keep a goat or cow these beans are an easily grown substitute for cattle cake.

FRENCH BEANS

The leading varieties now are Remus, which is the best of the new type of French bean without fibres down the back, Kinghorn Waxpod, also stringless and rather tastier, and the two old favourites The Prince and Masterpiece. Their yield depends on how often they are picked, for if the pods are allowed to grow large and tough, they will try to ripen seed and take the strength from late-developing bunches.

Sow them no earlier than the first week in May, 2 in. deep, 6 in. apart and with 2 ft between rows to allow plenty of room for picking. They should be ready about twelve weeks after sowing, when the lowest pods are 4 in. long. It is always better to have one row of French beans kept picked through the season than waste space on three that finish early from neglect.

French beans need potash just as much as broad beans, and on sandy soils it pays to water them with comfrey liquid manure (p. 59). Cut comfrey can be spread between the rows, or trodden into 6-in. deep trenches with 3 in. of soil on top before sowing on sands where French beans fail. Lawn mowings can be used on the surface or in trenches by those who are short of comfrey.

Haricot Beans

These are related to French beans, but with white or brown seeds to dry and store for winter cooking and vegetarian cookery. The old variety Comtesse de Chambord was valued for its thick foliage which made it, like all haricot beans, an ideal weed-suppressing and wire-worm-resisting crop for new allotments, but it is slower to grow than Brown Dutch, which is the tastiest of any and ready to harvest in September. The heaviest yielder is Purley King, a white 'baked bean' used for canning with tomato sauce, which has smaller seeds but is capable of producing 4 lb. of dried crop from 50 ft of row.

Because they need no picking room, haricot beans should be sown 2 in. deep, 6 in. apart and with 1 ft or even as little as 8 in. between rows, which should be staggered so that the foliage will fit closely together. Sow in May, or June where there is frost risk, and hoe off any crop of seedling weeds while the plants are small, with perhaps time for a second hoeing before the foliage meets.

They should be ready to harvest about mid-September. When the pods are pale light brown and the first are splitting at the tips, they are ready to cut at ground level with shears. The pods should be stripped and put to dry in potato sprouting trays, then threshed between sacks, or shelled if there is time. The plants are good compost material.

Those who have large gardens or can take a second allotment can use these beans for a fertility-building programme for sandy soils, which also defeats wireworm. Follow the beans with winter tares or grazing rye, dig these under in March or early April, then sow mustard and dig this under in May or early June before sowing beans again. Two or even three years' rest under this system will improve the poorest soils, while even a break under beans to make a four square rotation into one in which the greedy cabbages and potatoes come round every five years is a welcome holiday for a hard-working garden.

Before cooking, dried beans of all types need twelve hours' soaking, ideally standing in the refrigerator because this seems to reduce the 'windiness' that is the main disadvantage of this home-grown protein source. When they are fully soaked, bring them to the boil, and then simmer until tender (about an hour for Brown Dutch). A favourite recipe uses three cups of cooked beans, one of boiled whole rice, and bottled tomatoes or bacon scraps to taste, mixed and baked in a slow oven till really hot. Or make a bean soup with three cups of cooked beans, three pints of water, a sliced onion, three sliced carrots, herbs and salt to taste. Boil for about 15 minutes, put through the liquidizer, and heat up again for a really delicious vegetarian soup.

RUNNER BEANS

There are many varieties of runner bean, and Streamline, with pods up to 18 in. long, is a flower-show favourite. Enorma is even larger, nearly 2 ft, and produces a heavier crop, especially suitable for freezing. Fry is the first stringless runner bean, which means less to cut out and throw away, and can be picked from July till October. The fastest-growing variety is Sutton's Sunset, with pink instead of scarlet flowers, smaller pods and short joints, so it will make do with 5-ft rather than 8-ft bamboo canes.

Unfortunately, men with pony carts no longer hawk bundles of pea and bean sticks from door to door. Today we use bamboo canes 7–8 ft long, set out as in the diagram, with three tied together in a tripod at the end of each row, pairs of canes in inverted Vs at 4-ft intervals, and canes along the top to hold the structure together.

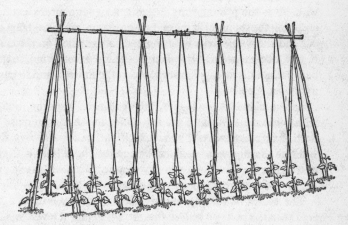

Runner bean supports

From this cross-bar, tie tomato string (3-ply fillis) leading down to pegs at ground level up which the beans can climb. There are gardeners who erect metal posts set in concrete and fasten stout wires to them to solve the problem of putting up bamboos every year and stowing them away for the winter, but this invites trouble from anthracnose fungus, for beans should rotate round the garden like most other crops.

Runner beans have a very large foliage area, so need plenty of material to hold moisture round their roots. Dig trenches 8 in. wide and deep and 30 in. apart and fill them with either rough material from the outsides of the compost heap, trodden lawn mowings or trodden comfrey, for there is plenty of this available before the beans are sown in May. Some gardeners prepare their bean trenches in the early spring by pulling their Brussels sprout and cabbage stumps, smashing these with an axe-back on concrete, and treading them into the trench bottoms, where they will decay more easily than in the compost heap and also get rid of the overwintering eggs of the mealy cabbage aphid and the cabbage white-fly.

Cover the filling material with 4 in. of topsoil, put up the bamboos with the pegs in the trenches and sow a bean about 2 in. deep by each of the 6-in. apart pegs. The tomato string, unlike plastic-covered wire, gives the plants plenty to grip; using wire means extra work stripping the stems off at the end of the season, whereas string can be cut and the whole mass of string and foliage piled on the compost heap. Choose a position for planting sheltered from wind, so that the bees are not discouraged from working the flowers, and so ensuring a good set of pods.

As the plants twine higher, they will need watering, but never with cold mains water on the leaves, for the shock can make beans drop their blossom. As the material in the trenches decays, the soil will sink slightly, which will leave a depression. Fill this with canfuls of water or by using a hose in dry weather. This will give an ample supply, with some trapped in the decaying material under the roots.

The secret of making one double row of beans feed a family is to keep the pods picked, so that stringy giants at low levels do not starve the later generations higher up the plants. If you need two double rows to supply a deep freeze, set the second pair 3 ft away from the first and spread lawnmowings between the two to keep down the weeds.

If you have a greenhouse it is simple to sow beans singly in plastic pots in late March, and have them ready to go out with a flying start in early May. Protect them with newspapers or brown paper tied to the strings above them like a topless tent.

Butter Beans

The grocer's butter bean is the Lima bean of America, more tender than our runner beans, which also come from Peru, but from higher in the Andes like potatoes and tomatoes. The butter beans we can grow are crosses with runner beans; they have the same white seeds, but smaller, and the habit of runner beans. White Achievement and White Emergo are the leading varieties, while Earliest-of-All is a climbing haricot with small white seeds.

The ideal places for butter beans are in the narrow bed next to the house, or where they can hide unsightly sheds or fences. It is much cheaper to borrow a ladder and use a masonry drill to insert vine-eyes, which are large screw eyes, at 1-ft intervals high up on the wall, or make S hooks out of stout wire to fit over the top of the fence and take strings, than to make a bamboo structure to support them. Butter beans do not need to be picked through the summer and all you need to do is cut the string to let them down at harvest time, so they may as well run up the side of the house like a temporary, white-flowered creeper.

A garden may contain several suitable places, but if there is only one, sow only half the site with beans and plant the other half with tomatoes. Change over so that neither grows the same crop two years running. Butter beans grow just as well on a bamboo structure, but if the odd corners in full sun are available, they may as well be used.

Give them a trench just like runner beans, water in the same way, but leave all the pods on till they turn light brown and begin to split. Cut the strings and strip the crop, and dry in potato sprouting trays. Store the beans in screw-top jars.

PEAS – GREEN

The hardiest pea of all is Meteor, which grows only 15 in. high and can be sown in January, if the weather is favourable and cloches are available, with the first pods ready in May. Perhaps the most popular kind of all is Kelvedon Wonder; sown from March onwards it will be ready to pick about eighty days from sowing. It grows about 18 in. high, and resists both wilt and mildew when sown in June or July for an autumn crop of fresh peas. Onward is a 30-in. maincrop, bred to produce pods over a longer period than the earlies, while Admiral Beatty is a heavy-yielding, fine-flavoured variety that grows up to 5 ft.

Sugar Peas, about 30 in. high, should be gathered young and cooked to eat pods and all. These are delicious shelled and eaten raw, and for the best nutritional value all peas are best uncooked in salads. Raw peas have about five times as much vitamin C, three times as much riboflavin, and four times as much thiamine as those canned or frozen. About half the value is lost in cooking, but cooked or raw, peas are one of the most enjoyable vegetables of all.

Tip all pea seed into paraffin and swirl it round before sowing, to repel mice without tainting the crop. If your soil has had plenty of compost in the past, spread another bucketful, and lime at 8 oz. to the square yard if needed, and dig them in, before taking out spade-wide trenches 2 in. deep and 2 ft apart. Then sow the peas 2 in. apart in two staggered rows with about 3 in. between them, spade back the soil and put up the pea wires.

As pea sticks are no longer available, modern gardeners use $1\frac{1}{2}$-in. mesh wire netting, so that the most popular peas are the dwarfs, which can be supported with the cheaper widths. Drive a creosoted stake in at each end of the row, cut a length of netting and take it along the row round both posts, joining it by hooking the ends together. Thrust canes through the meshes and into the soil at 3-ft intervals, to hold the wire apart at the bottom and prevent flopping. The peas can climb the wire from the inside, and the middle pods can be gathered by reaching down from the top. The netting is useful not only as a support – it also keeps the birds from pecking out the young pods when they look like small green bent nails.

Make the first sowing of Meteor in February in sheltered gardens, then sow a succession of Kelvedon Wonder, starting three weeks later and then every three weeks until mid-July, or sow one in March, and follow with a maincrop kind. Protect them all with the wire,

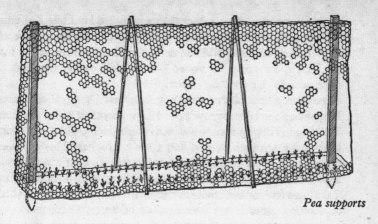

Pea supports

which rolls up and stores year after year. The stakes will last as long if you creosote them, otherwise they will rot off at ground level in only a few seasons.

If the soil is poor, sandy or chalky, use trenches like those for runner beans. Where rats are attracted by kitchen wastes in the compost heap in winter, when there is too little vegetable matter to decay them fast, it is a good idea to dig the first pair of pea trenches in November, empty the compost bucket in it each morning, add a scattering of lime, and cover with soil to keep the birds and dogs away. The first trench filled will take the early peas and the others can take the later sowings. If you throw away any green potatoes with the peelings, these can grow and become a 'weed' among the peas, so put these separately in the dustbin.

This trench system steadily deepens the humus layer in a garden as the peas and beans rotate round it. On sandy or chalky soils it is a good idea to line the trenches with four thicknesses of newspaper to retain more moisture. This raw kitchen waste in what are in effect long narrow compost heaps cannot rob the soil of nitrogen, because the peas have their own supply from their root bacteria. Runner beans can also use this type of trench.

PEAS FOR DRYING

Many gardeners sow rather more than they need of an early, round-seeded pea like Meteor, rather than a wrinkled kind like Kelvedon Wonder, and let the plants dry off, picking the pods when these are light brown and splitting like haricot beans. However, peas that are bred to eat green are not so good in pea soup as those which are especially designed for drying.

There is a new variety, Proco, and another like it called Alaska. Both are sold in bulk to growers who have a contract with a packeter. The original drying variety was Harrison's Glory, which is a dwarf kind about 2 ft high, hardy, and a heavy cropper. This has been rechristened Maro and is more easily bought. Another way to obtain a stock is to buy dried green peas (not split peas) in a supermarket. Take out a few and soak them overnight in cold water, then put them on blotting paper in a saucer half full of water. Leave them in a warm room, or on the warm spot at the back of the fridge, as though they were mustard and cress. If they do not grow they are suitable for eating but too stale for sowing. If they do, then you have bought one of the three varieties more cheaply than from a seedsman, and with less trouble.

Sow in March, just like green peas, but because you are going to let them dry off they do not need picking room, and the double rows need go only 1 ft apart. They should be ready for harvesting as July ends. Take up the wires, and strip off the pods for shelling by hand or threshing by beating between sacks.

The yield is about 4 lb. to 50 ft of row, and they have the advantage of clearing sooner than haricot, tic or daffa beans, so that there is a wider choice of crops to follow them. On the other hand, peas are attacked by birds, while all classes of beans escape. On a farm scale peas are as easy to grow as wheat, with automatic guns and tattered fertilizer bags keeping off the pigeons with the help of shooting, but farmers do not have neighbours who attract birds by feeding.

Dried peas are also a good protein source, nicer than tic and daffa beans, but with a small yield. They could also be the basis of a fertility-building rotation, if followed with winter tares or grazing rye sown in July and dug under in March. After they finish, they can be followed by a complete range of winter and spring cabbage in the firm soil left by hoeing off when the peas are cleared, instead of digging.

II The Fruiting Vegetables

Cucumbers, Marrows, Courgettes, Pumpkins, Sweet Corn, Tomatoes

We enjoy a number of vegetables which are not fully hardy, but can be sown after spring crops finish, or planted with protection until the risk of frost is past. There is a constant contest between plant breeders and our climate to produce varieties that will be hardy enough to start sooner, and grow fast enough to mature a crop before autumn closes in. Sweet corn and cucumbers are new victories for every gardener, even without a greenhouse, but so far the capsicum or sweet pepper has beaten British breeders.

Polythene bag 'cloche'

The polythene bag cloche is one of the cheapest and easiest methods of giving a flying start in April to everything in this group of vegetables except tomatoes. Dig out a hole about 1 ft square and deep. Fill it two thirds full of compost and one third with firmed topsoil, and plant any one of these large seeds edgeways in each, about 1 in. below the surface. Then take two 18-in. lengths of 20 gauge galvanized iron wire and bend them into staples or hairpins about 4 in. wide. Thrust the wire into the ground across the seed so that it makes a croquet hoop about 4 in. high, and put another one across it. Then stretch a polythene bag over the top, and keep it from blowing away with a rubber band at ground level.

Water the depression in the soil under the 'cloche' and leave the seedling to grow, removing the bag when the two rounded seed leaves are fully open and the risk of frost is past. Because the sun on this miniature cloche will warm up the weed seeds in the soil so that *these* germinate fast too, it is as well to take off the bag at intervals on sunny days for weeding, and if the weather is still terrible, make a larger pair of croquet hoops and put on a bigger bag.

These polythene bag cloches have several advantages over glass ones. They make protection possible for crops like pumpkins, which are planted 3 or 4 ft apart, which would mean two end glasses for every barn-type cloche. They cost very little, for the wires last five or six years and the bags at least three as they are only on for a short period and can be washed and put away. And above all, they do not spend the rest of the year on edge getting green with algae and risking a smash at every handling. Unfortunately, there is so much condensation inside that polythene bags cannot be used for lettuces.

Those who have a cold frame or greenhouse can sow their cucumbers, marrows, pumpkins or sweet corn singly in small pots of John Innes potting compost (a standard mixture, sterilized to kill weed-seeds and harmful fungi and pests) in mid-March. Water them well and cover with sheets of newspaper till the seedlings appear. These will be ready to plant in early May, but will be too large to go under polythene cloches.

Crops that spread flat, like cucumbers, marrows or pumpkins, can be covered at night with potato sprouting trays, removed in the morning, until frosts are past. Sweet corn and tomatoes are too tall for this easy protection, so collect cardboard boxes from a grocer or even a radio shop and place them over the newly planted seedlings with stones on their spread flaps in case of winds in the night. It is possible to snatch a useful fortnight's growing time by using these protection methods.

Tomatoes need more heat to start them, and the small electric propagators that save heating a whole greenhouse to the 55°F. they need are good value for these and for cucumbers. Sow the seed thinly in early April in the small boxes provided, using one of the seed composts available, and pot the seedlings carefully in John Innes compost, covering with newspaper for frost protection and to provide more humidity while they are taking hold in their new homes.

If the greenhouse or cold frame has no electricity laid on (oil-heated propagators can be bought), sow the tomato seeds three in a pot in early April, cover with paper, and thin to the best when they are growing well. In the South, three seeds can be sown $\frac{1}{2}$ in. deep under a polythene cloche in early May, and thinned to the best when this is sure. The idea of the three seeds is to make certain that one at least comes up. The greenhouse plants raised in heat will be the best, and so will bought ones, but this gives no choice of variety, and they can be surprisingly expensive.

OUTDOOR CUCUMBERS

The modern American cucumbers are bred from Japanese strains that look almost exactly like greenhouse types, entirely unlike the coarse and chunky ridge varieties that have not much taste and tough seeds. The best are the Burpless race, with edible skins, containing the vitamins A and C which are usually thrown away in the peel, and all are more digestible than the frame or greenhouse varieties.

Burpless Early is ready to pick in July, and Burpless Tasty Green starts in August. Burpless Green King also starts in August, and has resistance to mildew. Burpee Hybrid has a great quantity of fruit up to 1 ft long, and is ideal for those who are selling their surplus for the seaside salad trade in late summer.

Cucumber holes should be dug 2 ft apart each way and from an early April sowing they should be ready for polythene bag removal in mid-May. Water the seeds to start them, but once the bags are on they need none, because moisture will condense at night and run down the sides to soak back again. Greenhouse-raised plants can go out in early May, with the protection of cardboard boxes or trays at night. Seed can be sown outdoors without protection, but not until May.

When the first shoot has seven joints, pinch out the tip to make it grow sideshoots. If the latter do not fruit, pinch out their tips also, at the same distance. Keep a watch for ripe cucumbers lurking under the leaves, for if these are left unpicked they will try to ripen seeds and starve all the others that could be enjoyed right on until the first hard frost. If you want to save seed for next year, watch for one with a bulge at the far end and leave it till it goes yellow, then cut it open and take out the pale yellow seeds to dry on a pane of glass in the sun. These new hybrids do not come true from seed. If you want a variety that is easy from seed, grow the old Bedfordshire Prize, or Kaga, which is one of the original Japanese kinds, dark green with yellow stripes and a rather different taste.

MARROWS

These are grown exactly like outdoor cucumbers, but are hardier, and are very poor value for space because most of their weight is water. Those who like them can grow Long Green Trailing, Long White (which is the best to store for winter), or the many bush versions, which take rather less room.

Their holes should be 2 ft apart each way, and they can be useful to fill a space with thick foliage that suppresses weeds. Sow under polythene cloches in early April, or plant in mid-May, leaving a few marrows on the plants to grow monsters suitable for sawing across to make jam in October. Size is strongly inherited, so it pays to save seed from one of these monsters, which are often the pride of village flower shows.

Those who like marrows will enjoy this recipe for Marrow Stew:

1 small vegetable marrow	1 tsp. demerara sugar
2 medium-sized onions	1 oz. butter
2 medium-sized tomatoes	pepper and salt

Peel marrow and remove seeds, then cut into small cubes. Peel onions and skin tomatoes. Chop up roughly. Put a little water in the base of an oven-proof casserole and add the vegetables mixed together. Cover and place in a moderate oven (350°F., gas mark 4) for 15 minutes. Then add seasoning, sugar and butter and mix well. Cover, return to oven, and allow to simmer for 1½–2 hours.

COURGETTES (or Zucchini)

These are baby marrows, produced in a long succession of delicious sausage-sized fruit. You can grow either the bush varieties and pick the fruits when small, or one of the special kinds – Golden Courgette, which is bright yellow and should be picked at 3–4 in. long, Aristocrat which is green, and True French, which is also green and ready from July, when sown in April under polythene cloches like all this new and useful race.

Make their compost-filled holes 1 ft apart and allow 3 ft picking room between the rows. Their main need is to be picked frequently, because if they are allowed to grow to full size, one will race ahead and set seed, starving all the others. If you *want* to save seed buy only one kind to prevent crossing, and leave one large courgette on at the first picking.

PUMPKINS

The pumpkin usually grown is Hundredweight, which is grown for weight-guessing competitions, but the best are the Japanese hybrids, a cross between Belgian and Japanese varieties, which have about twice the dry matter of the American pie pumpkin, four times the vitamin A, nearly three times the protein and 25 per cent more calcium. Pumpkins are one of our best sources of calcium, even though spinach holds more, because they lack oxalic acid to lock it up, and therefore are excellent for milk-intolerant children.

They should be sown in April, just like outdoor cucumbers, under polythene cloches spaced 3 ft apart each way, or outdoors in May. When the first shoot has eight joints, pinch out the top to encourage side branches to grow, and when each of these branches has grown one plain-stemmed male flower after the first female one, which will have a tiny green pumpkin behind it, cut it short to make sure of more individual pumpkins rather than a single monster. After this first cutting back, however, the bed will get thick with shoots too quickly to thin, so let them roam, turning them inwards if they encroach on paths.

Colour is no guide to ripeness. The Japanese race is mainly orange, but it includes greens, greys and mixtures. Wait till October when the first frost takes the leaves, and cut off the pumpkins with about 2 in. of stout stalk left on each. Wipe the pumpkins carefully if they are muddy, leave in the sun to dry thoroughly, and hang them in the coloured nylon nets in which nuts, Brussels sprouts and other items are delivered to greengrocers – these are usually available free. Do not hang them by the stalks, for these will shrink and let the pumpkins down with a startling thud in the middle of the night. Store them in a temperature of 50–60°F. They need the warmest storage of any vegetable, and the space under a house roof is not too warm for them; in fact if there is fibreglass insulation between the joists they may need something in the way of a heater.

The main handicap pumpkins have in England is that no one knows how to cook them. Perhaps the best way of preserving pumpkins is as follows. Peel, dice and simmer 4 lb. of pumpkin in $\frac{3}{4}$ pt of water for 15–20 minutes. Drain and rub through a sieve. Add $\frac{1}{2}$ lb. butter, 2 lb. white sugar and 2 lb. brown (Barbados) sugar, and mix thoroughly. Add the juice, pulp, and grated rind of six lemons, discarding the pips and pith. Boil the mixture for 5 minutes, let it cool a little, and pack into jars, sealed like jam. It sets on cooling to what amounts to a vegan 'lemon curd', with the pumpkin replacing the eggs.

For an everyday recipe, try pumpkin soup. Scrub your pumpkin, cut it up into pieces about 3 in. square, and put in a saucepan with water to cover. Cook for 15 minutes, or until tender, then put the cooked pumpkin into a liquidizer with about a quarter of its weight of cooked potatoes. Add enough milk to thin it to the required degree and reheat, but do not boil a second time or the milk will curdle. Herbs may be added to taste. It is not necessary to remove the skin or seeds as everything will go through the liquidizer and make a good soup without using any stock.

Pumpkin can be peeled, cut in wedges and steamed or boiled with a little water as an ordinary vegetable. It can also be brushed with oil and cooked round a pot or oven roast. The American pumpkin pies 'like momma makes' are of course enriched with sugar and other fattening ingredients.

SWEET CORN

Our climate will grow what Americans call 'corn on the cob', but British gardeners spoil it by leaving the cobs on until they are almost as tough as the chicken maize we do not have sun enough to ripen. Though John Innes Hybrid and Golden Bantam are excellent varieties, there are newer and faster-ripening kinds including Sutton's First of All, the earliest of any, Kelvedon Glory, Earliking and North Star.

Spread at least a bucketful of compost or manure and 4 oz. of fishmeal to the square yard, and dig it under before sowing sweet corn in early April under polythene cloches. Sow 1 in. deep and 15 in. apart in short rows with 2 ft between them. It can be sown in May without cloches, and if the plants have been started in a cold greenhouse they can go out in early May with box protection. Sweet corn is greedy for phosphorus, showing a deficiency as dull purple streaks on the leaves, so 8 oz. a square yard of bonemeal before the *previous* crop will be appreciated. If the leaves turn rather yellow-green and the plants stop growing at about 1 ft high, give them a teaspoonful of dried blood each as a tonic.

At first they will need hoeing to keep ahead of the weeds, but otherwise need no special care, though in windy gardens some people spade soil round the bases of the plants to make them put out extra roots for a better hold. When the cobs feel plump and firm and the tassel beyond the green sheath that covers them begins to turn brown, they are ripe. Turn back the sheath, remove a grain and press it hard with the thumbnail, when the milky inside should come out. Try again when the tassel withers and cook a trial batch, for sweet corn is ripe sooner than you think and too good to let ripen past its best.

To pick them, hold the main stem of the plant and break the cobs out sideways with a sharp downward jerk. Do not cut them as this may damage the plants, which will go on producing till frost stops growth. If you take the big ones at the bottom first, this puts more strength into the others; ideally, pick them only half an hour before cooking. When they finally finish, the main stems should be bashed with an axe-back to make a very good foundation for an autumn compost heap.

TOMATOES

Harbinger is still the best all-round outdoor tomato. In the 1940s it led the trials by the John Innes Horticultural Institute by averaging the most fruit picked ripe before 6 September over five years. It has perhaps the thinnest skin and the nicest flavour of any outdoor variety, and has the quality of ripening best off the plant, which has kept it in cultivation on its merits as an amateur gardener's tomato for more than forty years. Another first-class kind is Outdoor Girl, new in 1961; this is rather faster to grow, with the same thin skin, but the fruits ripen rapidly all together for bottling, whereas Harbinger will ripen slowly until Christmas.

In Britain we average two good tomato-ripening years in five, and these two varieties, with their ability to ripen well off the plants so that most of the crop can be bottled and kept right round the year, make outdoor tomatoes one of the most valuable garden crops. Bush tomatoes like The Amateur are bred to lie on straw under glass cloches, and this means that slugs can eat more of the crop than you do in cold wet summers.

Dig holes for your tomatoes, just like those for cucumbers, 2 ft apart and 3 ft between rows, but drive a dahlia stake into the bottom of each hole so that it rises $3\frac{1}{2}$ ft out of the ground for Harbinger, and $2\frac{1}{2}$ ft for the less tall Outdoor Girl. Putting the stake in first and packing the compost round it saves damaging the roots by driving it in after planting.

If you wait till May and sow under polythene bag cloches, the clusters of three seeds can go beside the stake. Otherwise, put the plants in with a trowel, taking care to avoid breaking the ball of soil round the roots, then tie a string tightly round the stake and loosely round the plant to allow about $1\frac{1}{2}$ in. play for the stem as it thickens through the season. Water in thoroughly to give the plants a good start.

One of the best uses for discarded colour supplements is to secure them thoroughly with drawing-pins to the stakes, making a paper cylinder round the plants to keep off frost and cold winds. They can stay on for as long as a month without harm, and are more convenient than cardboard boxes, which must be handled twice a day. Use the latter, however, if the plants are becoming pale and drawn for lack of light in long-continued cold after the end of May.

As the plants grow, take out the side shoots, especially those near the base, so that no strength is wasted – ideally when they are small enough to remove by pinching. Tie the main stem to the stake at roughly 8-in. intervals, using green garden string or tomato string (3-ply fillis), which is made to hold up a heavy crop under greenhouse conditions, since good outdoor plants should carry about 10 lb. of fruit each. Do not use plastic-covered garden wire for it will cut into the stems, and avoid nylon because it lasts for ever in the compost heap and the soil.

When the first fruits begin to show, pale green and pea-sized after the first blossoms fall, water with comfrey liquid manure (p. 59), and spread cut comfrey between the rows, with a mulch of mowings on top, both to suppress weeds and add potassium for greedy tomatoes building a big crop. If you have no comfrey, use a seaweed spray on the foliage as directed by the makers.

Do not cut back the leaves or remove them unless they are broken, because it is temperature and humidity that ripen tomatoes, not direct sunlight. It pays to put pieces of wood under the bottom trusses to keep the fruit off the ground and away from slugs. Start picking as soon as the tomatoes are a real red, for the best flavour of all comes from ripening on the plant, but if there is risk of frost or blight (see Chapter 15 for this disease), or if the birds attack the reddening fruit, pick when they are changing from cream-white to pink and ripen them indoors.

When October comes, with cold nights and the first frosts, pick the whole crop, green ones and all, carefully avoiding breaking the skins or bruising the fruit, and leave the stalks on, for their removal leaves a wound through which bacteria can enter. The best way of ripening off the plant both in summer and for the main autumn batch is in the ever useful potato sprouting trays.

Line the trays with stout paper, such as thick and glossy colour supplement pages, set out the tomatoes with their stalks sideways and cover them with cut oblongs of draper's wadding, cotton wool, or old blanket. Stack the trays one on top of the other in a temperature of 54–56°F. in a greenhouse or sunny shed or room.

If the tomatoes stay in direct sunlight they will transpire quantities of water and wrinkle, but the blanket or wadding covering reduces the transpiration rate and condensation. The optimum ripening temperature will hold the most flavour, and finish the ripening process fast enough to keep the fruit ahead of the moulds and bacteria which usually mean only few and inferior fruits after Christmas. Lift the trays off the stack at weekly intervals, take off the wadding, which will not catch on the stalks if these have been turned sideways, and pick out the ripe ones for eating raw, cooking or bottling.

To bottle, slice the fruit in halves or quarters and stuff them into 2 lb. Kilner jars. Fill up with plain cold water, screw the lids tight, but give a quarter turn back to allow some expansion. Tie a strip of blanket, thin foam plastic or a rubber band round each so that they will not bang against each other when they boil, and pack them into a container deep enough for water to cover them.

Set the heat low enough to take 90 minutes to bring them up to 190°F., and then leave them at this for 15 minutes. Bale out some of the water so that the first top can be gripped through a cloth, and stand the jars on a wood or formica surface (not stainless steel, for this could chill and crack the jars). Give them a final tightening, and store in a dark cupboard or cardboard boxes with thick paper to stop light leakage through the folded-down flaps. This is to preserve the vitamin C which is destroyed by light. Stored in this way in an attic they will keep up to three years.

Bottling in this way has advantages over deep freezing because there is no risk of deterioration if a strike cuts off the electricity, and the jars can be stored anywhere frost-free. The capital cost of a cubic foot of freezer space is so high that it is best reserved for what cannot be bottled, such as strawberries, French beans or meat.

A dozen tomato plants can produce up to 1 cwt of bottled fruit, and they are far more easily stored than apples, pears or even potatoes, because the jars themselves are rat and mouse proof. Bottling without sugar costs only the caps or rings and the heat, so that a stock of jars is an investment for every family. Tomatoes contain fruit acids which tenderize tough meat, such as ox cheek and other cheap cuts, which is why they are used extensively in Spain to make even elderly goat go further, and real tomato soup made with your own tomatoes is just one of the many replacements for expensive tinned foods which prove that a garden grows better flavours than you can ever buy.

12 The Stem Vegetables

Celery, Celeriac, Kohl-rabi, Leeks, Rhubarb

There are root vegetables, leaf vegetables, seed vegetables, fruiting vegetables and finally those which have stems that we eat and enjoy. One of these is celery, of which I once grew a million a year to plant on 50 acres of black fen soil in Norfolk, where it grows best.

CELERY

There are two kinds of celery – Golden Self-blanching which needs no earthing-up and is eaten from August till the first hard frost, and the ordinary sort, eaten from October till about February. Most people prefer the white variety, but there are others with pink and red tints on the stems. Neither sort is of much nutritional value, for blanched stems contain no vitamin C or A, but many people like the taste.

Those who do not have a cold greenhouse or frame and an electric propagator would do better to buy their plants, which most local nurseries supply, than attempt to raise them without heat. With a greenhouse or heated frame, sow in early March in boxes of sterilized seed compost, and when the seedlings have two small celery leaves, space them out about 2 in. apart each way in other boxes of the same compost. Both kinds should be planted in the open in May or June.

Self-blanching celery is the easiest to grow, for it needs no trenches. Dig over the bed, which should have had compost the previous year. If it did not, give it a bucketful to the square yard, then space the plants 1 ft apart with 18 in. between rows, firming the soil round the roots with the handle of the trowel, which leaves a depression that will hold waterings while the plants get a start. They will need hoeing once or twice and watering if the weather is dry, but no more attention until they are dug for eating.

The usual way of growing the hardy kinds, which traditionally need a frost on them to bring out the taste, is to take out trenches like those for peas, but 1 ft deep and 3 ft apart. Tread 3 in. of compost or well-rotted manure into the bottom and cover with 3 in. of the top-soil from the trench. Then plant the seedlings 1 ft apart along the bottom. Water them till they start away and also during dry weather, and by August they should be about 1 ft high, ready to have any sideshoots broken off before earthing-up.

Gather the leaves and stems together in a bunch, and heap soil into the trench with a trowel, using one hand to hold the stems and the other for scooping the soil in. About ten days later gather the stems together and put a rubber band over them, then spade the soil round them till only the leaves are above it. Six weeks later your celery will be ready for eating.

CELERIAC

This is the turnip-rooted celery of which Giant Prague, Marble Ball and Globus are all good varieties. Sow it in March in boxes in a propagator and raise it like ordinary celery, planting it like Golden Self-blanching. It has the great advantage of needing no earthing-up, but as its base swells into a bulge, like half a turnip sitting on the soil surface, break away any side shoots. It needs plenty of water, and particularly copious supplies in a dry summer. About mid-November spade some soil over the bulges to protect them from frost.

The plants can be dug as required for grating the root and using raw to give a celery flavour to winter salads; the leaves and stems can be cooked for celery soups, and the roots can also be cooked when peeled and cut into inch-thick slices. The cooked slices can be fried in butter as a delicacy. Many writers consider this one of our tastiest vegetables and wonder why it is not more popular, when it is so much less work for the gardener than ordinary celery. The answer is that it is very time-consuming to prepare for eating, and plants are rarely for sale.

KOHL-RABI

There are two varieties of kohl-rabi, white and purple, the only difference being in the colouring of the swollen turnip-like stem, the edible part. Sow the seed in ½-in. deep furrows 1 ft apart and thin to 8-in. spacing, transplanting the thinnings to the same spacing to extend the season from each sowing. Make the first sowing in March, another in early May, and a final one in July or August to last through the winter until February.

Start eating the kohl-rabi when the bulged stem is cricket-ball size, pulling up the plants and cutting off the leaves and root for compost. Always eat them fresh, for the flavour is lost if they are dug and stored. It is a catch crop, to grow fast, not one to sow early and forget because, as it is a stem, it can easily grow woody. Kohl-rabi is at its best grated raw in salads, sliced into sticks to stand in a glass and eat like celery, or cut into ¼-in. thick sections and eaten as 'biscuits'. Never peel them for cooking, but steam or boil whole in their skins. Then slice and fry them in breadcrumbs, serve as a kind of turnip with a distinctive nutty flavour, mash them and make into rissoles, or liquidize the cooked kohl-rabi into a soup.

The yield can be as much as 1 cwt from 50 ft of row, but the value of this depends on how many are eaten. Time the winter sowing, in July in the North and August in the South, so that they mature as far as slicing hardness by October, and stay that way through the winter, for it is easy to grow woody weight by leaving them too long uneaten.

LEEKS

The leek is the best British winter crop, and when leeks are thrown on to the field when Wales plays a Rugby International, they are remembering the allotments of the unemployed miners in the 1930s. Clubroot was their problem, from cramming in the cabbages and savoys year after year to feed families on £2.50 a week, and leeks were the answer in Durham, Staffordshire, Lancashire and in Welsh valleys full of sordid spoil tips, mean terrace cottages and splendid voices.

The most famous leek is Musselburgh, but there are many others, and Sutton's Winter Crop is the hardiest of all and the slowest to run to seed in the spring, lasting until April. Early Market or Malabar are fast-growing varieties for those who want to eat leeks from September to November before the winter kinds are ready, but they need to be sown in heat in January.

Leeks are sown in the open in ½-in. deep furrows in March or April, depending on the weather, and remembering that there are 1,000 seeds in ¼ oz. – they keep four years. Sow them thinly, aiming at ½ in. between the small black seeds, which show up well against the soil, so that every plant will be a beauty from an uncrowded start.

Dig over the ground after the first early potatoes are lifted, with great care so as to pick up all the tinies and to leave the soil level; then firm it by treading. Make holes with a long dibber (make one by sawing off a broken fork handle and pointing the sawn end) 8 in. deep and 8 in. apart along a garden line, and drop a leek plant, roots first, down each. Fill the holes with water from a can without the rose on, to settle the roots in the soil, move the line 8 in. further down the bed, and repeat the process for another staggered row.

The earlier leeks go in the larger they grow. June is the soonest for the early kinds, July the best for winter, and August for late plantings that fill in empty space in winter, growing only as fat as candles, but good food from otherwise wasted room. Though leeks (and onions) are a useful source of sulphur, their best value in winter is from the vitamin A in the leaves, so merely shorten these to half their length, do not cut them hard back as greengrocers do and waste good winter green food.

RHUBARB

There are many varieties of rhubarb, and the favourites for flavour are Hawke's Champagne, Timperley Early, Early Albert and Victoria. The rarest rhubarb is Glaskin's Perpetual, which has the lowest oxalic acid of any, so it can be eaten right up to November without having a bitter taste, though this exhausts the roots. Rhubarb belongs to the spinach family, but the leaves should *never* be cooked like spinach, as some books recommend, because they contain so much oxalic acid that they can be poisonous.

A rhubarb bed should last about fifteen years, and then it should be dug and divided, by cutting up the black, gnarled roots into sections in January or February, each with 9 in. of stem, and a fat bud at one end. Prepare the site for a new bed in a different part of the garden well ahead of planting time, by digging in 2 lb. a square yard of *coarse* bonemeal, because it lasts longer than fine, and also, if possible, an old mattress stuffed with wool shoddy. Failing shoddy, dig in feathers from poultry plucking, as much as a barrowload to every 2 square yards, to provide nitrogen slowly released through the years during which the bed will live.

Plant the crowns, as the budded sections are called, upright and with the buds just below the soil surface, 2 ft apart each way. Pick nothing the first year, when radish or lettuce can be sown between the rows, and the plants will be ready for gentle forcing in their second spring.

The first rhubarb is always welcome, but after a final picking in June or July for bottling or jam, the stems should be allowed to die down on the plants after using the last strength of their leaves to gather and store the starches and sugars in the roots for next year's crop. Clear up their remains and scatter fine bonemeal at 8 oz. a square yard between the plants, and then cover them with dead leaves. Surround the bed with 1-in. mesh wire netting 1 ft high to stop the leaves blowing away and, in the spring, scrape them away so that the first shoots can be gathered.

The best rhubarb-forcing device for modern gardeners is a non-returnable oil or grease drum, usually obtainable free from a garage. Knock some holes in the bottom with a hammer and cold chisel, to provide the light for drawing aspiring rhubarb shoots upwards, clean out the drum with detergent, let it dry, and then paint inside and out with black bitumen paint. This not only preserves the tins from rust, but the black surface absorbs more sun heat and so the forcing effect is improved.

Rhubarb is sometimes available as seed, which should be sown very thinly in furrows $\frac{1}{2}$ in. deep and 3 ft apart on ground which has been prepared as for planting. Lettuce, radish or even carrots can be sown between these rows, which should be marked with a few labels along each one so that you do not step on the small red rhubarb seedlings when harvesting the catch crops.

Thin the rhubarb seedlings to 1 ft apart and plant cabbages or savoys between them through this first winter. In their second spring, the seedling rhubarb will begin to grow away, but they will still leave room for radishes between the rows. In the autumn cover the plants with dead leaves after a feed of bonemeal, and they will be ready to pick by the third spring.

13 Herbs

A herb, according to the dictionary definition, is a plant which dies down every year, as the plants do in a herbaceous border. But to gardeners a herb is an annual, biennial or perennial plant containing an essential oil or alkaloid that gives flavour in cookery, scent in the home, or has medicinal properties. Once there was a strong belief that herbs contained good spirits, or had magical powers. They do in fact contain vitamins and minerals but, because of their powerful flavour, it is not possible to eat enough of them to provide significant quantities. In many cases, their strong taste is a warning to us *not* to eat too much of them.

Parsley is a very good example of this. It contains as much vitamin C and A as kale, and more iron than any other vegetable, with a record 19.21 milligrams per 100 grams, but it also contains quite a quantity of apiol, an alkaloid which was once used to cause abortions and can have very unpleasant side effects. Yet in the quantities used in salads, as a garnish, with new potatoes and in cooking generally, parsley is perfectly harmless.

Most herbs used today come from the Mediterranean countries, and all these prefer full sun and a relatively poor soil. In fact, rich soils can reduce the quantity of the essential oils that give the flavour. So choose a sunny bed for a herb collection, preferably near the kitchen door for quick dashes for a leaf of something that will make all the difference to a recipe.

When drying herbs, never expose to sun or light as these extract or evaporate the volatile oils. Herbs are best dried in a warm, dark, ventilated but draught-proof place such as a shed that is out of the sun. Put them there as soon as possible after harvesting.

The following herbs can all be eaten freely in soups, salads and general cookery. The botanical name is given after every herb, because their popular names vary.

BALM (Melissa officinalis)

This is also known as 'lemon balm' and is an easy perennial which will thrive on moist soil. The leaves are used fresh or dried, cooked with fish, in chicken stuffing, in stews and shredded in salads. For drying, they can be picked when the first flowers are just open, dried in the plate-warming compartment of an oven, on a light-proof shelf in a greenhouse, or crisped off in an airing cupboard, and stored in screw-top jars for winter use. Either fresh or dried, they make a herbal tea.

Sow the very small seed in the open in April or May and transplant the seedlings in late summer 4 in. apart with 8 in. between rows to allow for hoeing. The following spring they will be ready for their permanent home 1 ft apart each way. Balm is quite a good weed suppressor to use for filling in an odd corner, and one packet of seed produces more than enough, however large the corner. It is also easily increased by division in spring or early autumn.

BASIL (Ocimum minimum)

Both this and Sweet Basil (*Ocimum basilicum*) are half-hardy annuals from tropical Africa and Asia. Sow them under glass in April in sterilized John Innes seed compost, space them out into boxes of the same compost when they have four leaves, and keep them in a greenhouse or cold frame until June, when they can be planted 8 in. apart each way in a sunny border. As soon as they flower, snip off the plant about 2 in. above ground and hang it to dry in a darkened corner of a greenhouse or shed, stripping the leaves off when these are crisp, to store for winter in a screw-top jar. In the South it may be possible to get a second cut from the plants.

Those who have a greenhouse can dig up the cut-back plants in early September, pot them and grow them on so that the fresh leaves can be picked for winter use in salads. The dry herb is excellent in all tomato dishes, in soups, and with meat and fish. It can also be used with egg, cheese and rice dishes. The handicap of this useful herb (there is little difference between the two species) is that very few people know that it is about as hardy as a tomato, and sow it in the open, or expect it to be a perennial like thyme. Grow it for drying to use round the year as a really useful herb.

BURNET (Sanguisorba minor)

A perennial with small leaves which are used to give a rather cucumber-like flavour to salads, and as a tea. It is almost evergreen so there is little need to dry it, though the leaves, like basil, can be hung in bunches in a darkened shed. Sow in March or April and transplant like balm, spacing it finally 1 ft apart each way. Once you have a stock, it can be increased by division.

CHERVIL (Anthriscus cerefolium)

This is an annual which runs to seed quickly, and is a member of the *Umbelliferae* family, like parsley. Sow in rows 8 in. apart, and thin to 9 in. between plants. The plants are ready to snip off close to the root from six to eight weeks after sowing and will provide a second cut, but let some run to seed and save your own because, like parsnip seed, it is useless after the first year. In fact, the best results come from letting some of the first sowing in March run to seed, sowing this in July and saving seed from this for the following season. If you like chervil, save your own seed because bought seed is so often stale that this herb is rare. Unlike most herbs, it will thrive in semi-shade, but it needs moisture, not the dry shade under trees.

Use it with fish, in soups, in salads and omelettes, also shredded and mixed with butter or potato salad. The flavour is best preserved by deep freezing rather than drying.

CHIVES (Allium schoenoprasum)

This small perennial onion makes a good border for a herb garden. It is increased by dividing the clumps in March or April into bunches planted 9 in. apart. If you have none to divide, sow the seed thinly and thin to 9 in., leaving the seedlings in groups of four to six. Snip off the small, thin, onion-type leaves at about 1 in. above the ground, and chop with kitchen scissors or put them through a hand chopper to mix with potato salads, omelettes, scrambled eggs, potato soup, and all other cream soups. A row of chives will take up to six complete cuttings, and should be divided every year. Chives will take a richer soil than most herbs. If they are attacked by rust, which shows as a yellow-orange powder on the leaves, dig them up, throw the clumps in the dustbin, and raise a fresh stock from seed.

FENNEL (Foeniculum vulgare)

This is a perennial growing up to 5 ft tall. It is best raised from seed, sown in April in pinches spaced 18 in. apart, thinned to the strongest in each cluster when this is certain. Fennel has towering flower heads and thick stems, so is best supported against a wall or fence. The stems, leaves and seeds all have a liquorice flavour and can be shredded for use in fish sauces, soups and salads. The seeds can be used in making fennel tea, and in bread.

GARLIC (Allium sativum)

Garlic is not so much a herb, it is more a way of life, and some who like it think it will repel all pests from the garden. Others are themselves repelled. It can indeed be said to grow more taste for its space than any other plant.

Grow garlic in full sun on light soil, digging in compost at the rate of a good bucketful a square yard before planting in March. Buy a few garlic bulbs from your greengrocer, and divide them into individual 'cloves' or offsets. Plant these 2 in. deep, 6 in. apart with 1 ft between rows. Keep them hoed and dig up the bulbs as July ends and the leaves turn yellow. Spread them in the sun for a week to dry, taking them in at night, and then hang in bunches in a dry shed to use as required.

Use garlic in soups, stews and sauces with caution. Some people run a clove round the inside of the salad bowl before filling it. Organically grown garlic is richer in sulphur, and can be grown for sale to a wholefood shop, as the bulbs are surprisingly expensive for such an easy herb.

MARJORAM, POT (Origanum onites)

This is usually propagated by division in spring or autumn. If you have none to divide, sow the small seeds in clusters 1 ft apart along ½-in. deep furrows with 1 ft between them. Then sow radishes along the furrows as they are up fast enough to mark the rows for hoeing, as well as giving a crop while the slower marjoram is still coming through. Thin these to the best and you will have all you need and plenty to give away. Use the fresh leaves in stews and soups, in vegetable dishes and shredded in salads. Cut some branches in September to hang up and dry for winter use, and cover the plants thickly with leaves to protect them during the winter. They can also be cut back, and later potted, to be grown indoors in winter.

MINT (Mentha spicata)

There are several species of mint and all are equally easy to grow. The most common one is *Mentha spicata* or Spearmint with pointed leaves, sometimes called Garden Mint. Another is Bowles' Mint, with rounded leaves that are grey-green and hairy, which is reputed to have a finer flavour. Apple Mint (*M. suaveolens*) and Pineapple Mint are varieties of this; there are many other mints, all of which are easily increased by division by those who like whatever they find in the jungle of a herb catalogue. Peppermint is *M. piperita* (of which I once grew an acre), and Pennyroyal is *M. pulegium*, and all these closely related species are grown in the same way.

Mint is almost always increased by division, splitting up the clumps into fragments of underground stem with growing points. These can spread far beyond the herb bed, and one way of keeping them in check is to obtain a plastic honey container, bucket or washing-up bowl, hold it over a lighted candle and melt holes in the bottom, and bury this in a suitable bed. Fill it with not too good soil and plant the root sections 2 in. deep and about 6 in. apart. Mint does not burrow deeply, and the underground stems will keep in their bowl, running round and round the sides but not going out through the drainage holes.

Use mint in salads, with new potatoes and peas, in mint sauce with sugar and vinegar, and in teas. Though it can be dried, it is better forced in winter in a frame or greenhouse, digging up a clump in October and potting it, or just taking in the plastic bowl full and keeping it watered in a temperature of about 60°F.

NASTURTIUM (Tropaeolum majus)

The flowers of this hardy annual make pleasant salad decorations, and can also be eaten, as can the young leaves. They have a really strong taste, so are best shredded and added as a 'trace element'. These climbing nasturtiums can be sown in late March and trained up apple trees, as there is a legend that they repel Woolly Aphid or American Blight (*Eriosoma lanigerum*). As the nasturtiums flower just as the winged form of this pest are about to migrate anyway, they are more valuable for salad and their vivid flowers. The young green seeds pickled are a good substitute for capers. The stems need tying round the trunk of the tree, when they make quite an effective show.

PARSLEY (Petroselinum crispum)

There are three kinds of parsley: the very curled type used for garnishing plates of sandwiches and decorating salads, the French parsley with leaves rather like small celery, which is the hardiest, and the Hamburg or turnip-rooted kind which is a root vegetable with a parsley flavour, and leaves that are just as good.

Sow thinly in March in furrows 1 in. deep, 15 in. apart if several rows are wanted, with radish seed in the furrows to mark the rows because, like parsnips, parsley takes four to six weeks to germinate at this time of the year. Thin the seedlings to 6 in. apart and do not pick any plant too heavily. In July make another sowing, which will germinate very much more quickly, to make sure of strong plants for winter; they can be dug in October and planted after tomatoes in a cold frame, or they can be potted and grown on a sunny windowsill for picking until the outdoor crop is ready again. Parsley is worth this trouble, because when it dries the flavour vanishes.

French parsley is hardier, and rather more tasty shredded and added to potato and other salads and to soups. Sow it in the same way, but in the South a single March sowing is all that is needed. If some of the row is left unpicked and allowed to flower, it will seed itself. This kind needs no winter protection and is usually available for picking even in December and January.

Hamburg parsley is a separate variety, *P. crispum* 'Tuberosum'. Sow thinly at the same spacing but with the seed only just covered, thin to 12 ins apart, and hoe to keep down the weeds through the summer. In November the roots, which sit on the surface and look rather odd, should be lifted and stored like beetroot in peat (see p. 100), and cooked like carrots or parsnips with a flavour which is a blend of parsley and celery.

There are gardens where parsley will not thrive, for reasons – ranging from the wife 'wearing the trousers' to the shedding of Campbell blood (in Scotland) – which are also applied to sage. The usual cause is a too acid soil, and 1 lb. a square yard of slaked lime dug in before sowing is the best answer. Soaking the seed overnight in urine will reduce the germination time to about a fortnight for all three parsleys; sowing seed in warm soil also speeds up germination.

ROSEMARY (Rosmarinus officinalis)

Rosemary is an evergreen bush which grows best against the wall of a house keeping off cold winds. A sprig of rosemary can be placed inside a roasting chicken, and added to the water when cooking peas, potatoes and turnips. There is no need to dry it.

Those who wish to take home 'Rosemary for Remembrance' from a friend's garden should break off a 6–9 in. shoot length between June and August and stand this in a jam jar full of water. After a few weeks it will grow a small white root or two at the bottom, and it can then be planted in the open in a sunny place, ideally on poor soil, and watered to give it a fair start.

It is also easy to grow from seed, sown in March or April, $\frac{1}{2}$ in. deep, but, as with many herbs, the result is a host of seedlings to plant 3 in. apart and 8 in. between rows, raising enough to give away on a grand scale. Herb seedlings are excellent 'bring and buy' gifts for good causes.

SAGE (Salvia officinalis)

Officinalis as a second name means 'the one used by herbalists' and it comes from the Latin *officina*, which was the room in a monastery where herbs were kept. Sage is a bushy perennial with grey leaves, which can be raised from cuttings about 6 in. long, broken off with a 'heel' or piece of the parent branch attached, inserted in sandy soil in May. It can be grown from seed sown in April with radishes to mark it, like parsley or parsnips. It is not a long-lived bush, and it is best raised from cuttings or seed every three years.

Use it in stuffing, with meat and fish, or in egg, cheese and bean dishes, or sprinkled lightly in salad. It will dry, hung up in bunches, and the leaves will crisp to store in screw-top jars for winter seasoning.

SAVORY, SUMMER (Satureia hortensis)

This is an annual with a taste rather like sage, used to add flavour to all the rather tasteless bean dishes eaten by vegetarians, and also with bread, gelatine and dyes by non-vegetarians, in sausages, meat-loaf and hamburgers. It is excellent in stuffings and soups.

Sow in early April in furrows $\frac{1}{2}$ in. deep and 1 ft apart, and thin to 6-in. spacing. Cut the plants down to leave 2 in. of stem when the flower stems appear, but before they open, and hang them up to dry and store. The pale lilac flowers in dense spikes are attractive, and the ancient Greeks used to sow savory near their beehives to flavour the honey.

The cut-down stems will grow again, and the second crop can also be dried, though its best use is as sprigs cooked with peas, broad beans and potatoes. It has been reported that Dutch gardeners plant it beside broad beans to repel blackfly, and it is possible that it could be grown as a border for a carrot bed or one of any crop attacked by a pest which hunts by scent. The problem is that herbs are often given the credit for repelling pests which were in fact also missing from gardens without that particular herb in the same area, because there were not many about that year owing to weather or some other cause.

TARRAGON (Artemisia dracunculus)

This is a part-hardy perennial to grow on poor soil next to a sunny wall. It can be increased by breaking up the clumps and replanting the rooted underground stems, or raised from seed sown in April and thinned to 3 in. apart. Pick the leaves from mid-June till the end of September to shred for salads, add to sauces and soups and to bean, egg, tomato, chicken and cheese dishes.

The flavour is at its best just when the flowers begin to open. Choose a dry day and pick the leaves, drying them slightly before a fire, or in an electric oven turned down to its lowest and with the door ajar, including the glass inner door if it has one. Tip the part-dried leaves, which should be flabby rather than crisp, into a jar and fill up with vinegar. Stopper the jar and leave it to steep for fourteen days. Strain through a jelly bag or discarded nylon tights, and bottle. It will keep for years if well stoppered. How many leaves go to how much vinegar is a matter of taste. It is possible to make a vinegar in this way out of the leaves of any herb you happen to like. Either malt or cider vinegar can be used.

THYME (Thymus vulgaris)

The problem with buying thyme today is that plants are expensive and a bush becomes straggly in about four years. An existing clump of the ordinary kind, or the lemon-scented (*Thymus* × *citriodorus*), can be filled in with soil in about April, covering the bare black branches in a mound like a large molehill, but leaving the growing foliage showing to pick for ordinary use. In July, August or September, dig up the clump, shake off the soil and tear the rooted pieces apart ready to grow into fresh plants for next year.

These divided plants, however, will always be more straggling than young ones grown fresh from seed. Sow thinly in April in a sunny border and plant the seedlings 3 in. apart each way, pinching out the tips when they are 2 in. high, and so grow hundreds of neat little bushes that should last at least five years.

Cut the branches for drying when they are just beginning to flower, tie them in bunches, protect with muslin and either hang them to dry slowly in an airing cupboard or, like tarragon, inside an oven with the temperature set at 110°F., which should take about an hour. When they are dried crisp, spread on a board and crush with a rolling pin, then store in screw-top bottles, which should ideally be brown glass, like those used for rose hip or other vitamin C tablets, to preserve the colour by excluding light.

Thyme is the most widely used herb in stuffings, soups, salads, bean and egg dishes, all meats, fish and poultry. It is also a very easy one for a windowsill, where the usual problem is finding enough light. All herbs are better in an *outside* box, and thyme, mint and lemon balm will grow happily in a city, in John Innes seed compost, which can be bought at most chain stores.

14 Soft Fruit

Soft fruits, fresh or bottled, are real value, both in terms of food for space and in vitamins and flavour. The bottling process is almost the same as for tomatoes (see p. 140), and the principle of keeping the bottles in the dark to preserve the vitamin C and colour is still more important. Almost every house has loft space for bottled fruit, which can be stored in any temperature. Though strawberries will not bottle, they freeze well, so those who can afford this relatively expensive storage should keep some space for these delicious fruits.

BLACKBERRIES, BOYSENBERRIES AND LOGANBERRIES

These are all powerful growers which put plenty of weight on their wires, needing strong support. The ideal material is pig fencing, which has oblong meshes of thick, galvanized iron wire 1 ft long and 9 in. high. This can be bought in 55-ft rolls 4 ft wide, and is vastly cheaper than chain-link for fencing, good enough to keep dogs in or out of a garden, and proof against farm livestock.

If a new garden is fenced by a contractor, it pays to have the posts for the supports of blackberries, boysenberries, loganberries and raspberries driven in by him, and the netting stretched and stapled between the posts. Concrete or metal fence posts can be bought, and it is a good idea to coat the latter with green bitumen paint to prevent rusting. Both are sold ready drilled with holes 1 ft apart to take wire, and the best is the insulated telephone wire advertised in most gardening papers. Blackberries and their two relations need 6 ft between their rows, for you need space not only to pick and prune, but for the sunlight to slant down between them and ripen the fruit.

The best blackberry for modern gardens is Oregon Cutleaf Thornless, which fruits in August, unlike the original thornless kind, John Innes, which waits till autumn, but has a first-class flavour and is a pleasure to prune. The best of the thorned varieties for flavour is Bedford Giant, which is ripe about the same time. This should go 10–12 ft apart, while the thornless kind will fit into 8 ft of fence space.

November is the best planting month, but these cane fruits can go in at any time in winter up to the end of March. Shorten the shoots to 15 in. long, and tie them to the wires in a fan so that they will grow leaves to feed the strong new basal growth which should be spread over the support fence and tied in to fruit the second summer after planting. If you leave the main shoots of any soft fruit unshortened for the first season, you will gain only a poor crop and stunt their growth for several seasons.

Blackberries blossom both on the shoots that grew the previous summer, and on older branches, so after the first year, pruning consists of keeping them under control. This is much easier with the thornless kind, for the others need stout gloves to protect your hands. In December when the leaves are off and you can see what you are doing, look first for any *thorned* shoots round the base of this kind and take them out by digging away the soil and cutting them off where they join the main root. Then cut out any dead or really old branches that are crowding the younger generation. Cut them out in sections, pulling them out from between the pig wire meshes and the other branches carefully to avoid breaking their neighbours. Any waste ground will show that blackberries fruit only on the outsides of their tangles – inside there is fruitless dead wood. The object of pruning is to have a blackberry wall, which is *all* outside, and a good windbreak as well as a fruit producer. The strongest variety of all is Himalayan Giant, which should go 15 ft apart; it has large fruit of poor flavour, but is a favourite windbreak among bulb growers in Norfolk and Lincolnshire. Bedford Giant is a better garden windbreak.

Blackberries have few pests and are hardy and easy to grow. They need no special manuring to start them, in fact they fruit best on a rather poor soil where they grow more slowly. This applies also to their relations, which need much the same treatment, but rather different pruning, though all should start with their shoots shortened to 15 in. and tied to the wires when they are first planted.

The thornless loganberry has long fruit like a dull red raspberry, which is deliciously acid, but has the disadvantage of not pulling cleanly off the central core or 'plug'. Pick them always with this in, and take it out as you eat, or before bottling. The plugs stay in the jelly bag when making loganberry and apple jelly to the same recipes as blackberry and apple. The best thorned loganberry is East Malling LY 59, with larger fruit and fewer pips than the older varieties, but the same plug problem.

Start all loganberries like blackberries, training in the young shoots the first season, but cut them off at ground level after they have fruited. The new shoots should be tied in place through the summer as they grow. Loganberries are a cross between a raspberry and a blackberry and fruit only on the shoots that ripened the previous summer, which makes them simple to prune.

Boysenberries are a cross between loganberries and blackberries, with rather less of the plug problem of the first parent, and the strength of the second. There is now a thornless variety which needs pruning like an ordinary loganberry, but without the disadvantage of the exceptionally savage thorns that have handicapped this easy and drought-resisting soft fruit. Boysenberries should go 12 ft apart on the support fence because they are as strong as a Bedford Giant blackberry.

Blackberries should be picked straight into the bottling jars, which are then filled up with cold water. Bring them up to 165°F. in 90 minutes and keep at that temperature for another 10 minutes, just like tomatoes, but 25°F. cooler. This temperature also suits loganberries, boysenberries and apples. Every year there are thousands of tons of windfall apples given away or dumped on rubbish heaps because they are bruised and will not keep. If these are gathered, wiped clean without peeling, cut up and the cores and bruised portions removed, they can be bottled on their own and stored for eating alone or combined with blackberries in tarts, jams and jellies.

CHERRIES

Morello, the cooking and bottling cherry, has the great advantage of thriving on a north or east facing wall in the narrow bed which is found against so many modern houses. It is self-fertile, so does not need another variety to pollinate it, and few people have room enough for two cherries when each needs twelve feet of wall width. Late Duke, a cooking and eating variety, is the nearest to self-fertility among the others, with deep red fruit in late August, but it is extremely rare. It needs a west wall as it is not as tough as a Morello, which is still the best all-round wall cherry. May Duke has black fruit in mid-June and is only partly self-fertile, though if there is room on the wall, it is reputed to be pollinated by Morello.

The best way of training cherries on walls is to bore into the brickwork with a masonry drill and insert vine eyes, which are extra-long-stemmed giant screw-eyes, in Rawlplastic asbestos compound, at intervals 1 ft apart up the wall. When these are set firm, thread telephone wire through them, which will last as long as ten years,

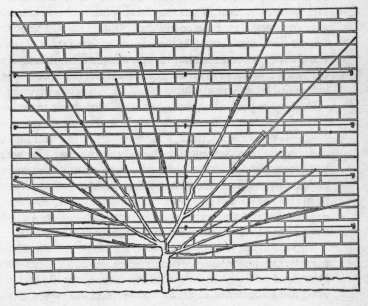

Cherry tree training

strain it tight and tie securely at the ends, so they give a good hold for tying in the branches. Use a long ladder and fit the wires right up the wall, for a ten-year-old Morello will reach the eaves of a two-storey house. The cherry-planting routine also serves for wistaria on a south wall, and the loveliest is the Japanese species, *W. floribunda macrobotys*, with magnificent hanging flowers as shown on willow pattern plates.

Narrow beds beside houses can have very poor soil, and as cherries are going to see at least twenty springs of snowy blossom, perhaps forty, they need good feeding. Dig the holes 2 ft deep, 3 ft long and 18 in. wide if there is room in the narrow border, taking out any builders' rubbish you come to and wheeling it away with the subsoil. Then mix 4 lb. of bonemeal and 6 lb. of oystershell chicken grit, and scatter about half this on the bottom of the hole. Fill in for about 6 in. with trodden topsoil, scatter the rest of the mixture, and then add 6 in. more topsoil, stripped from another part of the garden. This can be done by taking up turf, laying it grass-side down and treading it firm with no airspaces. If turf must be stripped to build a new house, have this stacked for bush or tree fruit planting holes. The object of this care is to make sure that the tree has a lasting stock of calcium and phosphorus, and a balanced supply of plant foods in the soil with the bacteria and fungi to make them available. On chalky soils the oystershell is unnecessary.

It takes two people to plant any tree, and they should never hurry. The tree will still be there when their new car is an old crock, their colour T.V. a museum piece, and their clothes ugly and odd with changing fashion. Set your fan-trained cherry in the hole with its roots spread and the main trunk three inches away from the wall. Hold it with the soil mark on the trunk (which shows how deep it was planted at the nursery) level with the soil surface, and shovel in the soil, working it between the roots with your fingers. When you have a depth of soil over these roots to protect them, tread this firm.

Tie the fan of branches to the wires and do not cut them back in any way. During the summer tie any sideshoots in, but pinch out any pointing away from the wall. Cherries fruit on the old and young wood like blackberries, so are not spur-pruned like apples, but on a wall they need more pruning than they do as bushes or standards. In

June when the trees are growing strongly, cut off the soft tips of the young shoots, removing about 3 in. of length. This takes off the softest part (to go on the compost heap) which the cherry aphid can attack, and puts more strength into forming blossom buds. Tie the shoots in when they are soft and bendy so that they grow to fit the shape of the walls and windows. Where a branch is dead, or intruding, always saw it out in June, never in the winter when die-back spores are blowing about and the tree will weaken itself by making gum. If any shoots are dead at the tips, wait till June and snip these short, looking for a brown stain in the middle. Snip again if there is still a stain, till the new wood shows white and clean.

In June, when the fruit has set and there looks a splendid crop, there will be a 'June drop' which is a natural 'thinning' to reduce the number of cherries to suit the moisture available. Beds against walls are often dry, and therefore it pays to run the hose near the tree to soak the soil thoroughly, which will keep the little cherries from drying and dropping. This is why everyone who plants a cherry, or any other fruit on a wall, should be sure that the soil level is well below the damp course. If it is heaped above it the water will soak up the brickwork and can go through, and the paper will peel off the walls of the room inside.

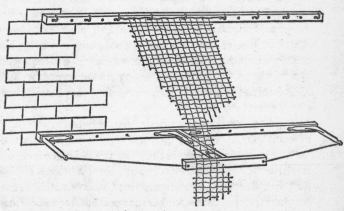

Support for cherry netting

Today, few people who grow standard cherries have any fruit because of the changing habits of birds who now associate houses with food. The fan-trained tree on the wall is the only answer to springs that may not be silent, but are fruitless without effective anti-bird measures. Use the masonry drill to secure to the wall a length of well-creosoted timber 2 in. by 1 in. (or nearest metric equivalent – ask for what you want in inches and you can usually get it). Secure shelf brackets to this as shown in the diagram, and lead a telephone wire through their end holes. Drive a row of 1-in. nails along the top of the timber to hook a nylon net on; this will be held clear of the fruit by the brackets and wire. The nylon net curtain will defeat the bravest bird, but it is essential both to prop it away from the wall at the top, and to hold it down away from the fruit with brick ends along the lower edge.

CURRANTS – BLACK

Blackcurrants are the best value in vitamins for the least trouble and space of all soft fruits, and if compact varieties are chosen to go 4 ft apart each way, even the smallest gardens have room for enough to provide plenty to eat raw with brown sugar and the top of the milk, or for bottling.

The variety that averaged the highest vitamin C over ten-year trials at Long Ashton Research Station was Baldwin, with 242 milligrams per 100 grams, but it does not suit all soils. The runner-up was Westwick Choice, with 235 milligrams, which resists big bud mite, so should be planted where this pest is common, and those who would like to spread the bottling or eating season can plant Wellington XXX, which fruits in July (204 milligrams) very heavily, but should go 5 ft apart each way.

Begin by digging the ground thoroughly to remove the roots of perennial weeds, because the blackcurrant bed will stay down for twelve or fifteen years before the yields fall and it needs replacement. It is better to dig out the docks and convolvulus before planting rather than fork about among the spreading blackcurrant roots later. The best start they can have is feathers or wool shoddy from old mattresses dug in generously to provide the slowly released nitrogen they need, with about a barrowload of manure and $1\frac{1}{2}$ lb. of bonemeal to 4 square yards.

Plant the bushes in holes 1 ft square and about 6 in. deep, so that their roots can be spread wide and the soil mark, which shows how deep the bush grew in the nursery, is at ground level. Then spread topsoil over the roots and tread firm, for there is no need to put any special food in the hole if the area has been well manured. Then cut back the long young shoots with light brown bark to above the third or fourth buds, whichever is pointing away from the middle of the bush. There will be no fruit the first summer while more strong shoots are growing from these buds, and from below ground, but the next season they will bear a full crop.

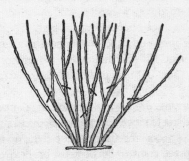

Blackcurrant pruning

The cut-back bushes will look very lonely at their wide spacing the first year, and it is quite safe to sow lettuces, carrots, radishes and any ordinary summer vegetable between them, because their roots will not have spread. This also makes it easier to keep the weeds down between the rows for the first two years.

Blackcurrants fruit best on these young one-year-old shoots, which should never be shortened, but they will also fruit from the two-year-old branches. Every November when the leaves are off go over the bushes and take out a third of the older branches to leave room for new recruits. Those with reddish-black bark and light markings grew the previous summer and will fruit well for another season, but take out the black ones down to the lowest light brown-barked sideshoots they have. If the oldest branches have no low shoots, take them right out, leaving only a 1-in. stump to grow new buds. Always take out the oldest and weakest branches really low, because the lower on the bush you cut, the greater will be the fruiting length of the new shoots that grow from them.

These prunings will include some young shoots that have grown high up on the old. Choose 6–8 in. lengths, cut them off cleanly with a sharp knife, and set them thickest end down, 6 in. apart, in a spade-cut deep enough to take them with only 2 in. showing above the surface. The very finest cuttings are from the pieces taken off the young shoots of new bushes when they are pruned immediately after planting. Tread the soil firmly round the cuttings and hoe the weeds from between the rows until the following November. Then dig up the new bushes, which should be well rooted and have two or three shoots 9–12 in. high. These should be cut back to three or four buds and replanted 1 ft apart and 18 in. between rows, to wait till the following November when they can be moved to their permanent homes and treated exactly like bought bushes.

Blackcurrants are always reputed to 'demand' nitrogen, just as some middle-aged men and women demand sugars, starches, mixed drinks and sweets, and the result of giving in to them is overweight bushes. Spread comfrey between the bushes every other summer, or compost every other spring, and cover this in April or May with a 2–3 in. coat of lawn mowings, which are tidier than the straw used by commercial growers and cost nothing. If the lawn is mown once every week or two there will not be trouble with grass from seed among the mowings.

The worms will take most of the mowings under by the autumn, and this build-up of humus will make many weeds easy to pull by hand. Other weeds, especially creeping buttercup and convolvulus, can be killed by spreading six thicknesses of newspaper between the bushes, weighed down with plenty of stones. The papers should be replaced as they go yellow and brittle with the sun and rain, and composted. They may not be beautiful, but they are cheap and effective, and modern newspapers have only about 12 parts per million of lead, unlike those of the past which held up to 215 p.p.m.;

so there is no pollution danger. Newspaper is more easily put on and more effective than black polythene, which harbours slugs under it, and is more inclined to be torn away by winter winds.

A fruit cage is almost essential for blackcurrants, and the only alternative to keep off the birds is tripods of long bamboo canes. Top them with 1-lb. jam jars to stop the canes thrusting through the green nylon netting. These should be put on in December because in hard weather bullfinches can strip off every bud and leave no crop at all. This protection should stay on until the crop is picked, or the blackbirds will have all the fruit.

CURRANTS – RED AND WHITE

Redcurrants are even more viciously attacked by birds than black, but it is possible to train them flat against a wall so that they can be protected with hanging nylon nets like cherries. Once it was possible to buy trained red and white currants for this purpose, but today the only way to find them is to visit a nursery and choose the flattest bushes.

The leading variety is still Laxton's No. 1, which is early, strong and upright, with a heavy crop in all districts. Red Lake follows it, with long bunches of rather larger fruit, and the latest of all is Wilson's Long Bunch, which is rather more straggling in habit. Radboud is also late, with shorter bunches but more of them, and resistance to leaf spot. If you like eating fresh redcurrants, try some of each, but if your aim is as much redcurrant jam and jelly as possible, plant only Laxton's No. 1, because it is the commercial favourite for a heavy crop. Whitecurrants are not as white as candles, but the colour of a white wine, with the same flavour and qualities as red and grown in exactly the same way. Versailles is about the heaviest yielder and the best all-round variety.

A currant wall can face north or east, and the bed below it need only be 9 in. or as little as 6 in. wide. Dig in 3 lb. a square yard of bonemeal along the bed for lasting phosphorus and calcium, because red and white currants live longer than black – up to twenty-five years. Drill the wall for vine eyes to take wires 6 in. apart and with eyes at 4-ft intervals along the wall, but there is no need to go higher than six wires at first, because these currants grow more slowly than cherries and their maximum reach up the wall is 6 ft.

Plant your bushes 3 ft apart, with their roots spread like black-currants, but do not cut the shoots back. Spread the branches in fan formation, tying garden string firmly round the wire and then loosely round the branch. Leave the young shoots at the branch tips to grow, but cut back all lesser shoots to two or three buds, whichever points along the wall or up it, for red and white currants fruit on these short spurs exactly as apples do.

In July, pinch out the tips of the new sideshoots which will have grown, to strengthen the fruiting buds round their bases. After the

Redcurrant pruning

leaves have fallen, shorten these shoots to three or four buds and the branch end shoots to their strongest upward pointing bud, which is rarely the one at the tip. Hose the bed as soon as the berries start to swell, and feed with comfrey under a mowings mulch, for these currants are not greedy.

Those without a suitable wall should plant their bushes 4 ft apart each way, on ground prepared as for blackcurrants. Shorten their small shoots to two or three buds but cut a third off all the smooth-barked young shoots at the branch ends. If you want to increase your red or white currants, take some of these leaders right off with a little of the old wood on each, and put the cuttings in as though they were blackcurrants. When they are transplanted in November, take back their strongest upward pointing shoot to its highest strong bud, and shorten the rest as described. This produces a cordon, with a single upright stem suitable for planting at 1-ft intervals along a wall and training higher and higher. If you want ordinary bushes, shorten to four buds and leave the cutting to grow as it will, ready for planting in the second November.

The bottling temperature is the same that applies to all bush fruits, 165°F. reached slowly in 90 minutes, with 10 minutes at this level, and both jam and jelly are delicious. The last, though famous for flavour, takes 6 lb. of fruit plus $1\frac{1}{2}$ lb. of sugar to each pint of juice to make 3 lb. of jelly. A more productive method is to add 3 pints of water to the 6 lb. of fruit and simmer until tender. Mash well and strain through a jelly bag for about 20 minutes. Then remove the pulp, boil it up again for about half an hour, and strain. Mix the liquid from both drainings, bring it to the boil, then add $\frac{3}{4}$ lb. of sugar to the pint, and boil rapidly until the jelly sets.

GOOSEBERRIES

The best gooseberries for small gardens are the upright kinds, not for instance the commonly grown variety Careless, which is grown commercially and inclined to sprawl. Choose Langley Gage, which can be picked early for cooking and then ripens pale yellow with a delicious flavour, Whitesmith with much the same qualities but almost white and with resistance to mildew, May Duke, which ripens red for eating raw and is reputed to be the best flavour bottled, or New Giant, green. There is unfortunately no thornless gooseberry.

When you buy plants at a garden centre or nursery, choose those with the longest distance between the soil mark on the main stem and the fork of the branches. This is called the 'leg', and the longer the leg the easier it is, if necessary, to dig both kinds of couchgrass out from under the branches. A 6-in. leg is a fair average, but if it is possible to find a 9-in. one, choose it every time.

In the past, cordon gooseberries were grown on walls just like red-currants, and if bushes are ordered from a good firm, they will select specimens suitable for training. If ordinary bushes are bought it is best to tie down the two main branches to the bottom wire, one on each side of the leg, and take out the others completely. Young shoots from these are trained up the wall, merely taking out the tips. Single cordons are planted 1 ft apart along the wall. The gain from this system is in easy weeding and picking, cheap protection from birds with a single nylon curtain, and early and complete ripening from the warmth and shelter of a wall, which will help mature a crop even in the Shetlands, provided the wall faces south. Prune the bushes exactly like redcurrants.

Take even more care than with the other soft fruits to get out perennial weed roots before planting gooseberries, which will benefit by having as much as 2 lb. a square yard of wood ashes scattered between the bushes in the April after the November planting, so that the new roots have a chance to absorb some of the potassium before it is washed away, as it is so easily from a sandy soil. Gardeners on sandy soil might find it worth buying a granite dust, which should contain between 3 per cent and 8 per cent potassium, or one of the ground felspars used in making crockery, if it contains at least 3 per cent, to help their gooseberries. Use either of them at the rate of 2 lb. a square yard every five years. Start them just like blackcurrants by using bonemeal, shoddy, feathers, compost or manure before planting. Seaweed meal is also good, but costly, and must be dug in at the rate of 8 oz. a square yard. Left on the surface, the alginates it contains will make a wasteful jelly there.

Plant the gooseberry bushes 4 ft apart each way, 3 in. deep, with the roots well spread out, and, after firming them in, cut back the light-brown-barked young shoots to between three and five buds, making the cut just above a bud that points upwards and away from the middle. The ideal shape for a bush is an inverted cone with the centre open, to let in the sunlight for ripening and your hands for picking, so always cut off shoots that grow into the centre, close to the main stems.

The bushes will not fruit the first year, while the roots are taking hold, but in October or November shorten the new shoots that grew at the ends of the main stems in the summer by a third, snip off all but about an inch of the smaller sideshoots, and remove any that are growing towards the middle completely. This is the normal routine pruning for all bush gooseberries.

It is possible to sow vegetable crops between the rows the first year, but not after that, and comfrey under a 3-in. mowings mulch will be necessary to keep up the potassium supply on a sandy soil. On clay soils this annual mulch is less important, and if the bed had a good start with plenty of compost, it may need no extra feeding for years. On clay the main need is to keep the grass down, and for this and all perennial weeds, the newspaper trick (p. 166) is an answer.

Gooseberries are often attacked by bullfinches, which peck out the buds in winter, sometimes starting in early November. To avoid the total loss of crop which results, protect the bushes with netting on supports, well above the bushes, for the whole winter. Put the netting back when the fruit begins to swell (or leave it on all the time).

RASPBERRIES

Raspberries and strawberries are perhaps the nicest of all our fruit, and fresh raspberries eaten with sugar and cream are probably the tastier of the two. So it is worth choosing varieties for enjoyment in succession, as well as for bottling.

The earliest raspberry is Malling Promise, which is ready in June, and crops well after the first two years – raspberry beds can stay ten to twelve years in the same place. Follow it with Malling Exploit, which is about three weeks later and a nicer fruit, and Lloyd George, which is smaller, but has kept ahead of the new Malling varieties for over twenty years. Then have Malling Jewel or Malling Enterprise if you can find it, with Malling Landmark, or Norfolk Giant to finish the season in November. The latter blossoms very late, like Malling Landmark, and is a favourite in Scotland and the north of England. The Malling varieties are much larger fruited than the older kinds, but be careful when picking, for the bunches have brittle stems and it is easy to tug at the first to ripen when it is not quite ready, break the stem and waste perhaps a whole dozen glorious fruit.

Give the same care to removing perennial weed roots as for all other bush fruit, and the same start with manure, wool shoddy or

Organic Gardening

feathers, plus bonemeal. Raspberries are unlike apples or cherries in that their roots spread wide and shallow, and therefore their lasting food should be dug in evenly all over the bed, instead of concentrating it in the planting holes. They dislike lime, so there is no need to supply any lasting form of this; what calcium they do want is in most soils in the quantities in which they need it. Bonemeal, as given for blackcurrants, will release some slowly in any case.

Raspberry canes are shaped like capital Ls when they arrive, and should be planted 1 ft apart along a 3-in. deep trench with the short arm of the L pointing along it. Tread them firm and shorten the upright part of the L, the cane, to 1 ft, for the only task this has is producing leaves to feed the strong shoots which will grow from the buried portion and fruit the second summer after planting. If you leave the main cane uncut in the hope of fruit the first season, it will be two more years before you have a real crop.

The temptation with raspberries is to try and cram extra rows into a small garden, but the minimum distance between rows should be 4 ft because the sun must get to the fruit. Raspberries need support wires to prevent them swaying and breaking in the wind, and the best kind, again, is telephone wire. Stretch this at 1-ft spacing between steel or concrete posts, and if the former, give them a coat of bitumen paint and bolt a wide, creosoted cross-piece at the bottom and another a foot above it. Both these should go underground with the soil rammed round them to transfer the pull of the wires to a wider surface. Without cross-pieces, tightening the wires merely pulls the thin metal fence posts through the soil like a knife through cheese.

Never use the thin, plastic-covered 'garden wire', because this is

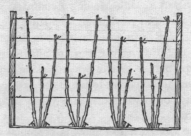

Raspberry supports and pruning

hard and the canes will rub their bark through against it as the wind fidgets with them through draughty winters. Twist soft green garden twine or tomato string twice to give a grip, then tie the cane loosely to it. Start by tying the 1-ft, cut-back canes to the first horizontal wire, and as the new shoots grow through the summer, support them with strings running from end to end of the rows.

Take off the original short canes at ground level in the first November and tie the new canes in firmly, shortening them to encourage three 'storeys' or tiers of fruit. The second summer cut out the canes which have fruited as soon as the crop finishes, and support the new canes with side strings until November when they are, in turn, shortened and tied in. The autumn-fruiting kinds like September are pruned by cutting the canes down to ground level every spring, and as the plants have a whole summer to grow new shoots in, it is possible to take a September crop from a spring plant-ing. Lloyd George can be pruned like the ordinary kinds, for summer fruit, or cut down in the spring for an autumn crop, and many gardeners prune half one way and half the other.

Keep the ground between the young canes clean for the first summer, which gives a second chance to clear perennial weeds, but in the second April or May, cover the soil with a 3-in. coat of lawn mowings, with a second layer in July or August. On poor soils some manure, comfrey or compost can be spread before the mulch goes on. After pruning in November, dig the remains of this under so that, through the years, the humus slowly builds up, suppressing the weeds at the same time.

Raspberries are attacked by birds when in fruit, but not in the bud stage by bullfinches, and will need to be protected by upright poles and nylon netting, allowing room to go inside for picking.

STRAWBERRIES

There are two types of strawberry – the ordinary kind which has been enjoyed with cream through about 300 summers, and fruits all at once, so that early and late kinds are required for a succession, and the Remontant or Everbearers, which start fruiting in July and continue into the autumn.

The best early variety, with the finest flavour still, is Royal Sovereign, and Red Gauntlet follows it as a heavy cropping, disease-resisting, good all-round mid-season kind. Grow Talisman as a late variety, again about the best of nearly fifty in cultivation. Most people want strawberries in June or July and these three kinds will cover the normal season.

There are now many Remontants, bred by crossing ordinary strawberries with alpine varieties, and two German kinds, Humi-Gento and Humi-Grande are popular because of the size of their fruit, but it is watery and tasteless. 'Climbing' strawberries are also in this class, and since a successful case was brought under the Trade Descriptions Act, they are now called 'Elevated', because they do *not* climb. They are a type of Remontant that fruits on its runners, and if these are tied up to a trellis or fence they will produce a crop, but rather a small one because of the work the plant has to do pumping the water up to them. On the flat they are simply an extra-runner-making strawberry, and poor value for space.

Perhaps the best small garden strawberry has the handicap of being called a Rollerberry, sold as a 'weed-suppressing plant of the strawberry family', when it is actually an old French Remontant variety. It is unpopular commercially because its berries are never ready altogether but ripen in a long succession between July and October, so that there are always some ready for tea. Because of the directions from the firms that sell it, most gardeners enjoy its fruit for about four years only and then blame it for the dwindling crop that appears among its close-growing foliage. Through the years it should be divided and replanted to give it a new lease of life. Two other good Remontants that fruit in flushes together for deep freezing or jam are Hampshire Maid and Sans Rivale, which can produce as much as 3 lb. of fruit to a plant.

Unlike other soft fruits, strawberries are grown on a rotation round the garden, replanting the bed every four years. This can be done with four small beds, so that there is one at every stage from newly planted to dwindling in vigour and ready for replacement. Or a new bed can be prepared in August or September to come into bearing the following summer. Some gardeners plant strawberries in spring, but these spring plantings give little fruit until the following summer, when the crop will be larger. Averaged over two seasons, however, August planting gives the best yield.

Dig thoroughly to remove perennial weed roots, and then turn in a good barrowload of manure or compost to 4 square yards, together with about 2 lb. of bonemeal to the same area. If there is time and space enough, prepare the ground in May and sow green manure lupins, which will help make available the phosphorus that strawberries particularly need, and be spaced widely enough apart for two or three useful hoeings to kill off some of the annual weed seedlings.

Strawberries need careful planting 1 ft apart and 2 ft between rows. Rake the bed finely and take out the holes 4 in. across and 2 in. deep, with a mound in the middle. Sit the plant on top of the mound with the roots spread down the sides, so that when the soil is firmed back over them with the trowel handle, the growing point (crown) is above ground level and the very shallow roots have plenty of hold and are distributed to grow in all directions. If you plant with the roots bunched together in a dibber hole, they are handicapped from the start by crowding and frost can heave the plants right out of the ground.

Hoe between the plants in the spring and then spread a coat of peat 1 in. or more thick between them to hold down annual weeds and provide surface humus. Never mulch with mowings because they harbour slugs, which peat repels. Though peat can powder ripening berries, it is cheaper today than straw and more readily absorbed into the soil. Those who can obtain straw and can take the time to get it under the foliage so that the berries will lie on it, can use it alone or in addition to peat, but today peat is replacing straw, especially as there is some risk from selective weedkillers used on the wheat. The peat should be renewed every spring, and when the bed is dug and divided, it provides useful humus for the crop that follows it.

Remontant strawberries fruit on a small scale in May and June and produce a main crop from August on into the autumn. Especially with new plantings, it can pay to snip out the early flowers to bring a bigger late crop for deep freezing or jam. Every year tidy up the bed in the autumn, taking off the bird protection and removing straw, weeds, old leaves, fruiting stems and runners to the compost heap.

Perhaps the best garden protection is to drive in creosoted posts,

2 ft tall, at 6-ft intervals round the bed and to staple wire netting to these. If the bed is a narrow one, make light wooden frames covered with wire netting to take on and off like cold frame lights for picking. The alternative is a row of taller posts down the middle, with jam-jars on top and nylon netting stretched over them like a tent, secured with clip-type clothes pegs at sides and ends. These can be un-clipped for picking, but it is a good idea to wear a special strawberry-picking overall, with no buttons to catch in the meshes. In the autumn, pull out the staples and roll up the wire netting, which should be replaced before June brings birds again greedy for fruit. If grass is allowed to grow through the wire, the oxygen and water transpired by the breathing blades will rust it very quickly. The nylon netting, too, should be stowed away for the winter and until the berries start to redden, because it goes brittle and breaks into holes with time in the sun. It should be treasured, for every time you buy a replacement of anything it costs about twice as much.

In the past gardeners took great care to snip off all the strawberry runners to put more strength into the parent plants, but many modern varieties, especially the Remontants, will fruit on these runners. So though it is a good idea to snip off any runners that form during the first summer, and even during the second one, it is less trouble to let the bed grow into a mat. When the new bed is prepared, dig up well-rooted runners, even in their second season, and plant as many as you need. Though the Rollerberry has been recommended even for growing as a weed suppressor between herbaceous plants, these rob it of water. Like all strawberries, it can do with a good soaking in a dry May, and generous feeding, which can include feathers or shoddy if available, at the start – both these retain moisture and leave plenty behind for the crop that follows.

15 Deficiencies and Diseases

In this chapter we look first at mineral deficiencies, then at safe remedies for diseases, and lastly at the diseases themselves, crop by crop.

It is difficult to tell the symptoms of deficiency of one or more minerals in a plant from those of plant diseases. We know that many human complaints can be caused by vitamin shortages in which vitamins are 'locked up' by other substances – for example, liquid paraffin can 'lock up' those that are fat-soluble. The same kind of effect in plants can be caused by chemical fertilizers used to excess.

Some organic gardeners are convinced that compost cures all plant 'diseases', either because it supplies trace elements in the forms in which they are most readily taken up by plants, or because it helps the bacterial and fungal allies in the roots to absorb them. Too much potassium can cause calcium and magnesium deficiency, too much calcium, boron deficiency, and too much nitrogen or phosphorus, potassium deficiency. Generally speaking, a healthy, well-balanced diet increases resistance to disease in both plants and human beings, as well as avoiding the conditions caused by mineral and vitamin malnutrition. If your soil is well fed, the main danger to your crops is your own horticultural hypochondria. There are many genuine plant diseases, and these are described later in this chapter, but first we will get the nutrient deficiencies out of the way. They are arranged in order of likeliness, not alphabetically, because it is easier to see the effect than to know what letter the cause begins with.

Magnesium Shortage

The symptoms of magnesium deficiency vary with the crop. It is commonest among crops which are greedy for potassium, especially tomatoes, because most gardens have only one good sheltered and sunny bed where these ripen well, and this is given sulphate of potash or wood ashes every year. The lower leaves turning yellow while the veins stay green will show a deficiency of magnesium because the plants have absorbed potassium in preference. Another cause is shortage of humus, which means that it is less easy for the crop to take up magnesium. This shows up on lettuces as yellowed outer leaves, with the veins still green, especially in dry summers.

The quick answer for the tomato bed or greenhouse is 1 oz. of Epsom salts (magnesium sulphate) dissolved in 2 gallons of water and applied with the rose to 2 square yards. An even quicker remedy is to spray this solution on to the foliage, for plants can take in missing minerals through their leaves in emergencies. Epsom salts are only a temporary cure because they wash quickly out of the soil. It is far better to dig in 2 lb. a square yard of ground dolomite limestone, which contains up to 45 per cent magnesium carbonate and lasts for years, especially with plenty of compost.

Magnesium deficiency in potatoes shows as brown patches in the leaf centres, with leaves withering prematurely, and a reduced crop. Gooseberries are equally likely to have it, again because of the chemical potassium in wood ashes and fertilizers, and their symptoms are broad, pale red-brown areas round the edges of the leaves which fade to cream and then fall early. In both cases water or spray with the Epsom salts solution and spread and fork in dolomite limestone in the autumn.

The cabbage tribe, including broccoli and turnips, show the familiar still-green veins and yellowing leaves, with brown patches on the older ones. Peas yellow in the same way, but the margins of the leaves stay green; runner and French beans go in for brown blotches between the veins of rather paler green leaves than normal; older leaves of carrots go pale yellow; and parsnips have bright yellow margins to their older leaves. All these 'symptoms' are 'curable' with dolomite limestone.

Raspberries suffer almost as often as tomatoes, because every year their fruited canes are cut out and burnt, taking away quantities of magnesium, and the immediately available stock can run out as the canes age. The leaves on the new shoots change to yellow with green veins, and this is often taken for a virus attack, so that the bed may be destroyed when it has perhaps five more fruiting years left. Dig in dolomite shallowly (see above) in the early summer when the new shoots are growing, for it is too late in the autumn when growth slows for winter. Blackcurrant leaves change to dull red-purple in the middles, with their edges still green.

Magnesium deficiency in soft fruit is far less common than in vegetables, because few fruit bushes are given heavy dressings of potassium fertilizers, including potassium chloride, 10 per cent of which is in all modern fishmeal used as fertilizer. Shortages due to these lock-up effects or because of lack of humus do not show up in soil tests. In theory a soil may have plenty of everything but still grow poor crops, therefore soil analysis needs expert interpretation.

Calcium Shortage

Calcium shortage is a problem on many sandy soils, especially those that grow pine trees, heathers, rhododendrons and azaleas well. It can also be caused by the sulphates from ammonium sulphate and potassium sulphate combining with the calcium carbonate that slaked lime becomes in the soil, and making calcium sulphate or gypsum which is only slowly available.

The crop most likely to suffer is, again, tomatoes, because of excessive use of potassium fertilizers. The blossom trusses die and any fruit that sets develops flat brown patches at the blossom ends; the growing points of the shoots die, and in extreme cases the leaves turn purple-brown. The fruit patches show first, and the immediate answer is to scatter lime at 1 lb. a square yard on the bed surface and hose it in, which may save the rest of the crop. Then lime in the autumn, applying the quantity required according to the results of a soil test.

The potato scab fungus enjoys lime, and many gardeners use very little of this in order to give themselves smooth-skinned and attractive tubers. Potatoes can, however, considerably lack calcium. The symptoms are pale green, stunted growth with thin stems, plus leaves curling up and in at the edges, and tiny tubers. If you have plenty of tubers but all are small, the cause is either potato eelworm (see p. 221) or calcium shortage. Potato eelworm, however, makes the foliage yellow and die off early. If a soil test confirms that the soil is acid, the remedy is to lime the soil generously, and use lawn mowings or comfrey in the potato trenches to give local acidity to beat the scab, instead of starving your potatoes of the calcium they need.

The cabbage tribe can suffer from calcium deficiency. This is shown by brown margins on the leaves, but is rare because most gardeners lime generously to combat clubroot. On broad beans that lack lime the growing points die, the young leaves fail to expand, the pods blacken and the seeds inside fail to grow. These are the symptoms for other beans too, while peas have their young tip growth turn pale and wilt. The symptoms are quite rare, for few soils lack calcium – it is mainly too much sulphate of ammonia and potassium causing little local difficulties that can cost a crop.

Boron Deficiency

Shortage of this essential trace element (so called because only a 'trace' is needed and any more than this is a disaster) is responsible for several quite serious 'diseases', mostly in vegetables. It causes crown canker in beet, with the centre leaves dying and the roots rotting from the outside inwards; hollow stem and curd browning of cauliflowers; brown heart in turnips; and fruit spot in tomatoes. The last is the most frequent in gardens and greenhouses, with fruit pitted with brown corky spots and ripening unevenly.

It is usually caused by heavy liming, or naturally chalky soils. The problem about correcting it is the very small trace of boron required, and on a greenhouse scale the best way to achieve the 20 lb. an acre of borax (a mixture of salt of boron and sodium, used for gargling and to make an ant poison) as advised by the Ministry of Agriculture is to mix $\frac{1}{2}$ oz. in 2 gallons of hot water, let it cool, and water it over 6 square yards. There is such a knife edge between too much and too little that the best answer is to use plenty of compost, which will contain a little; but use the borax obtainable from any chemist if you have this distinctive trouble with your tomatoes.

Potassium Shortage

This can be caused by too much nitrogen or too much phosphorus, and is one of the reasons why heavy manuring with dried sewage sludge or fishmeal, which are high in both, can be bad for both tomatoes and potatoes. Clay soils usually have plenty of potassium, and the most that chemical fertilizers can do is cause temporary shortages. Sandy soils, however, run out fast, as all potassium fertilizers, including wood ashes, are very soluble.

Gooseberries suffer soonest – leaves turn a rather blue-green and light brown bands appear round the edges, looking as if they had been scorched. They fall early, and the bushes become weak and crop poorly. Tomatoes have light brown scorching at the edges of the leaves, and the fruit ripens patchily, with green and yellow areas merging into the red surface (tomato mosaic virus looks very like this, but the yellower blotches are more sharply defined and the leaves are mottled yellow). Potato leaves turn a bronzy green with brown spots between the veins, and the foliage often dies down too soon for a good yield.

Beans suffer sorely from potash shortage – the chocolate spot fungus of broad beans attacks when this runs low. The symptoms in broad beans are very short joints and dark brown scorching at the leaf edges. Both runner and French beans show this leaf edge scorching, but light, not dark brown, entirely unlike the yellowing from magnesium deficiency. The cabbage tribe show that they are missing their potash by brown leaf margins which curl upwards, and this is also the sign with lettuce and beet.

The best immediate answer is to water with comfrey liquid manure (p. 59). Leave this to stand till it is clear, dilute 1 part of liquid with 3 parts of water, and spray on as a foliar feed for tomatoes. With plenty available this can be used to soak potatoes or gooseberries, but the best answer is more compost, or cut comfrey under a mowings mulch for bush fruit.

Phosphorus Shortage

Phosphorus is plentiful in most soils, for there is no other mineral nutrient which locks it out of root reach; however, it can be scarce on acid ones. Shortage produces stunted leaves in carrots with purple tints in the older foliage, entirely unlike the rich maroon-red which indicates carrot flies at work in the root. Lettuces lacking phosphorus are stunted, with dull green leaves, and the cabbage family can also suffer, showing dull purple markings towards the middle of the leaves. Sweet corn is greedy for phosphorus, as tomatoes are for potassium, and here the warning is dull purple streaks down the older leaves.

The remedy is a good dressing of bonemeal in the autumn, as much as 2 lb. a square yard dug in, or poultry manure if this can be obtained, for all bird droppings are rich in both phosphorus and nitrogen.

Iron and Manganese Shortages

Both these can be caused by excessive liming, but they can also occur on soils which are naturally very chalky. The symptoms of both are very pale green leaves too early in the year to be due to drought or natural autumn tints in a number of vegetables, especially in beet. Where iron is the trouble, it is the youngest leaves which lose their colour first. Manganese shortage also causes hollow centres in the seeds of peas and beans. Watering with a solution of $1\frac{1}{2}$ oz. of manganese (not magnesium) sulphate dissolved in 20 gallons of water, applied to 10 square yards, is the best answer; this rather rare chemical can be obtained to order from any good chemist. Apply it when the peas or beans are just beginning to come into flower, and again a week later. Generally speaking, more compost and less lime is the answer for mere leaf yellowing at the wrong time – hollow seeds show that the shortage is really bad. Even though your compost material comes from the garden that showed the shortage, enough of it can remove the symptoms, because it will recycle the supply made available by earlier root activity.

Another way round for these or any other shortages caused by too much lime is to use Epsom salts as directed earlier (p. 178) for magnesium deficiency, to lock up the excess lime as gypsum and release some of the 'missing' minerals.

The Seaweed Treatment

One safe treatment for any suspected mineral shortage is foliar feeding with one of the liquefied seaweed preparations. Seaweed contains a very full set of trace elements including boron, bromine, calcium, copper, iodine, iron, magnesium, manganese, phosphorus, potassium and sodium. Though plants would rather feed through their roots, they can take anything they badly need through their leaves, just as a man with his jaw shot away can be fed through a tube, but longs for surgery to help him eat normally again.

So if your plants have any of the deficiency symptoms described in this chapter, the simple answer is to spray with a seaweed preparation and the odds are that you will achieve a complete 'cure'. Like compost, seaweed preparations are effective when the condition is caused either by a mineral deficiency or by a fungus disease that can only get a real hold where a mineral is absent, like chocolate spot in broad beans. There is, however, not enough magnesium in a seaweed spray to replace the quantities locked up by too much potassium, so use Epsom salts, comfrey, dolomite or lime, with seaweed as a safe counter-measure against suspected unknown mineral deficiencies or possible diseases.

DISEASES AND SAFE REMEDIES

Genuine diseases need safe remedies, and the question is 'safe for what?'

The lime-sulphur washes of the past are unsafe for the gooseberry varieties that are 'sulphur-shy', and they also destroy those very useful pest eaters, the *Anthocoris* bugs. There are many more modern fungicides that can harm our friends, and however safe the spray, it costs money and is extra work to apply, so wherever possible the ideal remedy is a trick of pruning or evasion, or in-bred resistance to diseases or pests.

There are, of course, many new remedies produced every year by the chemical manufacturers which are tested for safety according to the regulations of the Departments concerned. This book, however, is written for those who wish to garden *without* these industrial products, and with as few *non-industrial* sprays as possible. The bodies of the organic movement have not the resources to test industrial products for their *full* effect on the environment, and therefore it is safest to assume that all are guilty until they are proved innocent. We regard all fungicides, pesticides and herbicides as being as safe as thalidomide, until proved otherwise.

Bordeaux Mixture

This was the first of the fungicides, and it is a preventative spray against potato blight. It can be bought as a powder, ready to stir into water for direct spraying, but here is the original recipe. Take 8 oz. copper sulphate, tie it in the toe of an old nylon stocking or tights, and hang it in 2 gallons of cold water overnight to dissolve. Use a plastic or fibreglass container, because copper sulphate can react with metal, and the wooden tubs of the past are scarce and dear. In the morning stir 10 oz. of slaked lime into another 2 gallons of water, mix the two, add 1 gallon more to make it up to 5 gallons, and spray it on to the potato or tomato foliage at once.

Burgundy Mixture

This is more powerful and should only be sprayed on trees or bushes in winter when they are leafless and fully dormant. It can also be used as a disinfectant killer of potato haulm in a blight outbreak. Like Bordeaux Mixture, it must be made up and used fresh, so gardeners should buy a store of copper sulphate (which can still be obtained to order through a famous chain of chemist shops) and keep it in a plastic container till required. It will corrode a metal one, like both the made-up mixtures.

Make it exactly like Bordeaux mixture, but instead of the lime stir 10 oz. of ordinary washing soda into the 2 gallons of water, mix the copper sulphate solution with it, add 1 gallon of plain water and you have 5 gallons ready for use. The soda dissolves much better than lime with no risk of lumps blocking the syringe, and the only precautions needed are to avoid getting any in your eyes, and never to use it after the buds start to swell, because it will damage young leaves and all foliage. Most soils could do with a little extra copper, so any spray that misses does no harm, and could correct a minor trace element deficiency.

Downy Mildew Mixture

There are two sorts of mildew: downy mildew which gets right inside the plant and can kill it, and powdery mildew, which remains on the surface, for instance in Michaelmas daisies and roses. Both attack the soft growth that is increased by too much nitrogen, and are particularly bad in dry summers. The long-term answer for either is more compost to retain moisture and provide a better diet.

The following mixture is effective against American gooseberry mildew and other downy mildew types. Dissolve 1 lb. of washing soda in 5 gallons of cold water, and stir in 8 oz. of soft soap. This used to be obtainable from ironmongers before it was replaced by modern paint strippers, but the grade used for enemas can still be bought from chemists.

Powdery Mildew Mixture

This mixture is effective against pea mildew in late summer and other mildews in the garden. Stir $\frac{1}{2}$ oz. of potassium permanganate into 3 gallons of cold water and spray on to the plants at once, taking care to wet both sides of the leaves. The left-over spray adds a little potassium to the soil and is entirely harmless.

VEGETABLE DISEASES

It is not possible to mention every vegetable disease in this chapter, and it is highly unlikely that any organic gardener using good compost and rotating his crops will have any but the commonest. With luck and good humus he will certainly have fewer than his neighbours.

Beans

The common disease of beans is chocolate spot fungus, which shows as brown markings on leaves and stems. If these show early, watering with comfrey liquid could help, but the best answer is more compost, and wood ashes at the rate of about 2 lb. a square yard before sowing in November. There is also a bean rust caused by another fungus, but this, like bean anthracnose which attacks French and runner beans, is favoured by poor drainage and waterlogged soil.

Those whose gardens have a wet end, where rushes grow and there is moss and water on the surface in winter, can attempt a modest drainage scheme. Dig out a soakaway 4 ft square and deep at the lowest point, with a trench leading to it, sloping down from 1 ft below the surface at the high end with a fall of about one in twenty. The trench can be beside the garden path, for it will draw water to itself for about 12 ft. The neatest drain is made by cutting the bottoms off 1-lb. jam jars with a bottle chopper, and fitting them with necks to open bottoms along the bottom of the trench. Cover the jars with rough material such as hedge clippings, and then fill in the trench, filling the soakaway with hard rubbish such as stones and old brick-ends. A drain and soakaway is a good way of disposing of this kind of rubbish, and stones, cinders and small clinkers can replace the jam jars along the drain itself.

Bean anthracnose is caused by a fungus. Its symptoms are black spots on the stems and pods which become round or oval pits edged with red, and brown spots on the leaves. It is carried by seed, so never save any from infected plants. If the attack occurs before the beans are in flower, spraying with Bordeaux mixture can stop the outbreak.

The main cause of bean diseases, however, is neglect of crop rotation, for fungi can live on as spores in the soil, waiting for a wet season. Never put in concrete posts or other permanent supports for runner beans so that they are grown in the same place each year, but use portable supports instead and move them round the garden.

Beet

All the beet family, including Swiss chard and spinach beet, can have beet rust (*Uromyces betae*) which shows as light and dark brown spots on the leaves. Always twist the tops off your beets over the compost heap. Rusts are killed at 120°F., and your compost heap should reach that, but put the leaves towards the middle, unless your heap is in a New Zealand Box or anything else which heats right out to the edges.

Broccoli, Brussels Sprouts and Cabbage

The cabbage family share their diseases, and the worst of these is clubroot. Clubroot is caused by a slime fungus, *Plasmodiophora brassicae*, which was known to the Romans and is present in almost every country in the world. The fungus was identified by Michael Stephanovitch Woronin of Russia in 1878, and his advice to gardeners is still as good as ever, though we are very little further than he was towards a complete cure. There are no cures that are economic on a farm scale, but farmers can control the disease by rotation, for the spores live up to nine years in the soil, and it is easy to grow, say, kale or cabbages on only 20 acres out of 190 every year. In the garden this is impossible, for we just have not *got* nine places for cabbages, and our four-plot rotations are too close for complete clubroot control.

The spores are tiny and chemical-proof. They sleep safely until we plant or sow any member of the cabbage family (the *Cruciferae*), broccoli, Brussels sprouts, cabbage, cauliflowers, kale, kohl-rabi, swedes or turnips. Radishes grow too fast to wake the spores, but if we leave them in to grow hot and woody, they may. Wallflowers, candytuft, arabis, and even aubrietia can all serve as an emergency diet for the spores, but the biggest allies of clubroot are the weeds belonging to the *Cruciferae* family. As long as you have shepherd's purse (*Capsella bursa-pastoris*), your clubroot spores are waking to a not very satisfying meal which will keep the generations going. They can also feed on charlock, wild radish, mustard and even docks and couchgrass, according to some authorities. This is why the gardener who takes over a long derelict allotment can still have clubroot as badly as his neighbours with cultivated plots.

Keep your weeds down, and try and concentrate your cabbage tribe crops so that three quarters of the garden enjoys a complete rest from them, with a proportion of the spores dying of old age each year. Kohl-rabi, kale, turnips, swedes and sprouting broccoli all have some resistance to clubroot; cauliflowers are the worst affected.

The cabbage wilts and starves as its roots are destroyed, and the legend that seaweed foliar feeding will cure clubroot arises from the fact that the mineral supply to the leaves takes the strain off the reduced root area. When the stump is dug up it will be found to break into fragments with a distinctive sour smell. If you pull up the stump, you leave this mess, which can be 28 per cent clubroot spores, each one with a nine-year life ahead of it, in your soil. So dig them up with care, and dump the plant whole in the dustbin. Do *not* put it on the compost heap, for this will not get hot enough to kill the spores, which can pass safely through the digestive systems of cattle. A load of manure from cows that have had uprooted kale with clubroot thrown to them, or who have trodden the mud from the field into their litter, can spread clubroot far and wide.

The other counter-measure recommended by our Ministry of Agriculture is lime. Spread as much as 2 lb. a square yard and dig it in, or better still, churn it under with a Merrytiller or other rotary hoe, for this distributes the lime evenly through the top 8–10 in. of soil. The spores wake to become mobile zoospores, which are of course microscopic, and dislike swimming through an alkaline soil solution, and the effect of the lime lasts for three years.

The Henry Doubleday Research Association has been testing a number of remedies through the years, and it is possible that they may have better news for gardeners by the time you read this book. One remedy they tried was 3-in. lengths of rhubarb stem dropped down the dibber holes at planting time. This can work very well, but fails if there is a late hatching strain of clubroot present, for though the decaying stem section masks the cabbage root secretions, the attack may come when the plant has run out of rhubarb. Another trick is to sow spinach as a green manure, which leaves still more oxalic acid in the ground to hide the secretions.

The most hopeful line of research now is growing cabbages in large 9-in. pots, standing these in bowls to collect the drainage after watering. This will be full of cabbage root secretions, and is watered on to the clubroot-infested area when it is sown with carrots, beet-root, or other *non-cruciferous* crops to wake the spores up to star-vation. This could be a garden-scale remedy, and synthesizing the secretions might be possible as a farm-scale cure.

There are mercury preparations such as calomel (mercurous chloride), but these are too expensive for farmers, and far too dangerous for gardeners, even inorganic ones. No one wishes to build up mercury pollution in his soil as the years go by, for the problem is that every zoospore has only 2–5 days of danger while it is swimming, so that the soil must be permanently poisonous to catch them. So stick to weed control, crop rotations and lime, and maybe the safe and simple remedy the world is waiting for will be found by a modern Michael Woronin.

Carrots

There are no carrot diseases which cannot be cured by crop rotation, but they can suffer from soft rots if stored in clamps in the open. This is why they are safer in a shed in peat.

Celery

Celery leaf spot is carried on the seed, and the answer is to buy from a good seedsman. Never grow your own. I once grew 2 acres for seed and know that seedsmen earn their money on this crop.

Cucumbers

The outdoor cucumbers described in this book are not subject to virus, and the fungus diseases of greenhouse cucumbers cannot develop without heat and humidity. If mildew occurs, use the powdery mildew mixture, given on p. 185.

Leeks and Onions

These have a number of fungus diseases, including downy mildew, white rot and rust. All show first with leaves turning yellow and dying back in June, well before August, the time when they do this as part of the normal ripening process; downy mildew also shows as a grey mould on the leaves; rust produces raised orange spots on the leaves, and white rot produces a white fungus on the bulb base. Though these can be cleared off with downy mildew mixture or Bordeaux mixture, the spores last up to eight years in the soil, so these three are hard to get rid of by crop rotation.

Luckily they are less tough than clubroot spores and, if there is part of the garden that grows a poor crop whenever its turn for onions comes round, it pays to sterilize. Mix ½ pint of commercial formaldehyde with 3 gallons of cold water, and apply this through a rosed can to each square yard. Cover it with old sacks or plastic bags to retain the fumes in the soil for 48 hours, then take them off and do not sow or plant anything while the soil recovers, and until all smell of the fumes has gone. This kills soil bacteria, and a number of carnivorous species (*Protozoa*), so the nitrogen-fixing kinds increase afterwards like deer in a lionless Africa, and there is a temporary *gain* in fertility as well as a loss of some unwanted fungi. Formaldehyde can be obtained from good horticultural sundriesmen or from chemists.

All fungus diseases in onions are worse where large quantities of nitrogen as manure, chemical fertilizers, or soot are used, and where potash is scarce. Good compost is therefore the best answer, and a policy of dumping in the dustbin any leek or onion that dies off or yellows out of turn will avoid trouble.

The best way of preventing onions from rotting in storage is to bend them over and dry them in the traditional way (see p. 103) before roping or storing. The fast finish that you get from using sets makes it easy to dry their troubles away. Sets also need less firm ground, which makes rotation easier.

Lettuces

These have many troubles when grown commercially under glass, but in normal gardens where they can be rotated and given plenty of compost, they have few problems. Never use manure or mushroom compost within a week of planting lettuces, because this can increase both the fungus and slug risk, which is why most gardeners prefer to manure in the autumn. The main lettuce disease is *Botrytis cinerea* or grey mould, and if this is bad, sterilization with formaldehyde is an answer, for this substance breaks down quickly in the soil and is cheaper than commercial soil sterilizers, apart from the consideration that what you are using has been used by growers for over fifty years without building up any problems.

Parsnips

The only real trouble that parsnips are likely to suffer from is canker. The commonest type produces reddish-brown patches on the shoulder of the root, and is mostly found where the soil is wet and badly drained. The variety Avonresister is resistant to this and to the other cankers.

Peas

Mildew (both powdery and downy) is the commonest pea disease, especially in dry summers, and if it attacks before the peas are flowering, spray with Bordeaux mixture or the two mixtures recommended for mildews (p. 184–5). There are a few stray fungi but these can be countered by crop rotation and better drainage, like those of beans.

Potatoes

We have grown potatoes in quantity for over two hundred years, and in this time they have accumulated a number of diseases, of which potato blight (*Phytophthora infestans*) is the worst. This was responsible for the Irish Potato Famine of the 1840s which starved between one and two million people. It is serious in dull wet summers, and causes a loss of potato crops by destroying the foliage too soon, so that yields are small, and by infecting the tubers, which then rot in store.

The disease overwinters in small infected tubers left in the soil, so all gardeners should dig up any 'wanderers' or 'travellers' (especially after a bad blight year), because these can spread infection. If everyone, including farmers, did this, the infection chain would be broken and we should have beaten blight. The main infection source is from farms, where mechanized harvesting means large quantities of left-in potatoes every year. Even one infected tuber on 200 acres can start an epidemic.

Look for dark brown patches with rounded edges starting from the sides and tips of the leaves, usually with a whitish mould on the underside of the leaf behind these patches, which are moist. If there are only a few, spray with Bordeaux mixture to stop it spreading, and if the weather turns warm and sunny you may save the crop.

With dull wet weather potato blight can spread very fast, with the patches enlarging until all the foliage turns black. Then the only remedy is to make up Burgundy mixture and spray it on to the leaves to kill the haulm. The alternative is to cut the haulm down with shears and compost it, because the spores die at 120°F., but this means carrying them across the garden which could spread the disease further. Wait a fortnight and burn the shrivelled remains of the foliage, then lift the crop and spread it on sacks to dry, and store as usual. A month later pick over the potatoes and throw any that have gone soft in the dustbin, and pick over again in another fortnight because, though the *blight* will not spread from tuber to tuber, its associated soft rots will. The safest policy is to use Burgundy mixture where you can see the blight symptoms, and to cut down any haulm that seems to have escaped.

This is why second early varieties that mature fast are always the best for gardeners. If blight strikes late, Duke of York for example can give an almost unreduced yield after haulm cutting. Better still, choose a blight-resistant variety, and as more and more farmers change over to these, there may be a big fall in the frequency of bad blight years.

Wart disease could have been even more serious than blight because this fungus, *Synchytrium endobioticum*, has spores that can last *thirty years* in the soil, and not even farmers can manage that kind of rotation. Fortunately, in 1908, Mr George Gough, a Ministry of Agriculture Inspector tracking down this disease, which appeared first in Cheshire in 1902, discovered that Golden Wonder, Snowdrop, Abundance, Conquest and Langworthy were immune to wart disease, and from these our immune varieties, still marked with an asterisk in many catalogues, have been bred. In 1972 there were only five cases of wart disease in the whole of England. As a result, very few gardeners have even seen the growths that look like black cauliflower curds on the tubers and round the bases of the haulm. If you see them, report to the Ministry of Agriculture (look under Agriculture in your telephone directory) because this is a notifiable disease, and means you will be obliged to grow only immune varieties for the next thirty years. This is no hardship, for most modern varieties are immune. The non-immune varieties which are available and popular are Arran Chief, Duke of York, Eclipse, Epicure, King Edward and Sharpe's Express.

Two other diseases, scab and blackleg, were so hated by the cottage-gardening trades unionists of the past that they used the names as terms of abuse for strike-breakers. The scab they hated was not *Actinomyces scabies*, our common scab, which is controllable with lawn mowings and by choosing resistant varieties, but corky scab, *Spongiospora subterranea*, which in bad cases can produce cankers on the tubers almost like wart disease, but smaller and brown, not black. Usually it shows as round pimples on the skins of potatoes at lifting time, but on wet soils it can produce large canker-like masses.

This disease is common on allotments and in gardens where potatoes have been grown too often, but it is possible to knock it out with flowers of sulphur at $2\frac{1}{2}$ oz. a square yard dug in before planting potatoes again, for six years is quite a long time to rest an infected garden from this essential crop.

Blackleg is a symptom of the bacterial disease *Bacterium carotovorum*, and it shows from June onwards, when occasional stunted plants with yellowed and rolled-up leaves appear in the rows. Later they wilt, and if you dig up the plants, the main stem at soil level will be found to be black and slimy, while the crop will be very small. The disease is carried by tubers which rot and spread their rottenness to others in the bag. Dig up and dump the plants in the dustbin. Blackleg is carried by the seed potatoes, and it is one of the many diseases which Ministry of Agriculture Inspectors now keep out of our gardens.

Good drainage, feeding the soil and crop rotation are the answers to the other diseases of potatoes. In fact it was the rise of the potato which really taught us the need for rotation on a garden scale.

Rhubarb

Rhubarb's one disease is crown rot. This is caused by the bacteria *Pectobacterium rhapontici*, which rots the terminal bud and progresses to a soft chocolate-coloured decay of the crown. The only answer is to dig up the diseased part of the clump and dump it in the dustbin. This is the best answer for anything else wrong with rhubarb. Grow a new plant from a newly bought crown, or raise some more from seed in another part of the garden.

Tomatoes

Tomatoes belong to the same family as potatoes and can catch potato blight from them, when the spores are being blown in the wind. It appears in cold, wet summers as large, russet-brown marbled areas on the green fruit, which slowly become brown and shrivelled, and as dark brown streaks on stems and leaves. If there is potato blight in the district, or the summer is wet and cold, spray with Bordeaux mixture at the end of July and at fortnightly intervals.

The spray is a preventative, so try and cover the leaves evenly. It will whiten them, and there will always be some splashed on the fruit which should be wiped off before bottling or eating, though the copper is harmless except in quantity. Any diseased fruit or leaves should be removed and burnt, which is worth doing, because the disease spreads so much more slowly in tomatoes than potatoes that there may be time to save the rest of the crop.

Tomatoes should rotate round the garden like other crops, which prevents the build-up of disease from always growing them in the same place; if you give up the idea that the only good tomato is a ripe one, then they do not need always to grow in the same sunny bed.

Turnips and Swedes

Clubroot is the worst disease of turnips and swedes, and should be treated as for cabbages. Keep the lime level at neutral (pH 7.0) and concentrate on the clubroot-resistant varieties from Scotland. The Wallace turnip is a yellow-fleshed variety and about the best; the swede Enector will give a crop on even clubroot-infested soil, but none is completely resistant to clubroot; the fast white kinds of turnip like Early Snowball can go in and out too rapidly for a serious attack. (Japanese and Chinese radishes are safe.)

Brown heart, though common, is not a disease but a deficiency symptom – the result of boron being locked up by too much lime, administered for clubroot. Cut open the roots, making a horizontal cut a little below the middle, and you will see a grey mottled zone near the centre. Dig in or ideally water on 1 oz. of borax to 8 square yards in the early spring, as suggested earlier (p. 180).

Soft rot is caused by *Pectobacterium carotovorum* which can also attack carrots. The outside of the turnip or swede often remains firm while the heart becomes a putrid white mass. It attacks mainly where there has been heavy manuring with chemical nitrogen or farmyard manure. Compost appears to give resistance by more balanced feeding, but rotation should not be neglected. Diseased roots and leaves should be dumped in the dustbin, as turnips and other roots cannot be heated in a compost heap to sterilizing temperatures.

FRUIT DISEASES

The problem of disease in bush fruit is that it is very easy to be persuaded by the next door 'expert' or one on the radio that you should dig up your bushes and destroy them in case they have something awful. A better policy would be to treat all symptoms as mineral shortages and spray as directed earlier, with a seaweed foliar feed if you are in doubt. If the symptoms do not disappear after several weeks of this treatment, then virus or other diseases may well be present, and removal will be the best answer.

Currants

The most striking disease of all three currants is leaf spot, caused by the fungus *Gloeosporium ribis*. The spots are dark brown, about $\frac{1}{12}$ in. wide and irregularly shaped, entirely unlike the coloured margins and zoning patterns resulting from mineral deficiency. In a wet season leaf spot can spread fast, until the leaves fall off the bushes completely in June or July and the crop withers. There is another leaf spot, *Septoria ribis*, with round brown spots, but it is scarcer and less severe. Both diseases have the same treatment. Rake up the leaves and burn or bury them 1 ft deep, for they will ripen to spread more spores, then spray the bushes with Bordeaux mixture. If there are only a few spotted leaves to be seen in June or July, pick these for burning and spray with Bordeaux mixture as before, and this will prevent the fungus building up.

A third disease is currant rust, *Coronatium ribicolor*, which makes light and dark brown spots on the undersides of the older foliage when picking is over. Again the answer is to burn or bury the leaves and spray with Bordeaux mixture.

These fungi attack worst where blackcurrants have been given plenty of nitrogen, as manure or chemical fertilizer, so the best preventative is compost, comfrey and lawn mowings.

The most serious currant disease is reversion virus, which makes the leaves grow longer and narrower than usual, looking less like a sycamore leaf and more like that of a nettle. The bushes have brighter flower buds than normal, but the crop dwindles rapidly, and the plants become worthless. There are no resistant varieties and the best policy in this case is to dig up the bushes at once and burn them. Strange as it may seem, it is safe to plant blackcurrants in the same bed, because the virus is not passed on by being left in the roots, but by the tiny Big Bud Mite, described in the next chapter.

The coral spot fungus, *Nectria cinnabarina*, attacks all currants. It shows as small coral red spots on dead twigs, branches and pruned-back stumps that have died. These will produce spores that can get right inside a bush and kill whole branches. Take off wilting or sickly branches with the secateurs back to where the internal wood shows clean and white. Make the cut just above a leaf-joint, remove the cut-off pieces, and burn or bury them. Another fungus, *Plowrightia ribesi*, has black pustules also on the dead ends and on elderly branches, and this, too, should be cured by removal of dead wood at pruning time.

Gooseberries

The worst gooseberry disease is American mildew, *Sphaerotheca mors-urvae*. This appears as a white mould spreading over the leaves, fruit and branches, and in this form carries the spreading spores that blow on the wind; this turns dark brown, almost like felt, especially on the shoots, and contains a second type of spore that lasts through the winter. Cut off the shoot tips, which will be twisted and stunted, with about 3 in. of stem in August, and burn them because they will hold most of the overwintering spores. As soon as you see the white mildew spreading, spray with downy mildew mixture (pp. 184–5).

The European gooseberry mildew, *Microsphaera grossularia*, is not serious, and attacks leaf surfaces only. It can be cured by spraying with the same mixture. Another fungus, *Botrytis cinerea*, causes die-back, which makes the margins of the leaves on affected branches turn first yellow, then almost white, before becoming brown and withered as the bush dies branch by branch. The fungus starts in a wound or pruning scar; it kills whole branches, and sometimes a complete bush. If a branch is attacked, cut it off below the affected area, or dig up the whole bush and burn it with the prunings. Dieback is like the currant fungi in that it increases where the bushes are overfed with nitrogen fertilizers. A slimming diet of compost and comfrey is the best preventative.

Currant leaf spot and rust can also attack gooseberries and the same control measures apply. Gooseberries have, however, a rust of their own, *Puccinia pringsheimiana*, which produces startling bright red or orange patches on the leaves and stems. Infected leaves and stems should be removed and burnt, and if the attack was a bad one, spray the bushes the following season with Bordeaux mixture, about a fortnight before they start to flower.

Raspberries and Other Cane Fruits

There are a number of raspberry diseases, including cane blight, which produces sudden wilting in summer, cane spot, showing as small round purplish spots on leaves and canes in May and June, and spur blight, which kills the buds on the new canes in summer. All three have the same treatment. Scrape away the soil from the base of the canes concerned, and snip them out for burning well below the surface, so that you do not leave a stump full of spores above ground. Spray the unaffected canes with Bordeaux mixture, and give another spray of this the following spring when the buds are beginning to open. There are two raspberry mildews, and both can be sprayed with the downy mildew mixture (p. 184). Other cane fruits infected by any of these diseases can be treated similarly.

Raspberry canes are relatively cheap, and if any disease attacks it pays to buy a fresh stock and start a new bed in another part of the garden. The two commonest causes of trouble, however, are poor drainage, and the magnesium deficiency that looks like a virus, best corrected with dolomite limestone or Epsom salts.

Strawberries

The main garden strawberry disease is grey mould, caused by the wretched *Botrytis cinerea*, and at picking time it is a good idea to take a small plastic bowl with you and pick any mouldy fruit into this for dumping in the dustbin. Dusting with flowers of sulphur is the simplest answer, and this also checks leaf spot. Redgauntlet is a variety that is reasonably resistant to grey mould, and should be grown where this is a problem.

Remontant strawberries are not so prone to disease as the ordinary kinds, and isolated beds in gardens, moved in rotation, are usually free from problems. Most virus diseases are carried by the plants, and if these are bought from reputable nurserymen they will have been inspected and certified free from disease by the Ministry of Agriculture. Good feeding, plenty of compost, phosphorus supplied in bonemeal, and rotating the bed round the garden – these are the secrets of successful garden strawberry growing.

16 Pest Control by Predators and Safe Pesticides

The sprays which organic gardeners use must be safe for birds, bees and humans, and must spare as many as possible of the predators which are the natural enemies of our pests. But however safe the pesticide, it costs time and trouble to use, so the ideal answers to pest problems are tricks of timing and cultivation, and other methods which can help our friends control our foes. Some of these methods are not as immediately effective as the more deadly chemicals, but the build-up of predators is of more value than 100 per cent perfection.

PEST CONTROL BY BIRDS

Thrust a 6-ft bamboo cane slantways into the rose bed, and tie a piece of fat so that it hangs about 1 ft above the roses and 1 ft below the cane tip. All kinds of tit – blue tits, coal tits and great tits mostly – will perch and peck on the fat all through November, December and January, but there will be room for at most three at a time. In hard weather as many as twenty tits will be waiting for a place on the fat, and while they wait they will search out the eggs of greenfly in the rough bark at the bases of the bushes. This means no greenfly to spray against next summer. The exact hanging distances are to prevent the starlings sidling up the cane like parrots, and reaching down to steal the fat, or perching on the roses and pecking up at it.

Both ornamental and fruiting cherries share the cherry blackfly, an aphid that is distasteful to most ladybirds. Hang fat for the tits from your ornamental cherries, and persuade your neighbours to do the same, as well as hanging some from the netting supports of your wall cherries, and the tits will solve the problem.

The blackfly of broad beans, which also attacks runner beans, dahlias and rhubarb, spends the winter on viburnum and euonymus bushes, and it is likely that your garden and its neighbours are providing winter quarters for your local pest stock, rather than having them blow for miles from wild species in hedges. Hang the fat above your *Viburnum carlesii* or *V. burkwoodii*, or your euonymus hedge, and you could save your broad beans and those of your neighbours too.

Do not, however, hang fat over the blackcurrants, for though the blackcurrant aphid spends the summer on nettles and returns in September to winter under the rough bark of the older branches ready to attack in the spring, if you leave the netting off in the depths of winter the hungry bullfinches will strip off every bud.

Almost every garden has its pair of resident robins, which watch with bright and beady eyes every forkful of soil we turn. These are specialized in picking out not only insects and larvae, but also tiny pupae which we cannot distinguish from small stones. If your carrots have suffered from carrot fly, or your cabbage family from cabbage root fly, dig over the bed in November, December or January. Ideally, do this twice or even three times, not deeper than 6 in., to give your robins a useful feed.

Robins are also helpful with the raspberry beetle, *Byturus tomentosus*. This emerges in May to feed on flower buds and blossom, and in June and July lays its eggs in the first formed fruit, producing the familiar grubs in the raspberries. When these are fully fed, they drop from the ruined fruit and pupate in the soil between the rows. They can also attack loganberries and blackberries, where the same counter-measures should be employed.

At pruning time for all three berries, dig over the soil and turn in the remains of the decayed mulch of lawn mowings, when you will be closely followed by your robins pecking up the pupae. These will be in the top 4 in., so that there is no need to dig deeply. A second turnover later in the winter is also worthwhile if there is time. The normal control of spraying the blossom with a derris and pyrethrum mixture, though safe for birds, will kill bees. The robin method is safer, even though it is harder work.

HELPING THE HOVERFLY

Everyone who has read organic gardening books will know of the classical examples of biological pest control. These mainly involve taking a predator from one country and releasing it in another to control a pest related to its natural prey. There are techniques that involve sterilizing males with radioactive cobalt, synthetic growth hormones that keep pests at juvenile stages, and imitation insect sex hormones, but all are unsuitable for amateurs. Releasing *Baccillus thuringiensis* as a kind of myxomatosis for caterpillars could, for example, exterminate all Britain's butterflies, some of which are rare and beautiful. So this kind of control is best left to the Ministry of Agriculture, who are very rightly far more cautious than any commercial firm.

However, there is no reason why we should not try to make life a little easier for our friends. Perhaps the easiest of these to help are the thirty-eight out of 260 species of hoverfly native to Britain whose larvae are efficient aphid eaters. Though both adult ladybirds and their larvae eat large quantities of aphids, the larvae search at random. If they meet other ladybird eggs they will eat these and continue searching, a habit which produces up to 70 per cent mortality. So beyond using sprays that spare them, there is little we can do to help ladybirds. Hoverflies, however, are easily helped. They look like slim wasps – almost everyone will have seen them poised like tiny humming birds as they hunt for aphid colonies amongst which to lay eggs. First they must feed on pollen and nectar for about six weeks after hatching but, unlike bees and butterflies which have long tongues to reach inside a wide range of flowers, hoverflies have short ones, like houseflies, and are therefore limited to flowers with an easy entrance.

Experiments with hardy annuals by the H.D.R.A. have shown that *Convolvulus tricolor* is by far the best for attracting and feeding hoverflies. Sow the small seeds thinly as a border in the vegetable garden, or anywhere in full sun where they will not be overshadowed by taller plants, in late March or April, so that they will have plenty of flowers ready for the hoverflies when these start feeding in May or June. Thin the seedlings to 6 in. apart and transplant the thinnings to grow on for a later crop, which will last well on into September. The flowers are shaped like those of the distantly related bindweed (*Calystegia sepium*), which is a perennial with wicked white roots, not a lovely and easy annual. They are deep blue or crimson, with a white inner ring and a yellow centre, and furl themselves at night like tiny umbrellas. They open at about 8 a.m. with a little dew condensed inside the petals, which dissolves some of the nectar and spreads it out in the middle of the saucer-shaped flower. From then until about 9.30 is 'hoverfly rush hour', when there can be as many as four flies at once filling their 'fuel tanks' for a hard day's flying and aphid hunting. The commonest kind is *Syrphus balteatus* which lays an average of 140 eggs per 'hen', spaced out among the aphid colonies in twos and threes to avoid competition with each other, each one capable of eating 600 aphids before it becomes a hoverfly.

If *Convolvulus tricolor* were to become as popular as the petunia, it is likely that many more hoverflies would achieve two breeds a season and more would pupate in time to come safely through the winter. The immediate advantage is that your garden is thoroughly searched for aphids every day through the summer, and your border may well support enough hoverflies to clear your neighbour's garden as well, unless he sprays and kills off the small and rather slug-like larvae.

PEST CONTROL BY HEDGEHOGS

The work of Dr E. J. Dimelow at Whipsnade Zoo has established that the favourite food of hedgehogs is the black millipede, *Tachypodo-julus niger*, which looks like a short length of armoured gas pipe and coils into a disc when picked up. This pest, like its relation the spotted millipede, *Blanjulus guttulatus*, eats potatoes, pea and bean seeds, carrots, lily bulbs and gladioli corms. Unless they are very hungry, hedgehogs will ignore *Lithobius fortificatus*, the 'ninety-nine bump' centipede, which is chestnut brown, flattened, and swift running, and *Geophilus linearis*, the thread-like pale brown one, both of which eat large quantities of slug eggs and insect larvae, especially young wire-worms. This makes hedgehogs far better allies than frogs and toads, which appear to have no taste-buds and merely grab everything that moves, because they spare our carnivorous friends and eat our vegetarian foes.

Our knowledge of the hedgehog diet comes from the work of naturalists who dry their black, rather rat-like, droppings and sort out the hard parts of beetles. But this can be rather misleading, for slugs, which form the largest part of their food, digest down to very little. Hedgehogs are the best slug controllers, and they eat large quantities of the leathery surface caterpillars which bite off seedlings at ground level. These are called cutworms and they are the larvae of the yellow underwing moth, the turnip moth and the heart and dart moth.

Hedgehogs should receive the same protection and help as birds; moreover, they have no bitten buds and slaughtered seedlings on the other side of the ledger, though they have been known to eat strawberries when searching for slugs. In the spring, round about March, before the slugs are about, hedgehogs get very short of moisture, and it pays to put out equal parts of milk and water for them in a dog dish which they cannot turn over. Undiluted cows' milk is too strong for them. Brown bread, bacon rind, tinned mackerel and any fish-based, tinned cat-food have all been used successfully for hedgehog feeding. They should always be fed at night when the only birds about are owls and nightjars, so that there is no competition. Those who feed their hedgehogs regularly will find that they become very tame and live contentedly in the garden for many years.

THE SAFEST PESTICIDES

There are a number of standard substances, mainly of vegetable origin, which have the merit of sparing predators so that these can get on with their job of pest control, with a better chance of overtaking the pest altogether when some of the work has been done by a timely spray. Usually these insecticides differ from organo-chlorine and other persistent poisons in not building up populations of resistant strains, like the DDT-proof malaria mosquitoes of many tropical countries.

Nicotine

The cheapest and easiest way to obtain nicotine is to collect 4 oz. of filter tip cigarette ends and simmer them in 1 qt of water for half an hour, topping up with more water as this boils away. Strain the brown liquid through a nylon stocking, dilute it by adding 4 parts of water to 1 of the solution, and spray it on to anything really hard to kill, such as caterpillars or weevils. Modern filter tips contain about 0.1 per cent pure nicotine, which should be kept off your skin and out of your eyes and always labelled Poison, because it is deadly to human beings. On the other hand, no one will mistake a hoarded tin of cigarette ends for sweets, and so long as it is boiled up as required, there is little risk.

Nicotine spares ladybirds and their larvae and hoverfly larvae, and unless a bird actually drinks it, which is unlikely, there is no risk to them. It breaks down within forty-eight hours, so there is no build-up in the soil. Always wash your hands after using it, keep it out of the goldfish pond, and use it with caution. Because it costs only a visit to the local cinema or bingo hall or pub, you can use it freely for any sudden and startling outbreak of caterpillars. Add 1 oz. of soft soap to 1 gallon of the final mixture, where a nicotine soap wash is required.

Derris

This is a fish poison used in Malaya which contains the alkaloid rotenone and is harmless to all warm-blooded animals. Unfortunately it kills ladybird larvae and eggs, though it spares the adult beetles, and the larvae of the lacewing fly. It also kills both bees and the friendly predator *Anthocoris*.

Pyrethrum

This is also non-toxic to warm-blooded animals, but it kills ladybirds, their larvae and other predators. Unlike derris, which stays toxic for about forty-eight hours, pyrethrum is spent in under twelve, so beekeepers can spray with it in the evening and be safe by the morning. Bees' bed-time is an hour before sunset on average, so look up the time of sunset in your daily paper. Pyrethrum can be sprayed on to fruit and vegetable crops, even just before picking, and it is the best pesticide against strawberry aphids.

Quassia

Quassia is made from chips of wood from the tree *Picraṣma quassi-oides*, which keep indefinitely. Simmer 1 oz. of chips in 1 qt of water, topping up as the water boils away, strain this through a stocking, and add 1 oz. of soft soap. Dilute the mixture by adding 3 parts of water to 1 of the boiled extract. It is effective against *small* caterpillars, like those of the gooseberry and apple sawflies, and all aphids. It spares bees, ladybirds, their larvae and eggs, and *Anthocoris*, but not hoverfly larvae.

HOME-MADE PESTICIDES

Aphids can multiply twenty or thirty times in a week, and it is better to spray quickly with something mild than to wait until you can buy something, or even gather cigarette ends. The easiest and cheapest spray for aphids is made by cutting up 1 lb. of rhubarb leaves until they fit easily into an old saucepan and simmering them in 1 qt of water for half an hour. Dilute with 2 qt of cold water and spray the mixture on to the attacked crop, but always use it within twenty-four hours of making. Elder (*Sambucus nigra*) leaves can be used in the same way, offering hydrocyanic acid in a dilute extract. Rhubarb provides oxalic acid. Both are safe for bees and both break down rapidly in the soil. Wormwood leaves are stronger, so $\frac{1}{2}$ lb. is enough, but always use an old saucepan, because the active principle is so bitter that it will take long washing to clean it.

Potassium Permanganate

This is a combined insecticidal and fungicidal chemical which is spent in four hours; it is easily bought at any chemist, and keeps if it is stored in a tightly screw-stoppered jar. Stir 1 oz. of permanganate of potash into 2 gallons of water and spray it on foliage against aphids and the powdery mildews. This is a very weak insecticide, sparing almost everything, but a good surface mildew and aphid killer. It is especially useful for strawberries when you are picking the crop, when even quassia will give the fruit an unpleasant taste.

Soft Soap

Unlike ordinary soap, which is made with caustic soda, soft soap is based on potassium carbonate and is rather more effective. The traditional recipe for use on cabbage white and cabbage moth caterpillars is 2 oz. dissolved in 1 gallon of hot water and allowed to cool. This is also effective against cabbage whitefly larvae (which suck the sap from the undersides of the leaves), as it will get through their waxy coats. In some areas it is still possible to buy the industrial grade of soft soap from ironmongers, or to order from chemists.

17 Pests and Their Control Crop by Crop

The pests which are common to a range of crops are discussed first in this chapter to avoid repetition. In every case the damage they do must be balanced against the trouble of spraying and the risk to predators.

Ants

Ants feed on the excretions of aphids, which they move from plant to plant like farmers driving cows from field to field, and they defend their herds from ladybird and hoverfly larvae as though they were wolves. The usual answer is to spray the aphids, but it is also possible to poison the ants, which can be done easily if they are a problem in the house. Mix equal parts of borax and icing sugar very thoroughly and sprinkle this near the places where ants are observed. If in the open, sprinkle on wood, slate or glass and cover with another piece propped on stones to keep off the rain. Because ants eat each other's droppings, sharing a digestive system as it were, a very small amount of the mixture taken back to the nest can destroy it completely without harm to anything else. Borax also kills cockroaches and crickets indoors. Keep it in a tin labelled Poison, because if you ate the tinful in mistake for sugar it would do you no good, though it has only recently been banned as a potted meat and sausage preservative after fifty years of use.

Aphids

There are very many species of aphid and these are described below under the vegetables and bush fruits they attack. Their life cycles are complicated – most of them are male or female for only part of the year. When winged, the females produce young directly without an egg stage, often at the rate of fifty a week. Their enemies, mainly hoverfly larvae and ladybird larvae, struggle to keep up with them, and therefore any sprays used should spare these useful allies.

Luckily aphids are easy to kill and therefore relatively weak sprays can be used – as long as you spray as early as possible. The rhubarb leaf and elderleaf mixtures described under 'Home-made Pesticides' (p. 205) are effective, and safe for the enemies of the aphids. With mealy cabbage aphid, which is in the winged stage in June and can increase to plague proportions in a dry summer, one or two safe sprayings will lower the numbers until the ladybirds can overtake the pests and fly off to other gardens. If you kill your ladybirds and larvae with toxic pesticides, you will have to keep on spraying the aphids. Derris and pyrethrum, though safe for birds and human beings, are both ladybird killers. Quassia and ordinary soapy water are safe. Keep nicotine for caterpillars and weevils.

Millipedes

Millipedes, like wireworms, live on the roots, bulbs and tubers of a range of crops, also on pea and bean seeds, and though hedgehogs will eat large numbers of them, we cannot all have hedgehogs, and their efforts need supplementing. Trapping is the best answer.

Cut an 8-in. wide strip of perforated zinc and roll it round a hoe handle to make a cylinder. Stitch down the side with thin wire to join it, and across the bottom, then make a wire handle. Fill it with potato peelings and bury it upright with the handle sticking out in the bed where the millipedes are working. Pull it out once a week and tip the peelings into the chicken run, where the trapped millipedes will cause great excitement, or tip them into cigarette-end nicotine. A 'trap-line' of a dozen, cleared regularly, will solve the millipede problem.

Tall tins of the type used for canned fruit can be fitted upside down over a round post and drilled with $\frac{3}{8}$-in. holes in the sides by those who have an electric drill. These are cheaper and rather more effective traps than those made by jabbing holes in the bottom of tins, because the millipedes mostly hunt horizontally.

Slugs

The problem of modern metaldehyde slug baits is that these are highly poisonous to hedgehogs, which are the best natural controllers, and to cats and dogs. The liquid types are worst, and if your pet suddenly has paralysed hind-quarters this is the effect of eating or drinking these wood-alcohol-based slug destroyers. There are so many cases of accidental poisoning from wandering cats and dogs finding other people's slug bait, that veterinary surgeons keep in readiness a special preparation for injection which is a quick cure if given fast enough.

The safe remedy for slugs, apart from having a hedgehog, is trapping. The traditional trap is a soup plate, wide and shallow, sunk level with the ground and filled with a mixture of 1 part of beer to 2 of water, sweetened with 1 dessertspoonful of Barbados sugar to 1 pt of the mixture. This can be cleared of dead slugs with one swish of a broom and the trap refilled from a can of the mixture, for you need a battery of traps and mass production methods – in one garden 60,000 slugs were trapped in a year.

The problem is that though beer is best, it is also expensive. An economy trap can be made by sinking a wine bottle into the ground with the mouth at soil level and only about $\frac{1}{4}$ in. of beer in the bottom. The slugs will be attracted by the smell, crawl inside, and be unable to crawl out. The filled bottles can be dug up and put in the dustbin.

An alternative is to sink a wider container such as a pudding basin level with the soil, and to half fill it with milk. The slugs will scent the milk, fall in, and drown. Another version is to fill the basin entirely with salt water and sprinkle the surface with bran or sawdust which will float. The slugs try to crawl on this and fall through. Plastic containers should not be used for slug traps, because these provide a rough surface they can climb out on, unlike smooth china.

Slugs are scavengers as well as lettuce eaters, and they feed on the droppings of a number of creatures as well as on the bodies of pests slain by pesticides. When these have been killed by organo-chlorine compounds, the persistent pesticides concentrate in their bodies until slugs can become crawling poison pellets. If a hedgehog, feeding to build up the 'mantle' or coat of fat under its prickles which stores food to support it during hibernation, has eaten a large quantity of these poisoned slugs, the DDT concentrates in this fat, as it does in ours, and is released into the blood stream on loss of weight. This means large hedgehogs dead for no apparent cause in spring. The danger extends to thrushes, which are also slug and snail controllers.

Surface mulches of lawn mowings should be used only under hard-wooded crops like blackcurrants, raspberries and roses, which are not attacked by slugs, and the 'no-digger' who spreads compost on the surface is providing decayed organic matter to feed a slug population. The theory is that the slugs will eat this and leave the crops alone, but this is only partly true, and the popularity of the Ruth Stout system of cultivation in the U.S.A. comes from the fact that in their generally drier climate there are far fewer slugs. In England, thick coats of hay on the soil surface make expensive housing (up to £100 a ton) for slugs.

When a mulch is sheltering slugs, or a soil is full of *Milex sowerbii*, the keeled slug which eats holes in potatoes, stir 1 teaspoonful of potassium permanganate and 1 of salt into a 2-gallon can and water this on over an area of twelve square yards. It will not kill slugs, it merely brings them to the surface, for the attention of robins, thrushes and starlings. Scattering fat or other food to draw a quantity of starlings is easy, and then you can water the soil with time for them to come back and finish the main course of slugs. Thrushes and robins are better birds for this job, and if your hedgehogs are about in the evening you can bring up slugs for them to eat. Do not use more than a teaspoonful of either substance or you risk bringing up the worms too.

There is a proprietary herbal slug destroyer, Fertosan, which can be watered on in a barrier round a lettuce bed or as a killer for keeled slugs. Another contact killer is 1 part of powdered alum and 7 parts of slaked lime, mixed thoroughly together and scattered on mild evenings when slugs are above ground. Neither substance is dangerous to hedgehogs or birds.

Wasps

Wasps will attack plums and peaches, and of course they can sting, and a sting on the lip or tongue is dangerous for children. The poisons employed against wasps, including cyanide, are also dangerous. A safer remedy is to add 1 tablespoonful of the quassia preparation (p. 205), undiluted, to 1 pt of water, stir in as much brown sugar or treacle as will dissolve easily, and paint this on a fence, or even a piece of planed plank near the wasps' nest. This will, of course, catch and kill a quantity of moths, but the wasps will scrape up the mixture and take it home so that they will be the main sufferers.

Wireworm

The wireworm is a pest not only of new allotments, but also of gardens with undisturbed grassy ground and tufts of grass as well as lawns or pasture. The methods of clearing them from new gardens and allotments by timing turf stacking and green manuring have been described on pp. 68–9, but there are smaller-scale methods for established gardens.

Buy linseed cattle cake from an agricultural merchant, smash it up with a spade, and fork it under at the rate of $\frac{1}{2}$ lb. a square yard where wireworm is likely, or bury pea-sized pieces with a dibber round your lily bulbs or tulips if these are what is being attacked. This is of course a variation of the 'feeding method' described earlier. On the other hand, trapping with potato peelings in perforated zinc exactly as for millipedes (p. 208) is cheap and simple.

Woodlice

Woodlice are mainly greenhouse pests. The best way to get rid of them is to wait till the house is empty, close the ventilators, sprinkle a bottle of cloudy ammonia on the floor and get out quick. This is about the cheapest and safest greenhouse fumigant, and it will also kill earwigs. Those who eat grapefruit for breakfast can leave the peel in domes beside the path as traps, but shaking the woodlice out is rather tedious compared with the ammonia method. On the whole they do not do much harm, for they mostly eat decaying rather than living vegetable matter.

If compost heaps contain quantities of woodlice it is a sign that moisture is lacking, and it would be better to turn the heap, watering the material as it is piled back. It is possible to gas them by cutting open enough polythene bags to cover the heap, mixing a bottle of household ammonia in a 2-gallon bucket of cold water, and then pouring this over the place where the woodlice are congregating. Spread the polythene on top to hold in the smell.

PESTS – CROP BY CROP

Generally speaking organic gardeners have fewer pests than inorganic, because the use of chemical nitrogenous fertilizers makes growth softer and more easily eaten. This also applies to heavy dressings of farmyard manure, which can increase the slug population considerably. Another advantage lies in sparing predators and their larvae, especially the ground beetles, of which the devil's coach-horse (*Staphylinus olens*) is the best known. All gardeners should buy the Ministry of Agriculture Bulletin No. 20, *Beneficial Insects* (85p from H.M.S.O., P.O. Box 569, London SE1), which gives coloured illustrations of all the leading British predators. In fact, this comprehensive guide to what not to squash should be the most important textbook for every school natural history class.

Artichokes

The only pest artichokes have is lettuce root aphid (*Pemphigus bursarius*), which looks like a grey greenfly, and lives on the tubers. It can be killed by watering round the artichokes with cigarette-end nicotine solution, in April or May, which has the spin-off effect of destroying the aphids in their winter home before they migrate and attack the lettuce bed.

Beans

The blackfly, *Aphis fabae*, attacks broad beans, runner beans, beet, rhubarb, spinach and turnips. The easy answer is to sow broad beans in November so that they come through the winter with skins too tough for the blackfly to attack, and have their pods set really early. Then when the aphids arrive and start on the new growth, this can be cut and dumped, leaving nowhere for them to settle.

On spring-sown Windsor beans, or other attacked vegetables, spray with the nicotine mixture, or whatever is available. This aphid can increase so fast that its feeding (by sucking the plant's sap) can damage the plants badly and reduce the crop greatly, so spray quickly, ideally at dusk so that the strongest effect of even nicotine is spent by the time the bees are again on the blossom.

Beet

The beet fly (*Pegomya betae*) lays clusters of up to six white eggs on the undersides of the foliage; these hatch to maggots which produce long blisters as they tunnel through the leaves. They drop to the ground and pupate for a short period, then hatch and repeat the process, with three or even four broods a summer. If only a few leaves are attacked, pick them and dump them in the dustbin, then give a tonic dressing of dried blood. With a really bad attack, spray with nicotine which will penetrate the thin skin of leaf over the maggots.

There is a rarer pest, the beet carrion beetle (*Aclypea opaca*), which is small and black and, together with its larvae which are also black and active, climbs the plants and eats the leaves greedily. Again, spray with nicotine, and use compost rather than nitrogen-rich manure. Both pests pupate in the ground and are good food for robins after winter digging.

Cabbage Tribe Pests

The commonest are what gardeners call cabbage caterpillars. These are the dark bluish or greenish black, yellow-spotted and hairy larvae of the Cabbage or Large White butterfly (*Pieris brassicae*), the velvety green ones with a narrow yellow line down the backs of the Small White (*P. rapae*), and the plain green, lineless, Green-veined White (*P. napi*). The first one lays yellow oval eggs in clusters of up to 100 on the cabbage leaves and these can sometimes be found and squashed in June and July for the first brood, and again in August or September for the last one.

All three butterflies are greatly attracted to the flowers of buddleia bushes, whose nectar appears to stupefy them, and they are easily caught with butterfly nets. It is frequently stated that spraying with 1 part of milk to 2 parts of water will repel the butterflies, but there is little evidence that anyone has tried it often enough to see if it makes enough difference to justify the trouble and the cost of the milk.

Normal spraying with nicotine and soft soap or, when the cabbages are near eating, with 2 oz. of common salt dissolved in 1 gallon of cold water, will control a bad attack. On a small scale, hand picking is also a useful method of control.

The cabbage moth (*Mamestra brassicae*) has smooth caterpillars, which can be light or dark green, brown or black, and which burrow right down into the heart of the cabbage and ruin it with their excreta. They should be sprayed with the salt water solution or nicotine, but once they have got well inside they are hard to kill. The moths are greyish brown, with black and white spots on the upper wings and light grey on the lower pair, but they are late-day fliers and rarely seen. Paint some short ends of planed plank with the treacle and quassia mixture suggested for wasps (p. 210) and put these out at night between May and September. Though this will catch a number of harmless creatures, most of the moths and butterflies attracted to the cabbage bed will be up to no good.

The mealy cabbage aphid (*Brevicoryne brassicae*) winters as small black eggs on cabbage stumps and such crops as sprouting broccoli, kale, and spring cabbage. Therefore the stumps of these should be smashed with an axe-back to go on top of the air channels at the bottom of the compost heap, in runner bean trenches, or stacked to dry until they can be burnt. Drought in May and June when the winged forms of this pest are migrating can produce an epidemic reaching its peak in September and October. The mealiness serves to protect the aphids from sprays, so use soft soap with the nicotine, and always a ladybird-safe spray because, as in 1975, this is one of the predators that can overtake the pest, with some assistance.

The cabbage gall weevil (*Ceutorhynchus pleurostigma*) produces galls on the roots which are often taken for clubroot, but they are usually round and firm, and if cut through they always have a maggot inside. The plants are usually stunted and can fail to heart. Chop the roots off and put them in the dustbin, or stack them to dry and burn. Dig over the bed, because the tiny pupae that hatch to $\frac{1}{8}$-in. long, black, snouted little beetles are among many which robins eat happily.

The cabbage whitefly (*Aleyrodes proletella*) was nearly wiped out in the hard winter of 1962–3, but a cycle of mild winters has made it a real pest of southern counties. It has immobile light brown or yellow larvae that sit on the undersides of the outer leaves and excrete copious sticky 'honeydew' on which grow the sooty moulds which prevent the leaves breathing. They mature into tiny white, moth-like flies resembling the tomato whitefly (*Trialeurodes vaporariorum*) which attacks the greenhouse crop. The best policy is first to break off any worn-out and discoloured leaves, which will have been attacked, and secondly to spray with 8 oz. of soft soap dissolved in 5 gallons of water. Spray at weekly intervals while the attack lasts because there will be successive broods of larvae coming on; the soap will kill these but not the eggs.

The worst pest of all is the cabbage root fly (*Erioischia brassicae*), which turns the leaves blue-grey with starvation from root and stem damage. The first brood of flies, like $\frac{1}{4}$-in. long house-flies, attacks in late April and May, laying eggs on the surface round the stems of the plants. These hatch and burrow into the stem, often causing so much damage that the plants blow over in the wind. When they are fully fed, the white maggots move out into the soil, become chestnut-brown pupae, hatch and turn into the late June-July brood; the final brood in August and September winters as pupae, and again these are robin food for those who dig their cabbage bed.

The traditional defence at planting time is to punch or cut a hole in a 4-in. square of tarred roofing felt, thread the plant through this and dibber it firmly home. The soil must be level and the hole should be about $\frac{3}{4}$ in. in diameter. The fly must have a soil surface to lay on, and so is completely defeated. Care should be taken to water the plant in with a spouted can, because the felt can keep off the rain.

A new version of this old trick involves collecting yoghourt or cream containers, or expendable plastic teacups. Light a candle and use the flame to melt a 1-in. wide hole in the bottom of each. Thread the plant root through the hole and dibber it in, digging the sides of the upside down container into the soil. The container baffles the fly as easily as the tarred felt, but has the following advantages: (1) there is no need to buy a whole roll of roofing felt and take the trouble to cut it up, when the plastic cups and containers are free; (2) watering is easier because the water and rain run down the sloping sides of the container; (3) the fly will not creep down beside the stem into the semi-darkness so the larger hole is safe, and a full-sized cabbage stem is tough enough to tear the plastic to fit it.

The last batch often lays eggs on the leaves, which defeats this trick, so spray with nicotine and soap if small maggots are eating your cabbages. Many areas escape this pest entirely, but the more inorganic gardeners there are who use pesticides which make their soils poisonous enough to kill the flies as they alight, the more Bembidion and other beetles they kill, the more cabbage root flies there will be, and the more pesticides will be sold.

Carrots

The carrot fly (*Psila rosae*) is about $\frac{1}{5}$ in. long, with a greenish-black body, looking rather like a small house-fly. However, you rarely see it – only the larger leaves of your carrots turning deep maroon-red from the damage to the roots by the slender, creamy maggots working inside them. They also attack celery, parsley and parsnips, and every roadside or waste land provides an inexhaustible supply of carrot flies from the roots of the hemlock and cow parsley on which they normally feed.

It is not possible to control carrot flies by killing, and attempts with aldrin have merely exterminated their natural enemies and produced resistant races. Professional carrot growers now hire a field for a season and move to another seven miles away next year, to keep ahead of the fly, which will travel this far to find carrots, drawn by the scent of crushed foliage at thinning time.

The normal March or April sowings are ready for thinning in late May and early June, just when the first hatch of fly is ready to attack. The eggs are laid on the surface of the loosened soil. They hatch to small maggots which bore *down* into the soil and then *up* into the root, so that no pesticide can be watered on to kill them in the tunnels. The only course of action when the leaves show that there is root damage is to dig up the attacked carrots, cut out the bad bit and use the rest. The maggots will escape into the soil, pupate and become the second hatch, laying eggs in August and September. The maggots from these will go on eating inside stored roots, which will not keep.

One solution is to use pelleted seed, which is large enough to sow individually 4 in. apart in the rows, thus cutting out the need to thin and avoiding any disturbed soil. However, it gives protection for only a few days. Like the many other tricks which depend on preventing the 'broadcast' of the scent message, or 'jamming' it with a different scent, it works well for distant carrot flies, but fails for those hatching in local gardens, because the flies are designed to hunt by sight as well as scent. It is effective for only a short period – simply cutting out the risk from the scent of crushed foliage at thinning time. In dry weather there is always a very poor germination from pelleted seeds.

If there has been a bad attack of carrot fly, the bed should be dug thoroughly about October and again in November, to give your local robin a chance to peck up the pupae, which look like tiny stones – only a skilled robin can tell them apart. Do not sow winter green manures or plant leeks or cabbage tribe crops where the carrots were, so that repeated diggings can feed the carrot fly pupae to your birds in winter. In an organic garden where persisting pesticides are not used, there will be plenty of ground beetles – the adult beetles eat up to 50 per cent of the carrot fly eggs before they hatch on the surface, and their larvae eat many more. If you come across any black, jointed, slow-moving six-legged creature in the soil, rather like a devil's coach horse beetle, as you dig in winter, spare it, and bury it out of reach of robins, for it is also pupae-hunting.

The scent 'jamming' methods are well known. One of the best is to sprinkle lawn mowings thickly between the rows, renewing them at every mowing. Sand soaked in paraffin is also suggested, and so is the creosote and tar-soaked string which can be bought for tree tying, run along the rows to a peg at each end. Planting onion sets or garlic between the rows is traditional, but less effective.

Another suggestion is based on the fact that the carrot fly has to see the top of the young carrot, or where the leaves join it, to judge when the root is large enough to hold the maggot. Ridge them by drawing the soil with the hoe over the top of the young carrot until the tips of the leaves just show. As these grow higher, ridge again. This is a promising method, especially as twenty rows at once could be ridged at tractor speed, but so far, like all methods, it is not 100 per cent effective. Neither are the inorganic solutions, which can produce large increases of carrot flies by destroying all their natural enemies. Digging over the bed in winter and giving your robins a useful meal is more effective than that.

Celery

The celery leaf miner, or celery fly (*Philophylla heraclei*), lays eggs on the undersides of celery and parsnip leaves between April and June, and the larvae make winding tunnels between the upper and lower leaf surfaces which show as light brown lines and blisters. Spray the plants with nicotine, and if there is a second hatch in September, spray again. The nicotine will go straight through the thin upper leaf surface and kill the maggot. This is a warning not to get nicotine on your hands, and to wash them after using – your skin is tougher than the leaf surface, but nicotine can penetrate a leaf's equivalent.

There is also a celery beetle (*Phaedon tumidulus*), which is about $\frac{1}{8}$ in. long and steely blue. It migrates in July and August, eating celery, parsnip and carrot foliage. The answer is derris dusted on the leaves as soon as the beetles are about.

Leeks

The leek moth (*Acrolepia assectella*) is brown, about $\frac{1}{2}$ in. across the wings, and lays eggs at ground level in April and May on leeks and onions. The caterpillars then bore long tunnels up leek and onion leaves, showing as white streaks which join and spread until the plants die from the damage. Spray with nicotine as soon as you see the first of the streaks, because they can produce a second brood that really will slaughter the bed. Digging over the cleared part of the bed gives the robins a go at the chrysalids.

Lettuce

One of the worst pests is the lettuce root aphid (*Pemphigus bursarius*) which, as mentioned earlier, can spend the winter as a pest of artichokes. It can also winter on most species of poplar. It begins the year by making galls on the young leaf stalks, hatching to a winged form in July, then migrating to the roots of lettuces, sowthistles and fat-hen (*Chenopodium album*). This is one of the reasons, as well as their robbing roots, why poplars should not be planted in gardens.

As soon as you see a lettuce plant wilting, water the row with nicotine, applied with a rosed can at the roots. The aphids are yellow at this stage and covered with white wool. They attack the collar of the plant, where the root is fattest just below the soil. Soak both sides of the row, for though you cannot save plants that have already flopped over, you can kill the aphids which are multiplying on the others. About half a teaspoonful of dried blood sprinkled round recovering lettuce and watered in will give them a quick tonic. Do not waste nicotine on the lettuce leaves, for this aphid only attacks the roots.

A less common cause of sudden wilting in hot weather is the chrysanthemum root fly (*Psila nigricornis*), which is a relation of the carrot fly. Its ½-in. long, white maggots, however, bore horizontally into the root instead of going down and then up, so there is a chance of killing them by soaking the soil round the root with nicotine wash. Market gardeners who grow lettuce where they have had outdoor chrysanthemums for some years can have their land full of the pupae of this awkward pest. An answer is to wire in the bed and run chickens on it, rotavating the land at intervals, to give the 'robin method' its maximum effect.

Onions

The onion fly (*Delia antiqua*) looks like a small house-fly. It lays eggs on the surface, like its relations the carrot and cabbage root flies; the resultant dirty white maggots bore into the bases of the onions, often as many as thirty to a bulb, reducing it to a rotting mess. There are three broods a year, and the last one overwinters as pupae in the soil. The answer is to grow onions from sets, for these need no thinning and there is very little scent message. If any do go soft, dig up the bulbs and dump them in the dustbin to get rid of the maggots before they have time to pupate. With luck this creature, which can also attack leeks and shallots, will become extinct as more and more gardeners change over to sets.

Parsnips

These have only one pest, the celery leaf miner, and nicotine as for celery kills this quickly.

Peas

The worst pest is the pea and bean weevil (*Sitona lineatus*), which is a ¼-in. long, light brown beetle with paler stripes. It eats notches in the edges of the leaves, giving them a scalloped appearance, and so reduces the leaf area when the plants are young, which can kill them in dry years when they are growing slowly. The weevils hibernate in hedges and grass lands through the winter and migrate to gardens in the spring. They feed and lay eggs from April until July, and the white, legless grubs burrow down and eat the pea roots, concentrating on the nitrogen-fixing nodules, and taking about six weeks from egg to adult.

The best control is nicotine watered along the rows to knock out the grubs before they mature – this is most effective if the peas are grown in trenches so that the solution soaks down into the humus layer. It will not harm the bacteria and is spent in forty-eight hours. The weevils are nocturnal, and spend the day hiding among clods and weeds. Hoeing between the rows disturbs them and robins can peck them up. Mulching with mowings between the rows provides easy shelter, and watering the dried surface of the grass with nicotine will catch the weevils sleeping. The boiled-up cigarette-end nicotine wash costs only the trouble of making so you need not stint its use.

The pea moth (*Laspeyresia nigricana*) is responsible for the familiar maggots in mid-season and late peas. The moths are flying from mid-June to mid-July, laying their eggs in twos and threes on the leaves, stems and small, still flat pods. They hatch in eight days and the tiny, pale green caterpillars can be killed then by spraying with nicotine and soap, before they get inside the pods. Spray about eight days after the first flowers appear, when the crop will be in full flower with the first-formed pods still flat. The problem is that the spray will also kill bees. Therefore make up the treacle and quassia solution as recommended for wasps (p. 210), and paint it on boards which can be propped against the pea rows at night and put in a shed early in the morning, thus avoiding any risk to butterflies in day time. On the other hand, they are likely to collect quite a few cabbage butterflies on unlawful expeditions. The alternative is to sow only an early variety of pea in March, for quick maturity in July, and miss the moth completely. It really depends on how bad pea moth is in your area – you may have too few to be worth extreme measures like treacle boards.

Pea thrips (*Kakothrips pisivorus*) are small and black, found on peas in May and June, and eat flowers, stems and pods, leaving silvery markings on them, while the tiny orange larvae feed on the pods and leaves. The adults hibernate through the winter in the soil. The best answer is to spray with the nicotine and soft soap solution, but as in the case of the pea moth, this gives a choice of bees or peas. The compromise is to spray at dusk to reduce the risk, which lasts about forty-eight hours.

Potatoes

The most serious potato pest is the potato eelworm (*Heterodera rostochiensis*), responsible for the condition called potato sickness which is found in many long-cultivated gardens and allotments. The symptoms are stunted haulm, which yellows, wilts and dies off early, with often abnormal fibrous roots below the surface, and tiny tubers. Lack of calcium means small tubers in quantity, and stunted, light green foliage, but yellowing and dying off early as well – sure signs of eelworm.

When these potatoes are dug, the swollen bodies of the female eelworms will be seen as white dots on the roots, about $\frac{1}{50}$ in. wide, just visible without a hand lens. They turn yellow and then brown before dropping off into the soil. Each contains between 200 and 600 tiny eggs containing living larvae. Therefore, dig up your plants with care and dump them in the dustbin so that they will be incinerated, starved on a refuse tip, or heated up enough in a municipal compost plant to destroy them. Otherwise burn them. *Do not* trust to the heating of your compost heap. In times of potato shortage it is safe to eat eelwormed potatoes, because the brutes attack the *feeding* roots and starve the crop; the cysts are merely resting on the outside of the skins, not *inside* the tubers like wireworms. Be sure to put the peel in the dustbin, not on the compost heap, for cysts on peelings are one of the ways in which potato eelworm is spread.

The best garden-scale solution so far is to grow eelworm-resistant varieties, especially Maris Piper, a good tasty maincrop, and Pentland Meteor or Pentland Lustre, two good earlies. These do not resist all strains of eelworm, but new potato varieties with better defences are under trial. Reinforce this with crop rotation, for every year a proportion of the cysts will die of old age and if potatoes are grown only every fourth year, this gives natural wastage a chance. This is the only farm-scale control, but farmers have more space and can wait eight or even ten years before growing potatoes again.

Radish

Radishes belong to the cabbage tribe, but are in the ground for such a short time that they are rarely a problem. They can suffer badly from flea beetle (*Psylliodes spp.* – there are eight of them), which also attacks all cabbage tribe seedlings, especially turnips.

The small, black, skipping beetles hibernate in hedges or among rubbish, then migrate. They appear in gardens about the first week in May, eating the leaves of cabbage tribe seedlings into holes, often attacking when they have only their rounded seed-leaves, and killing the whole sowing. On a farm scale they can clear a field of newly sown turnips or kale almost overnight, and are worst in dry springs. They lay eggs in June, and their larvae spend about three weeks eating the roots of cabbage tribe crops, three more as pupae, and are then back at work as beetles again. The larvae do relatively little damage, but the beetles themselves are a major pest.

Dusting with derris as soon as you see leaves with holes in is about the best answer, but the danger is greatest for crops sown between 10 April and 20 May. The traditional farm control is to sow turnips, kale and cabbage either on Grand National Day or Derby Day, but gardeners need their radishes for succession, and derris is the best answer, followed by a little dried blood as a tonic after a bad attack.

Tomatoes

Greenhouse tomatoes have plenty of pests, but those in the open escape most of them. If there are caterpillars, pick them off by hand, and if wireworms damage the roots and cause flagging, water round the plants with nicotine.

FRUIT PESTS

The pests described in the following pages relate to bush fruit and cherries. If apples, pears and plums had been included, accounts of their pest control would have expanded this book still further. There are many books on tree fruit growing, and dealing with their pests by organic methods is covered in my own *Grow Your Own Fruit and Vegetables* (Faber & Faber).

Cherries

The cherry blackfly (*Myzus cerasi*) is an aphid which resists all ladybirds except the fourteen-spot species, which is black with square cream spots rather like a tiny round chess board. Today, Japanese ornamental cherries are so popular that these harbour quantities of aphids, and their winged forms spread from these to attack wall cherries, which are the only type that can now be successfully grown because they can be protected from birds.

The blackfly can only attack the young shoot tips, so when the first of these aphids are seen on the growing tips, pinch off about 3 in. of shoot, drop the portion into a basket and dump it on the compost heap. This summer pruning system is also effective against apple aphids, and it puts more strength into the fruiting buds. The alternative is to spray with nicotine or quassia and soft soap wash, the soap helping to get the spray into any curled leaves. It is always best to use something simple, even plain soft soap, quickly, before the pest can spread with a birth-rate of about 20 per aphid per week.

The cherry fruit moth (*Argyresthia nitidella*) lays eggs in crevices and leaf scars in June and July, some of which hatch into tiny caterpillars in September and feed on the leaves for a short time before hibernating in bark cracks. They awake and burrow into the blossom buds as soon as these burst, and when the petals fall they bore into the developing cherries and destroy them. Spray with nicotine or derris in September to catch the caterpillars, and again just before the blossoms open, when the buds are showing white. The orthodox treatment is to spray with a winter tar oil wash, which will slaughter the predator *Anthocoris*, but this is useless for wall fruit. The pests which lay eggs which come through the winter in bark crevices go in between the branches and the wall, and *Anthocoris* prefers to spend the winter eating them just there, so the more care you take to squirt the tar oil behind the trunk, the more of your friends you kill.

The winter moth (*Chiematobia brumata*), which also attacks

apples, has flying males about 1 in. across the wings, and wingless females, which are normally baffled by putting a sticky grease band round any fruit tree. Wall fruits have the problem that these rather spider-like females can ignore the band round the trunk and walk straight up the wall. You can buy sticky grease bands but not the material to go on them, and any treacle mixture will wash off with the winter rains. An old-fashioned recipe uses 8 parts of powdered resin, 4 parts of turpentine, 4 parts of linseed oil, and $\frac{1}{2}$ a part of honey. Bring the mixture to boiling point over a slow heat, stirring well, and smear it along the wall while it is still warm. This mixture will also stop ants bringing aphids to pasture on the cherry, and it lasts at least a year.

The winter moth caterpillars are small green 'loopers', with six legs at one end and six suction pads at the other, which attack the blossom and young leaves. They are easily killed by derris or nicotine, provided you see them before they destroy the crop by killing the blossom.

Pear and cherry slugworm (*Eriocampa limacina*) is not a moth or butterfly caterpillar but the larva of a sawfly, which is at first yellowish-white and then turns green or black. It looks rather like a slug and crawls on the upper surface of the leaves, leaving them thin and skeletonized. It feeds from mid-June to September, producing two generations a season, and pupating in the soil round the trees. Spray with derris or even quassia or pyrethrum in June.

Currants

The winter moth larva attacks currants (and gooseberries), so if there are small green looper caterpillars eating the opening buds and blossom, spray with nicotine or derris. Bush fruit stems are of course too thin to take a grease band.

There are a number of currant aphids, all of which attack black, red and white currants. The official currant aphid is *Cryptomyzus galeopsidis*, but the currant-lettuce aphid (*Hyperomyzus lactucae*) and the lettuce aphid (*Nasonavia ribisnigri*) are rather worse because they double as pests of lettuces instead of migrating for their summer holidays to sowthistles and nettles. Unlike these two, the currant aphid just seems to relax and sunbathe without doing any real work before returning to the currants to lay eggs which last the winter, like its two colleagues.

All three feed on the undersides of the currant leaves, which they curl and distort to provide hiding places, from early April until June. Keep a watch for aphids on the currants and spray with derris or quassia with soft soap as soon as they are seen. Spray well on to the undersides of the leaves where the soft soap will help the spray to stick. The object of using the weaker sprays quickly is to spare the *Anthocoris* bugs, which are main controllers of currant red spider and big bud mite.

Big bud mite (*Cecidophyopsis ribis*) is one of the worst pests of blackcurrants, because it carries the reversion virus which is their worst disease. It is microscopic, and is responsible for the swollen buds on blackcurrants, and for buds drying up and going 'blind' without blossom on red and white currants (and also gooseberries). The mites work their way into the buds on the new wood in June and lay eggs that are even tinier. They breed safely inside the buds until April, when each 'big bud' contains hundreds of mites.

In spring, between late March and mid-April, they migrate and and are spread on the clothes of people walking through or by the bushes, on the feathers and feet of birds, and blown long distances on the wind. The most effective dispersal is on the bodies of bees, for the bee's habit of sticking to one kind of nectar and pollen at a time spreads the mites from bush to bush and garden to garden.

The obvious and easy answer is to look over the currants carefully in November or December when the leaves are off, and pick off any enlarged buds, but this is effective only when there are just a few, as there will be on the resistant variety, Seabrook's Black. A good organic gardener who has sprayed his bushes as little as possible and then with only the safest sprays should have plenty of *Anthocoris* on his currants ready to gorge on the migrants, and the best spray to reinforce their efforts is the potassium permanganate wash (p. 205). This is safe and simple, both for *Anthocoris* and the bushes, for the old lime-sulphur washes could also damage a number of sulphur-shy varieties, especially Davison's Eight.

Timing is important, because you have to catch the mites when they are outside the big buds and the migration season varies with the weather. Wait till the new leaves are about the size of 5p pieces, and the blossoms are like tiny pink bunches of grapes, with no florets open, and spray then for the best chance of success.

The currant clearwing moth (*Synanthedon tipuliformis*) and the currant shoot borer (*Lampronia capittella*) are both small moths that make slits in the bark for eggs which hatch to become caterpillars boring right up the centres of shoots and branches. The first signs of attack by either are wilting and yellowing of leaves, and fruit bunches drying up and failing. The only answer is to prune out the wilted branch for burning, cutting back until solid internal wood is reached, for the creatures can pupate in the abandoned tunnels.

Gooseberries

The worst pest is the gooseberry sawfly (*Nematus ribesii*), whose caterpillars have black heads, green and black spotted bodies and three orange-yellow patches at either end. The first generation comes in April and May, the second in June, and the third in August-September, any one of which can strip all the leaves off your bushes swiftly and completely. Organic gardeners are often asked the garden version of the conscientious objectors' question from every war: 'What would you do if you saw *your* gooseberries being eaten by ugly great caterpillars in football jerseys?'

The answer is spray with derris, pyrethrum, nicotine or quassia (the last for choice, because these are sawfly caterpillars and can be killed by this weak insecticide). Use any of these mixed with soft soap, and get it well under the leaves, where as many as thirty at a time of the newly hatched caterpillars will congregate along the midribs. If you have quassia ready when the caterpillars are small it is safe for predators – let them get large and you will need nicotine, which is dangerous for bees if used at blossom time.

The best controller of gooseberry red spider mite (*Bryobia ribis*) is *Anthocoris*, with the help of the potassium permanganate mixture, for red spiders, like big bud mites, are small, but tough. The red spider mite turns the leaves brownish in May, June and July, so these fall early, starving the fruit and weakening the bushes. The mite is just visible to the naked eye as rusty-red or grey patches on the undersides of the leaves. Another answer is to hose the bushes with a powerful jet, getting under the leaves and dislodging the mites, which are always worst in dry weather. *Anthocoris* can clamber back on to the bushes, while the mites may well starve before they return, and this serves to tilt the scale to the side of the predators. The hosing is a help to the bushes anyway. Red spider travels on the wind and hitches lifts on birds and bees, so the permanganate mixture should be used at once if the symptoms are seen.

The gooseberry aphid (*Aphis grossulariae*) attacks the tips of the young shoots, which it twists and curls so badly that it is very difficult to get a spray inside. Snip off these twisted tips and about 2 in. of soft stem and drop them in a basket to throw away. This acts as a summer 'pruning' and may gain a better crop next year by putting more strength into the fruit buds; it also gets rid of the aphids which attack only soft tips like those of cherries and broad beans.

The winter moth caterpillars can attack gooseberries badly, and so will those of the magpie moth (*Abraxas grossulariata*), which are black and white hairy loopers with a yellow stripe along the sides. The moth, which is equally psychedelically coloured, lays eggs in groups on the leaves until autumn, when the young caterpillars hibernate among dead leaves and in cracks in bark or woodwork. They awake in the spring as full-sized caterpillars and murder the leaves until the end of May, when they pupate in haste and become moths ready to start the sequence again. Spray with derris and soap, or nicotine and soap if possible, in late summer before they have time to do much damage.

Loganberries

Loganberries share the blackberry mite (*Aceria essegi*). It is white, and as small as the big bud mite. It spends the winter in bud scales and any dried-up fruits left on the old canes. In April it migrates to the undersides of the new leaves and increases rapidly until it moves to the flowers, where it is responsible for uneven ripening and some of the drupelets (the round segments of the fruit) turning light red. This pest is more common on wild blackberries than cultivated, because cultivated ones, like loganberries, should have their new canes trained in and their fruited ones cut out. If there is trouble with either berry when used as a hedge with old wood left in to keep it solid, spray with derris before the blossom begins to open.

Raspberries

The raspberry beetle (*Byturus tomentosus*) is best left to the robins, because of the problem of killing bees. If there has been a bad attack it is best tackled with pyrethrum or quassia. Spray ten days after the first blossom opens and again ten days later, always an hour before sunset when the bees have gone to bed. Pyrethrum will be spent before the bees are working again, and so will quassia. Derris is usually recommended but this is strong enough to kill beetles and bees for at least two days. The timing will catch the grubs when they are feeding on the outside of the blossom before tunnelling into the developing fruit, and they are small enough for these two quite weak pesticides to kill.

The raspberry moth (*Lampronia rubiella*) has caterpillars which get right inside the canes, which can be seen withered towards the end of April and in early May. Cut off the withered shoots at ground level and burn them. The moth measures only about $\frac{1}{4}$ in. across the wings and lays its eggs in the open flowers, just like the raspberry beetle, in May and June. The caterpillars bore their way through the fruit and when they have ruined it crawl down the canes and hibernate in rubbish and in crevices. They leave their cocoons in April, bore into the canes and feed on the pith. Digging in winter will expose some cocoons for the robins, like those of the raspberry beetle, but many cocoons will be found in the hollow stumps left from cutting out fruiting canes, and these should be snipped out and burnt, cocoons and all. As the moth flies in *daylight* and only during the last fortnight in April and the first in May, it is possible to catch quantities of this small purple-brown moth with yellow spots on the upper wings, by putting out treacle boards as for wasps (p. 210). Bees will not eat this kind of bait, but wasps will.

Strawberries

The strawberry aphid (*Chaetosiphon fragaefolii*) is the commonest of the aphids that attack strawberries, and the worst because it carries the yellow edge and crinkle viruses. They are not easy to destroy, but with care it is possible to get a nicotine and soap wash right underneath the leaves, and this is the best answer to most strawberry pests. Soak the crowns and under the leaves in April and again in May for the aphids, and for the blossom weevil (*Anthonomus rubi*) which lays eggs in the unopened blossom.

The strawberry moth (*Acleris comariana*) can have small green caterpillars feeding at this time, and the nicotine and soap wash will also hit them, but there is a second brood in August and September, and quassia and soft soap could be used then for the minimum bee risk. Those who are very seriously concerned about their bees should use pyrethrum or quassia, which are safer but less effective, in the evening. Allow forty-eight hours for the nicotine to be spent before picking fruit to eat.

CONCLUSION

Organic gardeners may feel that in this last chapter I have laid too much stress on spraying, and that with compost there is no need for such complex precautions – all that is needed is a bed of herbs to repel almost anything. The *inorganic* will insist that I have given too little space to the pests, and hastened over some of the worst problems. This is only to be expected, for the latter have the most pests and the compost gardeners have the fewest. This chapter has been written to provide the safest answers – safest not only for birds, bees and men, but also for the hard-working, unpaid friends of every gardener. They are cheaper, less energy-consuming and less hard work than even the safest sprays.

When a writer finishes a novel he draws the threads together, perhaps with a sentence reaching back to the first paragraph which established his main character. My main character is inflation, and I will say that since I began writing this book, prices have increased by 25 per cent and 40,000 acres of land have gone under concrete for roads, car parks, tower blocks, pedestrian precincts and civic centres. It is hard for those whose incomes still double every four years to realize that food matters, and that good food grown with compost matters far more because, provided we do not drive our soils too hard, the land will go on feeding us through the sunlit centuries when motoring is but a memory.

I am an organic gardener, and like organic farmers we differ from the inorganic in thinking further ahead into the future, when the fuel and the fertilizers will run out, when the pesticides, herbicides and fungicides will have built up to danger level in the soils and when other countries stop lending us money (this last unforeseen by the politicians who are most shortsighted of all). We have 'dug for victory' through two world wars in my lifetime, and now we must dig still harder for victory over inflation. Our task will be easier if we garden to build fertility for the future, to leave the land better than we found it, and to get some fun out of it.

Appendix 1
Organizations and Suppliers

Unlike the old-fashioned nurserymen and seedsmen, who were proud of the completeness of their catalogues, modern garden shops and centres tend to sell only varieties which are in mass demand. This is one reason for this appendix; it may also make it out of date, because the liking for cost effectiveness can easily remove just the variety I recommend from the catalogue of the firm that still stocked it when I wrote these final pages.

ORGANIZATIONS

Henry Doubleday Research Association, Convent Lane, Bocking, Braintree, Essex. Organic gardeners who buy for flavour have to hunt for their needs. The Henry Doubleday Research Association has now started a vegetable and fruit finder service for members. Non-members are entitled to one inquiry free for a stamped addressed envelope; members (subscription £5 a year) can use the service free.

The Association also sells green manure seeds in small quantities for gardeners, and a range of sundries such as ready-made compost containers, activators, pesticides such as Fertosan slug destroyer or quassia chips, comfrey plants, and some organic fertilizers. It is a registered charity, and sells to finance its work of research in the fields of organic farming and gardening. There is also an organic gardeners' advice service for members only (postal *not telephone*), a quarterly newsletter, and a great many publications of interest to all who garden without chemicals in Britain and overseas.

The Henry Doubleday Research Association of Australia, Greggs Road, Kurrajong 2758, N.S.W., Australia; The Doubleday Organic Research Association, 20 Heslop Road, Lesmurdie 6086, Western

Appendix 1: Organizations and Suppliers

Australia; The Henry Doubleday Research Association of New Zealand, P.O. Box 6416, Auckland, New Zealand.

The Soil Association, Walnut Tree Manor, Haughley, Nr Stowmarket, Suffolk. Subscription £5 a year. Concerned more with organizing lectures and courses on organic farming, runs a kind of organic employment agency for those who want to work on these farms and market gardens. Issues a quarterly newsletter.

Friends of the Earth, 9 Poland Street, London W1. Though this body is primarily concerned with fighting pollution, it campaigns actively for more allotments and runs a garden-sharing scheme, putting those whose gardens are too large for them in touch with others who need land to grow food. They have branches all over Britain and your nearest could be very helpful.

The Biodynamic Gardening Association, Rudolf Steiner House, 35 Park Road, London NW1. Spreads the gardening ideas of Rudolf Steiner.

'Practical Self-Sufficiency', Broad Leys Publishing Co., Widdington, Saffron Walden, Essex, is the only organic gardening magazine, but includes articles on goats, bees, chickens, small-scale dairying, windmills, etc. Six issues a year, £3.50 annual subscription, and about the best value in solid help and facts of the many publications in this field.

SUPPLIERS

Organic Farmers and Growers Ltd, Longridge, Creetings Road, Stowmarket, Suffolk, is the organic farmers' marketing cooperative. They can supply larger quantities of substances like gypsum, dolomite limestone, seaweed meal, and organic fertilizers, and are developing depots where these substances may be picked up by car, saving postage. These can often be obtained from your local agricultural merchant if you need smaller quantities such as 56 lb. (The H.D.R.A. supplies smaller amounts, and *Tagetes minuta*, see above. It also supplies soft soap, quassia and ready extracted nicotine, and other safe pesticides.)

Vegetable suppliers

Apart from the big commercial seedsmen, there are a number of small ones with interesting varieties.

Chase Compost Grown Seeds, Benhall, Saxmundham, Suffolk, supply standard varieties grown without chemicals. They include Japanese pumpkins and green manure lupins.

Thompson & Morgan, London Road, Ipswich, Suffolk, sell a very wide range of vegetable seeds, not organically grown, including Monarch cabbage, 'Burpless' cucumbers, and most herbs.

John McLean & Son, Dornoch Farm, Crieff, Perthshire, stock the largest collection of seed potatoes in Britain, about 150 varieties. Remember to order well before Christmas. They have the latest blight and eelworm resisters and the old flavour kinds as well.

F. Toynbee Ltd, Barnham, Nr Bognor Regis, Sussex, sell plants of Glaskin's Perpetual Rhubarb.

J. W. Boyce Ltd, Soham, Ely, Cambs, stock a range of flavour kinds.

Soft Fruit

The following all stock Morello and Duke cherries and a range of good soft fruit:

Messrs Hillier & Sons, West Hill Nurseries, Winchester, Hants; R. V. Rogers, Pickering, Yorks; John Scott Ltd, The Royal Nurseries, Merriott, Somerset.

Fernbank Nurseries Ltd, Benfleet Road, South Benfleet, Essex, sell the 'Rollerberry' strawberry.

Services

Messrs Aynsome Laboratories, Kentsford Road, Grange-over-Sands, Lancs. Soil analysis, manure analysis, pesticide analysis.
Messrs Battle, Hayward & Bower, Carrholm Road, Lincoln, Lincs. Suppliers of ammonium sulphamate.

Appendix 2
Further Reading

Lawrence D. Hills, *Grow Your Own Fruit and Vegetables*, Faber & Faber, 4th edition, 1975. Includes tree fruit and analysis of all fruit and vegetables.

Lawrence D. Hills, *Down to Earth Gardening*, Faber & Faber, paperback edition, 1975. Flower gardening, including trees and shrubs, alpines and herbaceous plants, for organic gardeners.

Lawrence D. Hills, *Comfrey, Its Past, Present and Future*, Faber & Faber, 1976.

E. D. Moreton, *Beneficial Insects and Mites*, Ministry of Agriculture, Fisheries and Food, H.M.S.O., 1969. The best book on pest control with the help of insect allies.

Home Preservation of Fruit and Vegetables, Ministry of Agriculture, Fisheries and Food Bulletin No. 21, H.M.S.O. The best value in practical help for every gardener.

T. Wallace, *The Diagnosis of Mineral Deficiencies in Plants by Visual Symptoms*, H.M.S.O., 3rd edition, 1961. The best book on its subject. Long out of print but worth looking for. Try to borrow it from your library.

Index

Index